PRAISE FOR *SUMMARY JUDGMENT*

"*Summary Judgment* is a compelling true story that exposes how conviction of innocents is not the only flaw to be guarded against in our criminal justice system—particularly in cases seeking to impose the death penalty. The book tackles the murky waters of justice for the guilty and will be of great interest to anyone who wants to know more about the legal and moral intricacies of defending a person facing a death sentence. With great honesty, Donald Cameron Clark, Jr,. offers an insider perspective and captures the complexities of a fascinating life-and-death case."

—Sister Helen Prejean, C.S.J., death penalty abolitionist
and author of *Dead Man Walking* (1994), *The Death
of Innocents* (2006), and *River of Fire* (2020).

"Loved the book! *Summary Judgment* is an extraordinary behind-the-scenes account of a dedicated legal team volunteering in post–death penalty litigation, including the lawyering that is involved. I recommend it for lawyers and nonlawyers alike as a tremendous example of lawyers upholding their oaths to ensure that justice, rather than retribution, is served."

—H. Thomas Wells, Jr., president, American
Bar Association (2008–2009)

"A meticulously detailed and often stirring account of one lawyer's dedication."

—*Kirkus Reviews*

"*Summary Judgment* is more than just a memoir—it is a primer on post-conviction practice in criminal cases, a "call to action" to all legal professionals to perform pro bono work, and a reassurance to those in the struggle to see a real-life example demonstrating that justice can prevail. It should also help the public understand that not everyone serving on death row is guilty or deserves to be there. Donald Cameron Clark, Jr., should not only be commended for this important work but also for his unwavering pursuit of justice."

—Sue Bell Cobb, chief justice, Alabama Supreme Court (Ret.)

"This memoir by Donald Cameron Clark, Jr., about representing a death-sentenced prisoner is exceptional in both its detail and honesty, providing a rare level of insight into one of the most important and yet least visible parts of our criminal justice system. By examining the moral and legal complexities of representing a prisoner who was factually guilty and yet wrongfully convicted, *Summary Judgment* marks an important departure from typical critiques of the death penalty system that focus on innocence. It exposes the deeply flawed reality of capital punishment law and procedure and makes a compelling case for taking action to protect those who are at the mercy of this broken system."

—Emily Olson-Gault, national expert on the appointment and performance of defense counsel in death penalty cases

"Donald Cameron Clark, Jr., has produced a fascinating account of exemplary lawyering which prevented the execution of a severely psychologically-damaged Alabama 'man.' In a narrative, accessible to nonlawyers, Clark takes the reader inside the system's difficult tactical, procedural, and doctrinal challenges which are designed to favor finality over justice. Most importantly, this book dramatically raises and explores the ethical and jurisprudential questions our country faces regarding the justifications for incarceration and execution."

—Rayman Solomon, professor and dean emeritus, Rutgers University Law School

"When Donald Cameron Clark, Jr., was a young lawyer, he and two colleagues mounted a long-shot effort to get the Alabama courts to overturn the conviction and death penalty of Tommy Hamilton, who had killed Lehman Wood during the commission of a robbery. The effort was ultimately successful. Clark's book, *Summary Judgment*, tells the story of the crime, the proceedings, and Clark's own professional growth as a courtroom attorney.

"The book is not the usual tale of a wrongly convicted man redeemed by newly discovered evidence of his innocence. Tommy Hamilton did murder Lehman Wood. But his trial was tainted by perjury and incompetence. Clark accomplishes something very difficult: helping us see the importance of making sure that justice is done even for the guilty. Along the way, he tells a gripping and fascinating story. He manages to delve into the minute and sometimes technical details of the case without ever losing the reader's interest. And he elicits our sympathies without trying to artificially tug at our heartstrings.

"Clark's decency, competence, and sense of conviction shine through clearly in *Summary Judgment*. He has obviously been pondering his role in Tommy Hamilton's case for decades. We should be grateful to him for finally putting the story in writing."

—Perry Dane, professor, Rutgers University Law School and former law clerk to Hon. William J. Brennan Jr., associate justice, United States Supreme Court (1982–83)

"*Summary Judgment* is fantastic. If you want to know what it's like to be a good lawyer, one who thinks client first / winning second, then this is the book for you. Clark's point of view of a lawyer defending a client facing the death penalty hasn't been created through the research most writers would need to do. He actually lived this. A fantastic story, swift page turner, and a smart, fun read. I love this book!"

—Timothy Busfield, actor, director, producer

"*Summary Judgment* offers an intimate, first-hand account of the professional life of a prominent Chicago corporate attorney who represented an Alabama man convicted of capital murder. Known for craving the challenge of an 'unwinnable' case, Donald Cameron Clark, Jr., uses his wit, intellect, and creative mind to strategize an outcome for an unsympathetic client whose life literally hangs in the balance, but who still deserves a fair shake at justice."

—Reid Weisbord, professor, Rutgers University Law School

SUMMARY JUDGMENT

SUMMARY JUDGMENT

A Lawyer's Memoir

DONALD CAMERON CLARK, JR.

Sgian
Dubh
PRESS

Published by Sgian Dubh Press, Glenview, Illinois
www.donaldcameronclarkjr.com

Edited and designed by Girl Friday Productions
www.girlfridayproductions.com

Design: Paul Barrett
Project management: Alexander Rigby
Image credits: cover © Dreamstime/Nexus7

ISBN (hardcover): 978-1-7368077-0-5
ISBN (paperback): 978-1-7368077-1-2
ISBN (ebook): 978-1-7368077-2-9

Library of Congress Control Number: 2021911573

First edition

To Ellen. Always to Ellen.

Humans have a responsibility to their own time . . . a responsibility to find themselves where they are, in their own proper time and place, in this history to which they belong and to which they must inevitably contribute either their response or their evasion.

—Thomas Merton

We have different gifts, according to the grace given to each of us. If your gift is prophesying, then prophesy in accordance with your faith; if it is in serving, then serve; if it is teaching, then teach; if it is to encourage, then give encouragement; if it is giving, then give generously; if it is to lead, do it diligently; if it is to show mercy, do it cheerfully.

Romans 12:6–8

CONTENTS

PROLOGUE

The Crime

On an ordinary summer evening in rural Alabama in 1984, Randall Curry and his coworker Randy Mitchell were driving away from the town of Moulton on Highway 33 to go to a bootlegger's house located atop a mountain in the Bankhead National Forest. Known as the "land of a thousand waterfalls," the William B. Bankhead National Forest, covering more than 181,000 acres, was a popular spot among the locals for hiking, hunting, and swimming.

Just inside the national forest, Curry noticed a blue Ford Maverick automobile stopped on a short spur off Ridge Road where it meets Highway 33. The Maverick had its hood raised. Curry leaned over the steering wheel of his truck and observed a woman sitting in the driver's seat of the Maverick, a woman sitting in the front passenger seat, and a child sitting in the back seat. Nothing about their demeanor seemed distressed or suspicious, but Curry took note of the group just the same.

Curry and Mitchell continued to the bootlegger's house and then left, traveling back toward Route 33 by taking Ridge Road. When they reached the spur road, they again noticed the Maverick with the same occupants. Curry and Mitchell then turned onto Highway 33 heading back to town. They passed a white Ford truck heading in the opposite direction toward Ridge Road. Soon afterward, for reasons unknown, Curry and Mitchell turned around and headed back in the direction of the bootlegger's house.

At some point below the intersection of Highway 33 and Ridge Road, Curry and Mitchell encountered the blue Maverick traveling toward Moulton. It now had three adults sitting in the front seat. When Curry and Mitchell arrived at the spur road, they found the white Ford truck and a man's body lying in front of it, covered in blood. They quickly realized that the man had been shot, so they flagged down a passing motorist to send for law enforcement.

Although I wasn't there, and I didn't know it at the time, my life would intersect with the people in that blue Maverick and be changed forever. This book is the story of how a trial lawyer from Chicago came to represent a death row inmate from Alabama. These are my memories. Most of them are true.

CHAPTER ONE

The Attorney

The first question was always the same. And there was only one acceptable answer.

"Did you win?"

The query was the post-court-appearance conversation starter directed at me by the partners at Isham, Lincoln & Beale, one of Chicago's most venerable law firms. It had been founded in 1872 by Edward Swift Isham, son of Vermont Supreme Court Justice Pierpont Isham, and Robert Todd Lincoln, the only surviving son of President Abraham Lincoln. Lincoln had met Isham at the time of the Great Chicago Fire. On the evening of Sunday, October 8, 1871, a fire started in the barn of Patrick and Catherine O'Leary on the city's West Side. The fire, which raged for three days, killed up to three hundred people, destroyed roughly three square miles of the city, and left some one hundred thousand residents homeless. Lincoln's law office burned in the fire. Isham's office was spared, and he graciously allowed Lincoln to share office space until the city and Lincoln rebuilt. Their relationship evolved from landlord and tenant to law partners. Together, they became the law firm of choice for notable individuals and significant corporations.

After seven years of working as an associate attorney, I was on the brink of being considered for partnership at this storied firm. My path to partnership was unusual. I had known that I wanted to be a lawyer, and specifically a trial lawyer, ever since I was in the seventh grade. I don't know from where this passion was born, as no member of my family had ever been a lawyer. Still, even as a child, I loved to argue and found it exhilarating to persuade others to share my point of view on topics large and small.

After completing my freshman year of college, I wanted to get as close as I could to the profession I aspired to join. I sought any job remotely related to the law. I ultimately succeeded by being employed to work in Isham, Lincoln & Beale's mail room. Besides delivering mail to the lawyers in their offices, I messengered their pleadings and documents to other law firms in the city. Not infrequently, it was my honor to get lunch for some of the lawyers to enjoy in their offices. After graduating from Williams College and law school at Rutgers University, I began working for the firm as an associate attorney in 1979. At the start, I was working hand in glove on cases and legal matters with attorneys to whom I had been delivering correspondence and lunch only a few years earlier. Seven years after that, I was in line to become the first person who had begun his career working in the mail room to become partner.

But first, I had to prove myself to the powers that be. A senior partner sent me to represent one of the firm's top clients at the Daley Center downtown, which had been named after the patriarch of the most powerful political dynasty in Chicago and was home to the Circuit Courts of Cook County, Illinois—one of the busiest court systems in the nation. Perched behind a six-foot-long mahogany desk on what appeared to be more throne than chair, in front of cabinetry that rose from the floor to the top of the almost fourteen-foot-high ceiling, the partner asked about the outcome of my efforts on behalf of his client. Sunlight poured through the curtain wall of windows that formed one side of the office. Green tweed side chairs flanked the desk. A hint of pipe smoke filled the air.

"Did you win?"

Making partner would be a significant accomplishment at a firm that had developed a reputation for gentility, if not stodginess. Sartorial distinctiveness within the firm, at least for the men, was largely defined by whether you wore a bow tie rather than a necktie finished with a Windsor knot. But in the latter half of the twentieth century, things were beginning to change. In 1956, Robert Helman became the first Jewish lawyer to be hired by the firm. Pioneering lawyer Sharon L. King, an Isham, Lincoln & Beale partner, was likely one of the first women to sit on the managing council of a major law firm, at a time when only 2 percent of attorneys were women. Reynaldo Glover, the firm's first Black partner, went on to become the President of the City Colleges of Chicago. And in 1973, former Illinois Governor Richard B. Ogilvie joined as a partner and became the public face of the firm.

By the 1980s, Isham had come to value powerful and connected corporate lawyers, but trial attorneys were underappreciated. Notably younger than many of the lawyers serving in other practice areas, Isham's trial attorneys were smart, energetic, and—most importantly—successful in representing their clients in court. Many of them would go on to have distinguished careers in politics, law, and business. James B. Burns, a former player for the Chicago Bulls professional basketball team, would become the United States Attorney for the Northern District of Illinois and vie, albeit unsuccessfully, for the Democratic Party's nomination for Governor. Pamela B. Strobel would become an executive at the energy giant Exelon (the successor corporation to Commonwealth Edison), and she would be touted in the local business press as one of the hundred most influential women in Chicago.

A few trial attorneys, such as David M. Stahl (a magna cum laude graduate of the University of Michigan Law School and a member of the honorary legal scholastic society the Order of the Coif), would go on to form their own blue chip litigation boutiques. Others, such as Vietnam War veteran Hugh R. "Rick" McCombs, a former Clerk for a Federal District Court Judge, and Paul W. Schroeder, a Phi Beta Kappa graduate of the University of Illinois and then a managing editor of its law school's law journal, would become noted litigation partners in some of the world's largest law firms. Ron Jacks, the former General Counsel for CNA Insurance Company, the first President of the Reinsurance Association of America, and the attorney who sponsored my own admission to the Bar of the Supreme Court of the United States, went on to head the international insurance practice at the law firm of Mayer Brown.

But in the 1980s, the members of this remarkable collection of legal talent were my colleagues at Isham, Lincoln & Beale. More than that, they were mentors and friends. I was as one with them, with my own office some fifty stories high in a modern office tower at the corner of Madison and Dearborn streets in the heart of Chicago's Loop, just a short walk from both the state and federal courthouses. My journey from the mail room had figuratively and literally brought me to the pinnacle of Chicago's legal profession. I could not have been happier at that moment, standing in the doorway of the partner and telling him about what had happened in court that day.

"Yeah, yeah . . . but did you win?"

When it was repeated for the third time, the partner's question became more of a demand than a query. He was not interested in hearing which legal arguments the Judge had found to be persuasive and which were deemed wanting. He just wanted to know whether the motion had been granted. He only cared whether I had won.

Trial lawyers are a distinct breed among attorneys. The measure of success for a trial lawyer is decidedly different than it is for a transactional attorney. Success for the dealmakers, contract drafters, and tax advisors is nuanced, if quantifiable at all, and it extends along a continuum of economic advantage gained over periods of time. But trial lawyers are gladiators, and the metric of success is unambiguous, often instantaneous, and always unforgiving. Whether arguing a pre-trial motion or an evidentiary objection, making a closing argument, or presenting an oral argument in an appeal, the range of outcomes is blunt and binary: you either win or you lose. While colleagues may appreciate the skills that produce the result, for clients it is the result alone that matters. The pressure to win is enormous.

"Yes, we won."

This outcome undoubtedly pleased the partner; he could report success to his client. But winning alone was no longer enough to satisfy me. Ambition and hubris had begun to fuel a desire to test myself with ever greater challenges. I felt a pull toward cases that seemed unwinnable. This does not mean that a case must be complex to be professionally challenging. There is perhaps no legal issue more straightforward and at the same time more challenging than one that turns on little more than which of two witnesses is telling the truth.

Maybe that is why I jumped at the chance to represent a minister who had been arrested for allegedly soliciting an undercover police officer to engage in sex acts. The residents of a conservative small town were upset because a public park where their children played had become the venue for secretive sexual liaisons between men. Facing intense pressure from the townspeople, the local constabulary had decided to set up a sting operation. An undercover male officer was assigned to loiter in the park; if he was solicited for a sex act, an arrest would be made.

Under normal circumstances, after several arrests, word would spread among the targeted offenders that the park was no longer a haven. Those arrested would have their lawyers negotiate deals by which they would plead guilty to a lesser charge, likely a misdemeanor of disorderly conduct, to reduce the penalty to a fine and mitigate the burden of their resulting criminal record. But there was nothing normal about the arrest of a minister in an undercover sex crimes operation in this tight-knit religious community. The harm to the reputation of the minister and his church, let alone the threat that the allegations posed to his marriage, far exceeded the criminal penalties he was facing. My client might as well have been charged with a felony, given the gravity of the consequences that would follow a conviction or a guilty plea to the underlying conduct of which he had been accused. The mere fact of the arrest was certain to generate media coverage. He was facing a reputational death sentence.

At first glance, the case boiled down to who was telling the truth: a minister of the cloth or a policeman sworn to uphold the law. They were the only two individuals who had been present and party to the events that transpired between them. Both could not be right; one of them would have to be doubted, if not disbelieved. As the defendant's attorney, it was therefore my job to convince a finder of fact that a police officer was not credible regarding the criminal charges he had made.

The first strategic decision in defending this matter was whether to request a jury. The pretrial publicity was likely to pollute the pool of citizens from which a jury would be drawn. Still, the degree of taint was probably not enough to successfully argue that the case should be tried in another jurisdiction to ensure an impartial tribunal for the defendant. At the same time, some preliminary investigation suggested that the arresting officer had a reputation for being the local equivalent of Deputy Barney Fife from Mayberry—a bit overzealous and a tad ineffective. While this assessment probably was not widely known in the community, I hoped that it might have bubbled up to the local judiciary. Thus, I made the decision to forego my client's right to a jury trial, placing his fate in the hands of a Judge at the conclusion of a bench trial.

My client vehemently denied that he had solicited the police officer for sex, but an early lesson learned by trial lawyers is that you should not overstate your case or any position you take in support of it. In short, do not take on more than is necessary to win. Since this was a criminal case, the prosecutor needed to prove her allegations beyond a reasonable doubt. I did not have to prove the policeman was a liar to win. I could win by sufficiently suggesting that he was mistaken. I did not have to risk hypocrisy by pleading that my client was innocent; it was enough to argue that he was not guilty because there existed a reasonable doubt as to his guilt.

I met with the minister at his home and asked him to tell me his version of the events. The arrest had occurred during the last weekend of his summer vacation. Although scheduled to return to the church on Monday, he had wanted to get a head start on the work that had piled up during his absence. A visit to the church office before Monday would leave him inundated with greetings and requests from welcoming parishioners, so he decided to drive his recreational vehicle to the park and attempt to make a dent in his work there.

He parked his RV in the parking lot and began to work. He told me that after a while, he heard a knock on the door. He opened it, and a stranger struck up a conversation and eventually asked the minister if he could come inside. The minster told me that he invited the man in. Immediately upon entering the RV, the man identified himself as a police officer and arrested the minister for soliciting a sex act.

I asked the minister whether anything the man was wearing indicated he was a law enforcement officer. According to my client, the officer was dressed in jeans and a T-shirt. Nothing in his appearance or behavior suggested he was a policeman. Then I asked the minister whether anything about his own attire indicated he was a minister. The arrest occurred on a hot summer day, and since the minister planned to work for a few hours, he did not want to run the vehicle's air-conditioning for a long period of time. After looking inside the RV for cooler clothing to put on, all he could find was a bathing suit. That's all that he was wearing when he opened the door of the RV.

I asked him if he still had the bathing suit. He told me that he did, so I asked to see it. The garment was boxer shorts in style, made of baby-blue pinstriped fabric. It had a drawstring and mesh interior, common in men's swimwear.

The rules of criminal and civil procedure vary from state to state and over time. In the jurisdiction in question at this time, criminal pretrial procedure offered me the opportunity to depose the arresting officer before the case went to court. A deposition is sworn testimony taken outside a courtroom that can either be presented in court as if the witness were present or used to impeach a witness whose in-court testimony deviates from his deposition. Taking full advantage of the opportunity to question the officer before the trial, I asked him most of the questions I had posed to the minister. My goal was to compare their stories about each aspect of the events on the day of the arrest.

The policeman recounted how he had been assigned undercover duty in the park to see whether solicitation for sex acts was occurring and to make arrests if anyone solicited him. He stated that while he was patrolling the parking lot, a man had opened the door of an RV and waved, as if to beckon the officer toward the van. The officer stated that when he approached the door to the van, the man invited him in and solicited sex from him. He promptly arrested the man, who he then came to learn was a minister, and told him to put on a pair of pants.

I asked the officer what the minister was wearing when he allegedly solicited the officer for sex. The officer said that the minister was wearing underwear. I asked the police officer to describe the underwear, and he told me that it was a pair of boxer shorts made of baby-blue pinstriped fabric.

It is no small challenge to get a local Judge to view the testimony of a local law enforcement officer skeptically, and to rule against a local prosecutor who (likely) appears in her courtroom on a regular basis. When an out-of-town lawyer appears in court, the reception is almost always cool. When a corporate lawyer from Chicago appears in a small-town court for a criminal case, it generates a kind of defensiveness. I wanted to use this to my advantage. I wanted to shift the attention away from my client—the defendant—and onto me and the prosecution's witness, the police officer. I needed to put the police officer on trial instead of my client.

Based on the deposition, I now had an angle with which to press my case. I took possession of the minister's bathing suit and stuffed it inside a four-foot-long cardboard tube, the kind used for storing rolled-up maps or posters. I used duct tape to seal the ends of the cylinder and prevent anyone from knowing what was inside, then I had it marked for identification as "Defendant's Exhibit A." During a preliminary hearing, I asked the court to take possession and control of the exhibit before any trial testimony had been offered so that there could be no assertion that this exhibit was created or obtained in response to testimony that was given.

Everyone in court, especially the prosecuting attorney, was puzzled by my request. This was a solicitation case, a case about what the defendant had said to a police officer. No one could understand how physical evidence of any kind might be relevant to an assertion that an undercover police officer had been solicited for a sex act, and no one had any idea what relevant evidence would be in a map tube. Nevertheless, without objection from the prosecutor, the Judge took custody of Defendant's Exhibit A.

The case for the prosecution was straightforward. The arresting officer testified as to the history of criminal solicitation problems in the park; law enforcement's plan to stem the tide; and his role as an undercover operative on the day of the minister's arrest. He testified that after a man in a motor vehicle matching the description of the minister's recreational vehicle entered the park, the officer approached the vehicle, and the occupant solicited him for sex. The officer identified the defendant as the occupant of the recreational vehicle and the man who had made the illicit solicitation in violation of the criminal code.

Of all the elements of a trial, I love cross-examination of a witness best. It can be the most dramatic portion of a trial. Done well, it can win your case. Generally, you never ask a question on cross-examination for which you do not already know the answer. Based on my pretrial questioning, I had the arresting officer committed to certain statements. The art of cross-examination includes presenting those statements through a series of questions that drive home your case. Your objective is to get the witness to agree or disagree with the statements that you, the questioner, are making. In doing so, you effectively become the one giving testimony. The witness is simply answering yes or no.

To be effective, my cross-examination needed to be short and sweet. Standing at the defense table, I asked the officer to confirm that he was present in the park as part of an undercover operation designed solely to arrest individuals soliciting sex acts, and not for the purpose of enforcing other laws. Because of the frequency of such behavior in the park, I asked the officer to confirm that he expected such activity to occur on the day he was assigned to his task and that he expected that he would be solicited to engage in sex acts. I asked the officer to confirm that he was alleging that he had heard the minister solicit him for sex in violation of the law:

> Question: You were assigned to patrol the
> park that day as part of an undercover
> operation to arrest men who solicited
> you for sex, weren't you, officer?
> Answer: Yes.
> Q: And that was your only assignment that
> day, wasn't it, officer?
> A: Yes.
> Q: And you devoted yourself to that
> assignment, didn't you, officer?
> A: Yes.

Q: You focused on your assignment and
   nothing else that day, didn't you,
   officer?

A: Yes.

Q: Now, prior to meeting the Reverend, no
   one had solicited you for sex in the
   park, had they, officer?

A: No.

Q: It was very hot that day, wasn't it,
   officer?

A: Yes.

Q: And you had been in the park, in that
   heat, for hours before you met the
   Reverend, hadn't you, officer?

A: Yes.

Q: And you had not yet made a single
   arrest, had you, officer?

A: No, I had not.

Q: It is your testimony, sir, that the
   Reverend waved at you from his RV,
   isn't it?

A: Yes.

Q: And you testified that in response to
   his wave you walked over to the RV and
   eventually entered inside, didn't you?

A: Yes.

Q: And it is your testimony that once
   inside the RV, the Reverend solicited
   you for sex, isn't it?

A: Yes.

With this foundation laid, I turned to what I proposed to make the heart of the matter. I asked the officer to describe what he saw the minister wearing at the time the alleged solicitation occurred.

> Question: Officer, what was the Reverend
>   wearing at the time that you allege he
>   solicited you for sex?
> Answer: He was wearing his underwear.
> Q: And what did this clothing look like?
> A: He was wearing boxer shorts.
> Q: And what material were these boxer
>   shorts made of?
> A: They were made of baby-blue pinstripe
>   fabric.

I paused. And then in a louder voice, I stated: "Your Honor, may I please have Defendant's Exhibit A, which we previously placed in the care of the court before this trial began and before the officer began his testimony."

The Judge directed the bailiff to retrieve the exhibit, and the bailiff handed me the four-foot-long cardboard map tube. I could feel all eyes upon me as I slowly removed the duct tape from one end of the tube and removed the garment that was inside.

> Question: Officer, I am holding in
>   my hands a garment that has been
>   previously marked for identification
>   as "Defendant's Exhibit A." It is a
>   garment that is boxer shorts cut in
>   style and made of fabric that is baby-
>   blue pinstripe. Do you recognize this
>   garment?
> Answer: Yes.

```
Q: What do you recognize this garment to
   be?
A: It is the underwear the defendant was
   wearing inside his RV.
```

After getting the exhibit admitted into evidence, I asked the Judge: "May I approach the witness, Your Honor?" The Judge granted my request. I moved from counsel table to the witness stand. I was now mere inches from the police officer. All eyes were on the two of us.

```
Question: Officer, I am going to hand you
    Defendant's Exhibit A, the clothing
    the Reverend was wearing when you say
    he solicited you for sex. And I ask
    that you examine that clothing.
Question: Officer, Defendant's Exhibit A,
    the clothing you say the minister was
    wearing when he solicited you, is a
    man's swimsuit, isn't it?
Answer: It appears to be.
Q: It appears to be a swimsuit because
   it is a swimsuit, isn't it, officer?
   It has a drawstring and it has a mesh
   interior, both commonly found in a
   man's swimsuit, doesn't it, officer?
   And it is in fact a swimsuit, isn't
   it, officer?
A: Yes.
Q: It is not underwear, is it, officer?
A: No.
Q: On the day you arrested the Reverend,
   you thought you saw him wearing
   underwear, you testified today that
```

```
            he was wearing underwear, and until
            just a moment ago you believed he was
            wearing underwear, didn't you, officer?
         A: Yes.
         Q: But now, you see that it is not
            underwear, you recant that it is
            underwear, and you no longer believe
            it is underwear; isn't that right,
            officer?
         A: Yes.
         Q: And your testimony that the Reverend
            was wearing underwear at the time you
            allege he solicited you for sex is
            wrong, isn't it, officer?
         A: Yes.
```

My closing argument was direct and to the point. The arresting officer had one task in mind that day in the park. He was there to arrest men for soliciting sex. And he wanted to be successful in performing that task. He wanted to make an arrest. And so, when he approached the good Reverend in pursuit of his assignment and struck up a conversation in pursuit of his task, *he heard what he wanted to hear, just like he saw what he wanted to see.* But he was wrong. The minister was not wearing underwear. And the minister never solicited sex.

The Judge found my client not guilty, with a glance that made it clear to me that she shared my understanding of the difference between a criminal defendant being not guilty and being innocent.

———

Winning cases like the minister's can be intoxicating. But while I loved the challenge of winning a seemingly unwinnable case, I also wanted to do something to serve the cause of justice more explicitly. I searched for a case in which I could do both, and that's what eventually led me to rural Alabama.

Lawyers are sometimes defined by others in terms of economic greed. The story goes that the prospective client asks the lawyer: "How much would you charge me to answer just three questions?"

The lawyer responds: "I would charge you one thousand dollars."

"One thousand dollars!" the prospective client reacts. "Isn't that kind of expensive?"

"Yes," the lawyer replies. "What is your third question?"

Isham, Lincoln & Beale charged hourly fees that reflected the standing of its clients and the importance of their legal interests. In 1979, a fee of two hundred dollars per hour was as typical as it was breathtaking. As a first-year attorney, I was paid the enormous salary of twenty-five thousand dollars per year. Profits per partner, one of the principal metrics of law firm financial health, were a staggering two hundred thousand dollars.

Yet, the legal profession also has a storied history of generosity. Indeed, doing legal work *pro bono*—without charging a fee—is part of the ethic of being a lawyer. The term *pro bono* comes from the Latin *pro bono publico*, which means "for the public good." When society confers the privilege to practice law on an individual, he or she accepts the duty to promote justice and make justice accessible to all people.

Following reinstatement of the death penalty in state after state beginning in 1976, America's death row population increased rapidly. Yet these convicted and sentenced prisoners—the majority of whom were illiterate and indigent—were effectively deprived of the assistance of a lawyer in mounting challenges to their convictions and sentences. There was an overwhelming need for lawyers who were willing to represent these defendants, especially during their final appeals.

A death penalty trial is the composite of two proceedings. The first determines guilt; the second decides the punishment. When a defendant is convicted of a capital offense—one that is death penalty eligible—the prosecution may seek imposition of the death penalty rather than years of imprisonment, if the case includes at least one "aggravating factor." Aggravating factors vary by state, but they commonly include the killing of a law enforcement officer acting in the line of duty, the killing of more than one person, or murder committed during a robbery.

Once the prosecution has established guilt of a capital offense beyond a reasonable doubt, the prosecution presents aggravating evidence—that is, reasons to execute the defendant. These might include prior violent acts. The defense presents "mitigating factors," reasons to punish with imprisonment rather than death. These may include family history or mental or physical health issues. After hearing the evidence of aggravating and mitigating factors, the jury makes a sentencing recommendation to the Judge. The Judge is the final arbiter of what sentence is imposed.

A defendant convicted and sentenced to death may appeal the guilt determination, the sentence, or both. Such appeals, often referred to as direct appeals, are heard by the appellate court. An unfavorable outcome on appeal may be further appealed to the state's highest court. After the state's final tribunal has ruled on a case, the defendant may ask the United States Supreme Court to review the case.

Most people know that criminal defendants have the constitutional right to have an attorney appointed for them at trial and during direct appeals if they are unable to afford one. Few people, however, are aware that additional legal remedies—known as collateral remedies—remain available to those convicted of crimes even after they have unsuccessfully exhausted all direct appeals of their convictions. And fewer still know that indigent convicts are orphaned as far as having legal representation provided so that they can meaningfully pursue these collateral remedies.

In general, the right to contest a criminal conviction and a sentence that have been upheld on direct appeal can be traced to the ancient writ of *habeas corpus*. A petition to a court for a writ of habeas corpus asserts that someone is being imprisoned unlawfully. If the court is sufficiently impressed by the claim, it issues the writ—which is essentially a summons addressed to the prisoner's custodian—demanding that the prisoner be brought before the court and that the custodian present proof of its authority to detain the prisoner. If the custodian is acting beyond its authority, then the prisoner must be released.

The United States inherited habeas corpus from English common law. The U.S. Constitution specifically includes the habeas procedure in the Suspension Clause, Article One, Section 9, Clause 2, which states: "The privilege of the writ of habeas corpus shall not be suspended, unless when in case of rebellion or invasion the public safety may require it."

For a convicted criminal, it is an appeal of virtually last resort. Thus, some of the most controversial presidential acts in history have been the suspension of habeas corpus by President Lincoln during the Civil War, by President Grant during Reconstruction, and by President Roosevelt during World War II. And it decidedly is not an opportunity to retry a case. Generally, in these post-conviction proceedings, it is permissible to raise only issues that were not or could not have been raised at trial or on appeal—such as the ineffective assistance of trial or appellate counsel, or matters arising from newly discovered evidence.

In the historic case of *Gideon v. Wainwright*, the Supreme Court read the Fourteenth Amendment as extending the Sixth Amendment's guarantee of a right to assistance of counsel to state court criminal defendants. In his unanimous opinion for the Court in *Gideon*, Justice Hugo Lafayette Black, who was a United States Senator from Alabama for a decade before assuming his role as an Associate Supreme Court Justice, held that the Constitution requires state courts to appoint attorneys for defendants who cannot afford counsel to defend them at trial.

The Court, however, did not extend the right of appointed counsel to prisoners seeking relief *after* trial, conviction, and direct appeals. This was made clear in the case of *Murray v. Giarratano*, which involved indigent Virginia death row inmates seeking to pursue post-conviction remedies. A plurality of Supreme Court Justices overturned rulings by a District Court Judge and the Fourth Circuit Court of Appeals sitting as a whole, holding instead that provision of counsel to pursue post-conviction, habeas-type relief was not constitutionally required.

The concurring opinion of Justice Kennedy nonetheless recognized not only the critical role that post-conviction proceedings play in death penalty litigation, but also the importance of counsel to an inmate's meaningful access to those proceedings:

> It cannot be denied that collateral relief proceedings are a central part of the review process for prisoners sentenced to death. As Justice Stevens observes [in dissent], a substantial portion of these prisoners succeed

in having their death sentences vacated in habeas corpus proceedings. The complexity of our jurisprudence in this area, moreover, makes it unlikely that capital defendants will be able to file successful petitions for collateral relief without the assistance of persons learned in the law.

Although some have lamented that the post-conviction appeal process is prone to abuse, the history of collateral review of capital cases has demonstrated its critical importance to the fair administration of justice. The number of death sentences that have been vacated at the federal level because of constitutional infirmity in state proceedings is notable. Some studies have shown that in noncapital cases, federal courts have granted relief less than 7 percent of the time, whereas in capital cases, the success rate has been estimated at 60 to 70 percent. This suggests an epidemic, rather than episodic, rate of error in capital cases. Given the finality of the penalty, the importance of meaningful access to post-conviction review cannot be overstated.

In 1986, the American Bar Association created the Death Penalty Representation Project to address this need. Headed by Esther Lardent, the Project sought to convince lawyers to volunteer on a pro bono basis to represent death row inmates in challenges to their convictions or sentences. Lardent, the daughter of Holocaust survivors who had emigrated to the United States, was driven to help others by a desire to repay the help her parents had received in this country. In Boston, Lardent worked for a low-income legal clinic, then headed the Boston Bar Association's Volunteer Lawyers Project, after which she moved to Washington, D.C., to lead the Project. She then became the founder of the Pro Bono Institute in 1996, where she served until her death at age sixty-eight in 2016. She was known as the "Queen of Pro Bono."

In a letter that was sent in the late 1980s to all members of the American Bar Association's Litigation Section, of which I was one, Esther Lardent acknowledged that some of the ABA's members favored the death penalty and some opposed it. Still, she argued, as lawyers we should all be in favor of the ability of individuals to meaningfully pursue rights that are available to them under the law. Thus, she asked counsel to volunteer to represent someone on death row: an inmate who had been tried, convicted, and sentenced to death and who had already lost all of his or her direct appeals.

The solicitation to meet my professional responsibilities in this manner had a trifecta of appeals to me. First, providing representation in such cases aligned with my moral beliefs. Second, few lawyers wanted condemned convicts for clients. And third, these were cases that most everyone thought could not be won. I sought permission from the leadership of Isham, Lincoln & Beale to volunteer. I shall forever be grateful that the firm fully endorsed the idea. I immediately volunteered to take one of these cases.

Would I be selected by the ABA's Death Penalty Representation Project to serve? I was an associate at a white-shoe law firm who had never tried or appealed a violent crime case, let alone a death penalty case. If I was selected, who might be my client? For what crime might my client have been sentenced? Where might my client be located while awaiting the state to put him to death?

All my questions would soon be answered.

CHAPTER TWO

The Client

On July 11, 1984, Tommy Hamilton killed Lehman Wood in Bankhead National Forest. That fact was well established before I ever heard about Tommy's case.

Tommy Lee Hamilton was born on May 24, 1964. He was raised in Hillsboro, Alabama, a rural town of no more than six hundred people, located a few miles west of Decatur. It is one of two majority-Black communities in its county. The Hamilton family was white.

Tommy was the youngest of Lucille and J. W. Hamilton's four children. He had two older sisters, Janice and Joyce, and one older brother, Jerry. Tommy had received the equivalent of a sixth-grade education, possessed an intelligence quotient that placed him in the category of borderline intellectual functioning, and had a history of minor trouble with the law—although none of those convictions had involved violence. His father, an alcoholic who worked for traveling-carnival operations, was often absent. When the father was home, he was physically and emotionally abusive. In one drunken outburst, he killed the family dog with a baseball bat before his children's eyes, made Tommy drag the dog's body away, and then tried to force Tommy to burn it. Many nights the family sought shelter from him by sleeping in a cotton field adjacent to the family home. The father often singled Tommy out. Noting that Lucille had broken the sequence of first-name alliteration in naming their youngest child and that Tommy's hair color differed from that of the other children, his father often questioned Tommy's parentage. On October 29, 1978, J. W. Hamilton died at age fifty-one, when he passed out from drinking and suffocated on his own vomit.

On July 3, 1984, Tommy Hamilton, age twenty, married his fifteen-year-old girlfriend, Debbie Gatlin. Because Debbie was a minor, under Alabama law she needed the permission of her mother to wed. To induce Debbie's mother to give them that permission, Tommy and Debbie told her that Debbie was pregnant by Tommy. It was a lie—but a lie that worked.

A little over a year earlier, Tommy had been convicted of third-degree burglary, and, while serving one year of his sentence in the Lawrence County Jail, he was granted the status of a "trusty." In general, a trusty is an inmate who has been sentenced to serve time in a county jail for a nonviolent crime and who has proven himself to be trust[worth]y. While usually housed in a jail cell with other inmates at night, trusties may run errands, assist with administrative tasks, or do work for the county outside the jail during the day—in effect, a work release program. While doing county time, Tommy was required to work for county official Lehman Wood. After being freed on parole, Tommy continued to perform odd jobs for Mr. Wood.

Lehman Vester Wood was a prominent if not beloved citizen of Moulton, Alabama—the county seat of Lawrence County, a mostly rural enclave nestled in the Tennessee River Valley in northwest Alabama. Moulton, a city of thirty-five hundred people, is concentrated along Alabama State Route 33, southwest of Decatur, and is just fifteen miles from Hillsboro. The median income for a family living in Moulton was modest, and about 15 percent of its population lived below the poverty line. The racial makeup of the town has always been predominantly white. Lehman Wood was white.

Wood, originally from Oneonta, Alabama, and Imogene A. "Jean" Allen, of Douglass, Alabama, met in June of 1944 and married a year later. They both graduated from Blount County High School. Wood was a World War II veteran. He was a gunner on a B-24 Liberator—an

American heavy bomber—in Italy. The four-engine aircraft was notorious among aircrews because it was difficult to fly and earned the moniker the "Flying Coffin." Wood was shot down in Austria in 1945 and was awarded the Purple Heart.

Wood, his wife, Jean, and their eight-year-old daughter, Charlotte, moved from Oneonta to Moulton on June 16, 1955. At that time, Wood was a Farm Bureau insurance agent. He then became a rural mail carrier for the post office, which brought him into daily contact with the residents on his route, and he became very involved in the community. He was an active member of the local Lion's Club and the American Legion. He was Vice President of the Moulton Boat Club. He also was a First Lieutenant in the Moulton National Guard Battalion and a member of the Moulton Rescue Squad.

By 1959, Wood became the owner of Moulton Sporting Goods, a retail store prominently located on the northwest corner of the town square. In August of 1962, he was appointed a Trustee on the Lawrence County High School Board of Education. Wood became the county's first full-time Civil Defense Director in February of 1977. Thereafter, he was given the title of Director of the Emergency Management Services Agency—the position he held at the time that Tommy Hamilton worked for him.

Lehman Wood died of two .30-30 gunshot wounds: one to the neck and one to the chest. The first bullet tore through the right side of his lower jaw, passed through his throat, and exited below the angle of his jaw on the left side. The second bullet went through his chest and straight into his heart. Either wound alone would have been fatal.

When Lawrence County Sheriff's Investigator James Ferris arrived at the scene of Wood's murder, witness Randall Curry, who had found the body and driven by the scene before the murder, described the occupants of the blue Ford Maverick he had seen parked by the road before Wood had arrived. From this description, Ferris somehow determined that the persons in the car were Tommy Hamilton; his fifteen-year-old wife of just seven days, Debbie Gatlin Hamilton; and one of Tommy's older sisters, twenty-seven-year-old Janice Hamilton Glasco. An all-points bulletin was issued for the Maverick and its occupants. At 7:00 p.m., Johnny Norton, a police officer from Trinity, Alabama, about thirty miles from the scene of the shooting, located the car and its occupants at a convenience store. Officer Norton advised his Chief of Police, Mike Durbin, and at approximately 8:30 p.m., the officers arrested the three suspects. As officers put Tommy and Debbie into separate cars, Tommy yelled to his wife: "Don't tell them a damn thing. Don't answer any questions."

At some point, Lehman Wood and his wife Jean had separated. A war hero and county official, there is reason to believe that he had a somewhat showy personality and reveled in his social status in Moulton. He was in the habit of carrying a quantity of money and had been seen with a large roll of currency, which included some hundred-dollar bills, both the day before and on the day of his murder. When his body was searched, there was only some change in a front pocket. A search of Janice Glasco's purse after her arrest revealed $226, which included two hundreds. A search of Debbie Hamilton revealed ten hundreds and one fifty. Tommy was found to have a single hundred-dollar bill.

A shotgun and some beer were discovered in the trunk of Janice's car. Hair found on the hood of the Maverick matched that of Lehman Wood. Blood and fatty tissue the same as that of Lehman Wood was also found splattered on the car. Blood stains consistent with Lehman Wood's blood type were found on the Maverick, on a Budweiser T-shirt found in the car, and on the denim jeans worn by Debbie Hamilton.

Officers at the Lawrence County Jail spoke to Tommy's seven-year-old nephew, Jason, who directed them to the Hillsboro residence of Tommy's mother, Lucille Hamilton. Mrs. Hamilton gave consent for the officers to search her property. Jason then led the officers to a log in some woods behind Lucille's house, under which they found a .30-30 caliber deer rifle and a box of .30-30 ammunition. A bullet from a test firing of this rifle was compared with a bullet found near Lehman Wood's body, and it was determined that both bullets were fired from a rifle with the same barrel characteristics. The bullet found at the scene, the bullet used in the test firing, and the box of ammunition found with the rifle were all the same brand of ammunition.

As the suspects were being questioned, the crime scene was investigated by Ed Weatherford, an investigator with the Lawrence County District Attorney's Office. Weatherford observed a large spot and a trail of blood on the ground where Wood had been dragged across the road. The distance from the blood spot to Wood's body was eight feet and eleven inches. There were blood splatters on the grill of Wood's truck, indicating that Wood had been shot the second time after he was dragged across the road. When officers recovered the .30-30 rifle, it was found to contain six rounds. Fully loaded, the same gun would hold eight rounds.

On September 26, 1984, Tommy Hamilton was indicted by the Grand Jury of Lawrence County for the murder of Lehman Wood during a robbery, a capital offense punishable by death. One month later, on October 24, Tommy—who had turned twenty years old in May—was denied treatment as a juvenile offender and required to face trial as an adult.

Tommy's trial took place in the Lawrence County Courthouse, which stood as the focal point of Moulton's town square. It was the third courthouse to be built in Lawrence County. The first, constructed of logs in 1820, consisted of three rooms and was destroyed by a fire in 1859. It was replaced with a two-story brick building that at one point housed Union soldiers who had been captured by Confederate forces. The current structure, built in 1936, features a main temple flanked on either side by a wing. The south side of the main section features a parapet with the following inscription: "The Eternal Laws of Justice Are Our Rule and Our Birth Right." The north side of the main block of the courthouse carries a similar parapet inscription, which reads: "Let Us Remember That Justice Must Be Observed Even To The Lowest."

The new courthouse in Moulton had seen some notable trials in its fifty-year history. Just four years earlier, sisters Marita McElwey and Robbie Jean McCorkle were found guilty of kidnapping and assault charges for tarring and feathering the fiancée of McElwey's ex-husband. Only hours before she was due to walk down the aisle with sixty-two-year-old physician John McElwey, forty-year-old registered nurse Elizabeth Jamieson, who had previously worked for the doctor, was viciously assaulted by the two women. Marita, fifty-three, had been married to Dr. McElwey for thirty years before divorcing him in 1976. She and Robbie Jean, forty-nine, forced their way into the home that the happy couple planned to share and held the bride-to-be at gunpoint. Thus began a brutal ritual of humiliation. First, the two sisters hacked off Elizabeth's dark waist-length hair. Then they stripped off her bridal clothes from the waist up and smeared thick black roofing tar on her body. Next, they emptied the feathers from a pillow over her head. Finally, the two women bundled their pathetic victim into their station wagon and abandoned her at a garbage dump seven miles out of town. The two assailants cackled with laughter as they were hauled off to jail. Two days after her horrifying ordeal, Elizabeth—free of tar and wearing a short brown wig—became the new Mrs. John McElwey. On September 23, 1981, the assailants were criminally convicted and sentenced for the attack.

On the date of Lehman Wood's murder, retired minister Jewel Dutton was south of Moulton at Smother's Store, a grocery with an attached lawnmower shop. At Tommy's trial, Dutton testified that Lehman Wood had stopped by Smother's at 5:00 p.m., bought a Coca-Cola and a pack of cigarettes, and told Dutton that "Janice and them had had some car trouble up on the mountain," and that they had called him and wanted him to go out there.

At trial, Tommy was represented by court-appointed defense counsel and testified in his own defense. His testimony established that he worked for Lehman Wood and that his sister Janice had dated the fifty-nine-year-old victim and lived with him for a time. Tommy testified that he hadn't gone to work that day for Wood as he was supposed to do. Rather, he was drinking and taking pills and riding around with his sister, his wife, and his sister's son, Jason. He stated that he had put some beer in the trunk of his sister's automobile—along with a gun that he intended to sell.

Tommy testified that Janice had called Wood because she wanted to spend the afternoon and have a few beers with him in the forest at Brushy Lake. They were to meet him at Ridge Road. Tommy testified that when they got to Ridge Road, he hid the gun in the woods because he did not want Wood to ask for a beer and see the gun in the trunk. Tommy was afraid that if Wood saw the gun, he would turn Tommy in for violating the terms of his parole.

Tommy testified that when Wood arrived, they got into an argument over what Wood had paid Tommy when Tommy had done work for him. According to Tommy, Wood told him that "a sorry son-of-a-bitch like you don't deserve no more" before suddenly saying "I'll kill you" and putting his hand in his pocket. Tommy testified that he ran into the woods, picked up the rifle, and shot Wood. Tommy could not recall shooting Wood a second time.

Also testifying at Tommy's two-week-long trial was Jimmy Dale Owens, a trusty at the Lawrence County Jail when Tommy was there awaiting trial for Wood's murder. Owens testified that while he and Tommy were in the jail together, Tommy confided that when Wood "got out of the truck, I shot him. I shot him in the neck. It was a damn good shot, wasn't it?" Owens also testified that Tommy revealed that after he shot Wood, he had his wife, Debbie, and his sister Janice drag the body out of the way. According to Owens, Tommy also said that Janice told him that she didn't believe Wood was dead—so Tommy shot him again to make sure. According to Owens, Tommy proclaimed that "[the] son-of-a-bitch deserved dying" and that he would do it all over again.

On August 30, 1985, the jury of eight men and four women charged with hearing the guilt phase of Tommy's trial deliberated just thirty-five minutes before handing in its verdict form to Judge Billy C. Burney. Tommy grimaced, then looked at the jury, as Judge Burney read the unanimous verdict finding Tommy guilty of the capital offense of intentional murder committed during a robbery.

Two sentences were possible for conviction of a capital crime in Alabama: life in prison without the possibility of parole; and death. In the sentencing phase of the trial, Tommy's mother, Lucille, his brother, Jerry, his sister-in-law, Faye, and a family friend named Alvie Little all offered testimony about Tommy's upbringing in an attempt to spare Tommy the death penalty. Tommy burst into tears when his mother testified that her husband "died drunk" in 1978 when Tommy was fifteen years old. "He was just an ordinary teenager without a father," she said. "If he hadn't been drinking and drugged up, he would have never hurt nobody. That's no excuse but he would have never hurt nobody."

Whereas a unanimous jury verdict was required to convict Tommy, Alabama law required that only ten of twelve jurors needed to recommend a death sentence for it to be considered and possibly imposed by the Judge. A bare majority of jurors could recommend a sentence of life imprisonment. After less than thirty minutes of deliberation, the jury returned a sentencing recommendation of death by electrocution by a vote of 10 to 2.

It takes longer than thirty minutes to do many mundane things: to get a crown on your tooth, to get your driver's license, to wait for the Chinese food you just ordered to be delivered to your house. But in less than half an hour, a jury had voted to recommend that the state should end this twenty-one-year-old's life.

Tommy's fate now rested solely in Judge Burney's hands.

CHAPTER THREE

The Punishment

Only a decade before Judge Burney weighed his decision about Tommy's fate, the death penalty would not even have been an option. Despite the brief hiatus from 1972 until 1976, though, capital punishment has a long and checkered history in American jurisprudence.

When the first European settlers came to America, they brought their practice of capital punishment with them. Laws regarding the death penalty varied from colony to colony. In 1612, Virginia Deputy-Governor Sir Thomas Dale expanded the list of capital offenses covered by the *Articles, Lawes, and Orders, Divine, Politique, and Martial* to provide the death penalty for offenses such as stealing grapes, killing chickens, and trading with Indians. The New York Colony instituted the Duke of York's "Code of 1665," which made several Puritanical offenses, such as striking one's mother or father, or denying the "true God," punishable by death.

The first person known to be executed in the territory of the future United States of America was Captain George Kendall of Jamestown, in the colony of Virginia. He was accused of spying against Britain for Spain, and a firing squad shot him to death in early 1608.

Jane Champion was the first woman executed in the new colonies. In 1632, a Virginia grand jury indicted Champion on charges of slaying and concealing the death of her child, who was allegedly fathered by William Gallopin and not Champion's husband. Gallopin, who aided in the infanticide, also was sentenced to the gallows.

While thousands of extra-judicial lynchings of Indigenous and Black people occurred in early American history, the first legally sanctioned execution of a Native American occurred on October 30, 1639. Military authorities hung and then beheaded Nepauduck, a Pequot, in New Haven County, Connecticut, after he allegedly confessed that he had killed four white settlers, severed their hands as trophies, and abducted a white child during the Pequot War between 1636 and 1638.

In doing research for this book, I was unprepared to discover that one of my own ancestors was among the first settlers to be executed in Colonial America. William Cheney, Jr., a seven-times great-grandfather on my mother's side of my family, voyaged to America as an infant with his parents. They came from either the Netherlands or England and settled in Roxbury, Massachusetts, in approximately 1635. He married Deborah Wiswall, daughter of John Wiswall, sometime before 1661. Cheney had an affair with Sarah Daniels, the daughter of Robert and Elizabeth Daniels, resulting in the birth of a child, William (probably surnamed Daniels), on August 3, 1666. Cheney and Deborah seem to have separated for a time, given that his father's will (dated April 20, 1667) left all his land in Medfield to his son on the condition that William "and his wife Deborah be reconciled and live together." The will provided that if William rejected this condition, then twenty pounds were to be paid to John Wiswall of Boston instead.

In August of 1681, Cheney was indicted for raping an unmarried maidservant "contrary to the peace of our Soueraigne Lord the king his Croune & dignity the lawes of God & of this Jurisdiction." The indictment helpfully added that he failed to have "the feare of God before thy eyes," and his actions were "Instigated by the divill." The alleged victim, Experience Holdbrook (daughter of Joseph and Elizabeth), had been living with the Cheney family. When he was arrested, Cheney allegedly compounded his crime by stabbing the constable and attempting to escape on the official's horse. During his trial, Cheney pled not guilty, and his wife portrayed Experience Holdbrook as a "lying wench." Nevertheless, the jury found Cheney guilty of rape, and the Governor sentenced him to hang on September 21, 1681.

Unbeknown to Cheney, the authorities had arranged a reprieve for him conditioned upon his showing remorse. When Cheney refused to listen to the execution sermon preached by Reverend Cotton Mather—not yet a famous Puritan minister, only seventeen years old, and serving as an assistant to his father at Boston's North Church—his fate was sealed. He was hanged as much for his obstinacy as for his crime.

With the encouragement of the selfsame Reverend Mather and in reliance on Exodus 22:18, which commanded that "Thou shalt not suffer a witch to live," fourteen women and five men were hanged for the crime of witchcraft at Salem, Massachusetts, between July 10 and September 22, 1692. The suspects, who ranged in age from five to nearly eighty, had been accused of sorcery by mischievous girls who hysterically told juries that they were being tormented by ghosts summoned by the defendants. Those of the accused who admitted consorting with the Devil were spared, leaving only those who professed innocence to be hanged. The first to be hanged was Bridget Bishop, who protested that she did not even know what a witch was; she was followed to the gallows by five more women, including Rebecca Nurse, a seventy-one-year-old invalid mother of eight.

The 1700s saw an increase in human rights advocacy, and Europe became a hotbed of opposition to the death penalty. An abolitionist movement found its roots in the writings of European philosophers such as Montesquieu, Voltaire, and Bentham, and the English Quakers John Bellers and John Howard. However, it was Cesare Beccaria's 1767 essay, *On Crimes and Punishment*—which posited that there is no justification for the state to take a life—that had an especially strong impact throughout the world.

In 1779, the first attempt to reform the death penalty in the United States occurred when a committee led by Thomas Jefferson submitted Bill 64 to the Virginia Assembly, as Virginia made the legal transition from colony to commonwealth. The legislation put its primary objective right in the title—"A Bill for Proportioning Crimes and Punishments in Cases Heretofore Capital"—and then plainly stated that the death penalty "should be the last melancholy resource against those whose existence has become inconsistent with the safety of their fellow citizens." The bill proposed that capital punishment be available only for the crimes of murder and treason. It was defeated in the Virginia House of Delegates by a single vote. (The prospect of punishing horse thieves with only three years at hard labor rather than death seems to have played a large role in the outcome.)

Dr. Benjamin Rush, a Philadelphia physician, signer of the Declaration of Independence, and founder of the Pennsylvania Prison Society, also sought reform. Rush challenged the belief that the death penalty serves as a deterrent. He gained the support of Benjamin Franklin and William Bradford, Pennsylvania's Attorney General. Bradford, later appointed by George Washington to be the young nation's second Attorney General, led Pennsylvania to become the first state to consider degrees of murder based on culpability. In 1794, Pennsylvania repealed the death penalty for all offenses except first-degree murder.

In the early nineteenth century, some Americans began advocating for abolition of the death penalty. The high-water mark of their efforts came in the 1830s with the enactment of statutes barring public hanging by Rhode Island, Pennsylvania, New York, Massachusetts, and New Jersey. The public character of executions had been thought to be central to their expressive power and deterrent effect. From the beginning of the Mexican War in 1846 through the Civil War and its aftermath, a nation preoccupied with its self-preservation paid little attention to the subject of capital punishment.

National interest in the issue was revived when New York chose electrocution to replace hanging as the means of execution. In 1888, a state commission searching for a humane alternative to hanging deemed electrocution "instantaneous and painless" and "devoid of all barbarism." It proved otherwise for William Kemmler who, on August 6, 1890, in Auburn, New York, was the first person to die in an electric chair. Kemmler had been convicted of murdering a woman with a hatchet. A *New York Times* reporter who covered the execution deemed it "a disgrace to civilization." The correspondent for the *Boston Daily Globe* deemed it "[m]ore fearful than anything ever beheld at the most barbarous hanging."

A new wave of reform followed. On March 29, 1897, Colorado abolished the death penalty, leading a march of nine other states that followed suit in the ensuing two decades: Kansas in 1907; Minnesota in 1911; Washington in 1913; Oregon in 1914; North Dakota, South Dakota, and Tennessee in 1915; Arizona in 1916; and Missouri in 1917. The onset of World War I reversed this trend. Animosity toward foreigners, fear of radicals, and anticipation of an increase in crime induced states to reconsider. By 1920, eight of those states—all but Minnesota and South Dakota—had reinstated capital punishment.

In the 1958 case of *Trop v. Dulles*, the United States Supreme Court found that the Eighth Amendment's prohibition against "cruel and unusual punishments" embraced an "evolving standard of decency that marked the progress of a maturing society." *Trop* was not a death penalty case; rather, the Court ruled that stripping a military deserter of citizenship constituted cruel and unusual punishment. Nonetheless, the introduction of an "evolving standard of decency" analysis provided the intellectual basis upon which to formulate the jurisprudence governing administration of the death penalty in the United States.

The Supreme Court thereafter became a key player in America's evolving stance on capital punishment. The Court tackled problems associated with the role of jurors and their discretion in capital cases by deciding the consolidated cases of *Crampton v. Ohio* and *McGautha v. California* (1971). The defendants argued it was a violation of their Fourteenth Amendment right to due process for jurors to have unbound discretion in deciding whether capital crime defendants should live or die, and that such standardless decision-making resulted in arbitrary and capricious sentencing. Crampton also argued that it was unconstitutional to have his guilt and sentence determined in a single set of deliberations, as the jurors in his case were instructed that a first-degree murder conviction would automatically result in a death sentence. The Court, however, rejected these claims, thereby giving its blessing to unfettered jury discretion and a single proceeding to determine both guilt and punishment. The Court stated that it was "beyond present human ability . . . to provide a rational basis for distinguishing [the] characteristics of criminal homicides and their perpetrators which call for the death penalty."

The constitutionality of the death penalty was revisited by the Supreme Court in 1972 in the cases of *Furman v. Georgia*, *Jackson v. Georgia*, and *Branch v. Texas*. Furman, like McGautha, argued that capital cases resulted in capricious sentencing. Unlike the *McGautha* case (a due process claim under the Fourteenth Amendment), the *Furman* case was a challenge brought under the "cruel and unusual punishment" clause of the Eighth Amendment. This approach proved more fruitful for the challenger.

Notably, each of the nine Justices wrote his own opinion in *Furman*. The collection of opinions comprised 66,233 words spread over several hundred pages—the longest decision handed down by the Court at the time. While most of the four dissenters joined in each other's opinions, the five-person majority was united in the outcome of the case but shared no common rationale. The Court found that Georgia's death penalty statute, which was typical of those throughout the country in that it gave the jury complete sentencing discretion, produced arbitrary outcomes. The result was an irreversible punishment capriciously applied. The majority therefore held that the process by which capital punishment was imposed under the statute was "cruel and unusual" and violated the Eighth Amendment. Thus, on June 29, 1972, a majority of the Supreme Court effectively voided forty state death penalty statutes, thereby commuting the sentences of 629 death row inmates around the country and suspending the death penalty in new cases because existing statutes were no longer valid.

Although the opinions of Justices Brennan and Marshall stated that the death penalty was inherently unconstitutional, the overall holding in *Furman* was that the death penalty statutes as written were unconstitutional. The Court thereby invited states to rewrite their death penalty statutes to eliminate the capriciousness cited in *Furman*. As Chief Justice Burger noted in his dissent, the states had "the opportunity and indeed unavoidable responsibility" to reconsider their death penalty statutes. Advocates of capital punishment quickly proposed new statutes that they believed would remove the obstacle of arbitrariness in capital sentencing. Led by Florida, which in a special legislative session passed a new law less than six months after *Furman* was decided, thirty-five states proceeded to enact new death penalty statutes.

To address the unconstitutionality of unguided jury discretion, some states removed all discretion by mandating capital punishment for those convicted of capital crimes. To no avail: the Supreme Court held this practice to be unconstitutional in the 1976 case of *Woodson v. North Carolina.*

Other states sought to limit discretion by providing sentencing guidelines for the Judge and jury when deciding whether to impose death. The guidelines allowed for the introduction of evidence of aggravating and mitigating factors in determining sentencing. These guided discretion statutes were approved in 1976 by the Supreme Court in *Gregg v. Georgia, Proffitt v. Florida,* and *Jurek v. Texas,* collectively referred to as the *Gregg* decision. This landmark ruling upheld new death penalty statutes in Florida, Georgia, and Texas as constitutional. The Court also held that the death penalty could be a constitutionally permissible penalty under the Eighth Amendment.

In addition to sentencing guidelines, three other procedural reforms were approved by the Court in *Gregg.* The first was bifurcated trials, in which there are separate deliberations for the guilt and penalty phases of the trial. Only after the jury has determined that the defendant is guilty of capital murder does it decide in a second trial whether the defendant should be sentenced to death or given a lesser sentence of time in prison. Another reform was the automatic appellate review of convictions and sentences. The final procedural reform from *Gregg* was proportionality review, a practice that helps the state to identify and eliminate sentencing disparities.

Despite the invitation extended by the "evolving standard of decency" analysis in *Trop,* the Supreme Court and the nation seemed to be engaged less with the moral appropriateness of the death penalty and more with the means and manner by which the death penalty would be imposed. True, subsequent cases would occasionally preclude imposition of the death penalty as *per se* "cruel and unusual" and therefore unconstitutional for certain categories of crime (for example, *Coke v. Georgia*—death penalty is an unconstitutional punishment for rape of an adult woman when the victim is not killed; and *Ford v. Wainwright*—execution of an insane person is banned). Still, both the Court and popular culture focused more on the mechanics of death. For example, Oklahoma in 1977 became the first state to adopt lethal injection as a means of execution. And public support for the death penalty surged after *Gregg*, undoubtedly because the public then believed that the Court had "fixed" the death penalty system.

As a college student from 1972 through 1976, I was engaged by the intellectual debate about rationales for the death penalty. I read countless essays by Ernest van den Haag and others arguing the merits of such utilitarian justifications as incapacitation and deterrence. I devoured rebuttals by Hugo Bedau and was fascinated with *Cruel and Unusual*, Michael Meltsner's history of the NAACP Legal Defense Fund's campaign against the death penalty. I absorbed theological and historical interpretations of God's command to Noah in Genesis 9:6 that "whoever sheds human blood, by humans shall their blood be shed;" the *Lex talionis*, or law of retaliation, whereby a punishment resembles the offense committed in kind and degree, such as the *"eye for an eye, tooth for a tooth . . . life for life"* of Exodus 21:23–24; and the dictate of the Ten Commandments that "thou shall not murder." I was fascinated by arguments over whether the retributive extinction of a human life could ever be morally justifiable. But even if there existed cases where the death penalty might be warranted, I felt strongly that the accused must be granted every possible protection afforded under the law before the state meted out such a cruel and final punishment.

———

When *Furman* was decided in 1972, there were twenty-three people on Alabama's death row who had been convicted under a death penalty statute that allocated significant discretion to the jury. Forced to apply the new *Furman* standard, the Alabama Supreme Court had no choice but to find that statute unconstitutional and commute the twenty-three sentences from death to life imprisonment. Afterward, the Alabama legislature passed and Governor George Wallace signed (on March 25, 1976) a revised death penalty statute. The first execution under the new law was carried out in 1983.

John Louis Evans III was born in Beaumont, Texas, on January 4, 1950. After his 1976 parole from an Indiana prison, Evans and fellow convict Wayne Ritter embarked on a crime spree. Evans admitted to committing over thirty armed robberies, nine kidnappings, and two extortion schemes in two months and across seven states. On January 5, 1977, he and Ritter robbed and killed Edward Nassar, a pawnshop owner in Mobile, Alabama. They fled but were captured on March 7 by FBI agents in Little Rock, Arkansas. Among the evidence recovered was the gun used to shoot Nassar in the back and another gun stolen from the pawnshop.

Although Evans gave a detailed confession, prosecutors refused to accept his plea of guilty because they wanted him sentenced to death— something allowed under Alabama law only following conviction by a jury. On April 26, 1977, Evans was tried in Mobile Circuit Court for first-degree murder committed during a robbery. During the trial, Evans again admitted to his crime, stating that he did not feel remorse and would kill again under the same circumstances. Furthermore, in an act that would reasonably call into question his sanity, he threatened that if the jury did not sentence him to death, he would escape and murder each of them. The jury convicted Evans of capital murder as charged and recommended a sentence of death after deliberating for less than fifteen minutes. The trial Judge sentenced Evans to die, and this sentence was confirmed by both the Alabama Court of Criminal Appeals and the Alabama Supreme Court. His execution was scheduled for April 6, 1979.

Just four days before he was scheduled to die, Evans's mother, Betty, acting as a "next friend," petitioned the United States District Court for the Southern District of Alabama for a writ of habeas corpus, arguing that the conviction was unconstitutional because the jury had not been offered the possibility of finding Evans guilty of a lesser included offense. The District Court dismissed her application on the grounds that she did not have standing to bring the claim. She appealed to the United States Court of Appeals for the Fifth Circuit, which overturned the District Court's decision. But this favorable outcome was in turn reversed by the United States Supreme Court, and Evans was once again scheduled to be executed. Justices William Brennan and Thurgood Marshall dissented in part, because they outright opposed the death penalty on the grounds that it was cruel and unusual punishment and therefore prohibited by the Eighth and Fourteenth Amendments to the Constitution.

In July, Evans fired his attorneys and filed a motion to dismiss all further appeals. The courts acceded to his request on October 19, 1982. Despite this, Evans still almost avoided execution.

Alabama's Governor, George Wallace, was greatly changed following Arthur Bremer's attempt to assassinate him in 1972. After recovering from his wounds, Wallace declared himself born again. He recanted his segregationist views, and his private reservations about the death penalty evolved into complete opposition. On the eve of Evans's execution, a tearful Wallace telephoned Lieutenant Governor Bill Baxley to say that he had been up all night "praying the Bible" and could not bring himself to sign the warrant authorizing Evans's execution. Baxley told Wallace that if Wallace called off the execution, he would hold a press conference in the morning to brand the commutation a farce. A cowed Wallace signed the death warrant, and Evans was executed at Holman Prison near Atmore, Alabama, on April 22, 1983.

The execution was botched. It was carried out using an electric chair that had been constructed in 1927 at Alabama's Kilby Prison by inmate Ed Mason, a master carpenter by trade who was serving a sixty-year sentence for theft and grand larceny. The chair was nicknamed "Yellow Mama" because of its distinctive traffic-yellow coat of paint, which was used because it was readily available from the Alabama Highway Department. The first use of Yellow Mama had been to execute Horace DeVaughan on April 8, 1927. The chair had not been used since 1965 due to the effective moratorium on the death penalty imposed by the United States Supreme Court.

Two months after the state of Alabama executed John Evans, his electrocution was described this way by his attorney, Russell F. Canan:

> . . . the first jolt of 1,900 volts of electricity passed through Mr. Evans' body . . . A large puff of greyish smoke and sparks poured out from under the hood that covered Evans' face. An overpowering stench of burnt flesh [pervaded] the witness room. Two doctors examined Mr. Evans and declared that he was not dead.

This horrific scene was also witnessed by reporter Mark Harris, who wrote a first-person account for United Press International that was published on May 4, 1983. He reported what transpired after what was supposed to be an instantaneously lethal dose of electricity:

> Two doctors filed out of the witness room to examine the body and pronounce Evans dead.
>
> The prison doctor, dressed in a blue surgical costume and tan loafers with tassels, placed a stethoscope to the smock, turned and nodded—the natural sign for "Yes, he's dead."
>
> But the nod meant that he had found a heartbeat. The other doctor confirmed the gruesome discovery.

Evans's attorney recorded what happened next:

> At 8:33 p.m. Mr. Evans was administered a second thirty-second jolt of electricity. More smoke emanated from his leg and head. Again . . . he was still alive.
>
> I asked the Prison Commissioner . . . to request clemency on the grounds that Mr. Evans was being subjected to cruel and unusual punishment. The request was denied.
>
> [A] third charge of electricity . . . was passed through Mr. Evans' body. At 8:44, the doctors pronounced him dead. The execution of John Evans took fourteen minutes.

It was this potentially grisly manner of death that Judge Burney was forced to consider after the jury's verdict in Tommy Hamilton's case. The Judge was not bound by the jury's sentencing recommendation; he was legally obligated to independently review the case and consider both aggravating and mitigating circumstances before passing sentence. However, apparently Tommy's jailers were confident as to what Judge Burney would decide. On September 6, 1985, while still waiting for the Judge's decision, they moved Tommy from the Lawrence County Jail to a cell on death row at Alabama's Holman Prison. And they did not put Tommy in just any death row cell. They housed him temporarily in *the* death cell, the cell immediately adjacent to the electric chair, where condemned prisoners are housed the week before their scheduled execution.

After conducting the sentencing hearing—with the jury's recommendation in mind and a mental health evaluation of Tommy, conducted by the staff at the Taylor-Hardin Secure Medical Facility, in hand—Judge Burney found two aggravating factors. First, the capital offense of murder was committed by Tommy while he was already under a sentence of imprisonment. Second, the murder was committed by Tommy during a robbery. Regarding mitigating circumstances, Judge Burney found that "there were none shown, nor proven." And the Judge stated that he gave the jury's advisory verdict "solemn deliberation in determining the weight to be attached" to it.

On September 25, 1985, a mere three months after Tommy's twenty-first birthday, Judge Billy C. Burney sentenced Tommy Hamilton to death by electrocution.

Although Debbie Hamilton and Janice Glasco were also indicted for the capital murder of Lehman Wood, each was treated differently and prosecuted separately from Tommy. Having seen her husband convicted of capital murder and sentenced to death, Debbie Hamilton—now sixteen years old—undoubtedly was terrified about her potential fate, especially since she had dragged Wood's body across the road and had been found in possession of the most stolen money. She likely also did not relish the idea of life in prison without the possibility of parole, the only sentencing alternative to death following conviction of a capital offense.

Debbie had been sexually exploited by jail personnel since the day of her arrest. After Debbie informed Tommy about what was happening, the couple hatched a plan to use Debbie as literal "jailbait" to escape. Shortly before 3:00 a.m. on October 16, 1984—about three months after the murder—Debbie uncharacteristically did not object to a jailer entering the women's cell where she was being held. When the cell door was opened, she evaded the guard and locked him inside the cell, after which she proceeded to free Tommy from a two-man cell on the second floor. Barefoot, Tommy and Debbie scrambled down the fire escape and fled.

Law enforcement immediately launched a manhunt for the fugitive couple. About twelve hours later, Sheriff's Deputy Kenneth Goodwin found Debbie and Tommy crouching under a bush in a wooded area of Moulton, about a mile from the jail. Tommy hollered, "Don't shoot; I'm not armed!" They were quickly reincarcerated. Perhaps to avoid having to explain a 3:00 a.m. entry into Debbie's cell and mitigate the embarrassment of the ensuing escape, jail staff concocted a story that Tommy had overpowered them with a black broom handle disguised as a gun.

Debbie, like Tommy, was represented by court-appointed defense counsel. She pled guilty to the lesser charge of murder (as opposed to capital murder), agreed to testify during Janice's trial, and was sentenced to life in prison. Under the terms of her agreement, conviction, and sentence, Debbie was eligible for parole, but it was not likely to come until after years, if not decades, in prison. And it was certainly not guaranteed.

Janice Glasco had somehow retained Don Holt, one of the most experienced and successful criminal defense attorneys in the state of Alabama, to represent her despite her indigent status. On October 26, 1985, after trial before a jury, she was found guilty of manslaughter. "None of the evidence substantiated" a conviction on anything more serious than manslaughter, said jury foreman James W. Jones, a Methodist minister. On November 20, she was sentenced to ten years in prison. Under the terms of her conviction and sentence, Janice also was eligible for parole.

Under Alabama's new death penalty law, all capital sentences had to be reviewed by a higher court. On September 9, 1986, the Alabama Court of Criminal Appeals unanimously affirmed Tommy's capital conviction and sentence of death. On January 27, 1987, it denied a request to rehear the case. That judgment was subsequently affirmed unanimously by the Alabama Supreme Court on November 6, 1987. On February 12, 1988, it too declined to rehear the case. On October 3, 1988, the United States Supreme Court declined to hear Tommy's case.

With all his direct appeals exhausted and the United States Supreme Court denying his petition for review, only one judicial avenue remained by which Tommy could challenge his conviction and sentence of death: post-conviction review. However, with no money to retain private counsel and no right to have an attorney appointed to represent him, he faced the prospect of instituting this complicated, multilayered legal process—and of death, should the process prove unavailing—alone.

CHAPTER FOUR

The Legal Team

A s Tommy's situation worsened, my professional life was in tumult. Perhaps ominously, on Friday the 13th of June 1986, the then biggest law-firm merger in Chicago history was announced. While retaining its name, the century-old firm of Isham, Lincoln & Beale, with 180 lawyers, combined with the eight-year-old firm of Reuben & Proctor, with 80 lawyers.

An unwelcome amalgam of contrasting cultures and personalities, the combination of Isham, Lincoln & Beale and Reuben & Proctor was doomed from the start. Reuben & Proctor was the child of the bold— some would say brash—managing partner Don Reuben, who had so alienated his partners when he was at the law firm of Kirkland & Ellis that they effectively dismissed him one day as he vacationed in Europe. After the merger, an Isham partner is said to have smirked: "It was a shotgun wedding of first-rate introverts with second-rate extroverts." Indeed, little thought and even less effort went into merging the divergent personalities of the two firms.

The merged firms unraveled within a year amid rancor, recriminations, and remorse. I was one of the last lawyers to leave. Loyal perhaps to a fault, for months I had observed with increasing frustration the exodus of colleagues and friends who sought professional shelter at other law firms in the city. It became increasingly apparent that Chicago's blue-chip legal community had only so much capacity to absorb the more than two hundred lawyers who might be exiting from the new (and not improved) Isham, Lincoln & Beale. I had a wife and two children, ages six and three. I had corporate clients of my own and aspirations to do litigation of significance. So, in January of 1988, I moved my practice to the firm of McDermott, Will & Emery.

Founded in 1934 by attorneys Edward H. McDermott and William M. Emery, McDermott, Will & Emery initially specialized in tax law. A corporate-law department was established when Howard H. Will joined the firm in 1941. By the time I joined the firm as a litigation partner, McDermott, Will & Emery had over 150 lawyers and was a full-service law firm. Headquartered in Chicago, the firm also had offices in Boston, Los Angeles, Miami, and Washington, D.C.

After 116 years of distinguished service, Isham, Lincoln & Beale, the law firm born from the ashes of the Great Chicago Fire of 1871, went up in flames of its own making and formally dissolved on April 30, 1988.

It was amid this professional chaos and personal upheaval that Esther Lardent of the ABA Death Penalty Representation Project contacted me. Tommy Hamilton had lost his appeals to the Alabama Court of Criminal Appeals and the Alabama Supreme Court, and just a few days earlier the United States Supreme Court had refused to hear his case. She told me that, if I remained willing to volunteer to represent a death row inmate in post-conviction proceedings, I had been selected to represent Tommy Hamilton. An execution date had yet to be set. The twenty cells on death row at Holman Prison, where executions were performed, were full, so Alabama had created a second death row with an additional twenty-four cells at its West Jefferson Correctional Facility in Bessemer, Alabama, near Birmingham. That is where I would be able to find Tommy.

Esther Lardent had done her job. She had found a lawyer willing to be lead counsel on a pro bono basis to represent one of the more than twenty-six hundred convicts then on America's death rows. Now it was time for me to do my job.

I was thirty-four years old, and nine years out of law school, when I agreed to serve as Tommy Hamilton's post-conviction counsel. The leadership of the McDermott law firm was less than enthusiastic about my decision. At a meeting of its Pro Bono Committee, a motion of approval passed by a single vote—contingent on the understanding that I would have to do the work on my own time and not let it materially reduce the number of hours that I billed to clients of the firm. Also, I would have to cover any expenses in defending Tommy out of my own pocket. Luke DeGrand was a junior associate whom I highly respected. He had obtained his bachelor of arts degree from the University of Illinois in 1982. He graduated magna cum laude from the university's law school in 1985 and served as an associate editor on its law review. Luke was as smart as they come and had followed me to the McDermott firm from Isham, Lincoln & Beale. He joined me on Tommy's case as well.

While I was licensed to practice law only by the Supreme Court of Illinois, I was accustomed to representing clients in other states. My work for corporate clients with nationwide interests had already led to my being admitted to appear before the federal Circuit Courts of Appeals for both the Third Circuit (with jurisdiction over federal district courts in Delaware, New Jersey, and Pennsylvania and the territorial court of the Virgin Islands) and the Seventh Circuit (with jurisdiction over federal district courts in Illinois, Indiana, and Wisconsin). Motions *pro hac vice* ("for this occasion only") for permission to appear in a state court located outside the state of licensure were regularly granted. Those courts usually required a representation that this would not be a frequent occurrence, as well as affiliation with a local attorney who was admitted to practice law in that state.

Beyond the ethical and regulatory requirements, engaging local counsel was just plain wise. These attorneys provided invaluable insights into the practices of local courts and the preferences or demands of their Judges. And even beyond strategy, engaging local counsel in Tommy's case was imperative for logistical reasons. I needed someone in Alabama who, on a moment's notice, could attend a court appearance, file a pleading, and simply lessen the number of trips I would have to make to Alabama—thereby saving some of the attendant expense.

Esther Lardent had explained to me that her efforts to procure an Alabama lawyer as Tommy's lead counsel failed for two reasons. First, Alabama does not provide meaningful compensation for attorneys who volunteer to represent clients in capital post-conviction proceedings. Second, the cases are so notorious, and so politically charged locally, that any Alabama practitioner handling such a case risks becoming a pariah. Nevertheless, I strongly believed that it was imperative to have the assistance of local counsel, so I begged Esther to find me someone. Of course, just like the state of Alabama, neither I nor my client would be able to pay that "someone" for these services.

After a bit of time passed, Esther contacted me with the good news that she was able to find an Alabama attorney who was willing to help. She introduced me to Lynn McKenzie. More completely, she introduced me to *Sister* Lynn McKenzie, a Benedictine nun at Sacred Heart Monastery in Cullman, Alabama.

The Benedictines, officially the Order of Saint Benedict, are a monastic Catholic religious order of monks and nuns; it was founded in the year 529 by Benedict of Nursia. In 1852, a small group of Benedictine sisters from St. Walburg Abbey in Bavaria (then a kingdom, now a part of Germany) traveled to St. Marys, Pennsylvania, where they formed the first Benedictine women's community in the United States. Other communities of Benedictine women in the United States were founded in turn, including in Kentucky and Florida. Eight sisters from each of these two communities came together on April 20, 1902, to form the Benedictine Sisters of Cullman, Alabama. On March 21, 1903, the sisters in Alabama purchased 123.5 acres and broke ground that October for the construction of their convent's first building.

Verse 17 in chapter 58 of the Rule of Saint Benedict states the solemn promises, known as the Benedictine Vow, that candidates for reception into a Benedictine community are required to make: a promise of stability, that is to remain in the same community; conversion to a monastic manner of life; and obedience to God, as particularly expressed through the community's superior.

The Benedictine Sisters of Cullman, Alabama, embody the spiritual wisdom and monastic tradition of St. Benedict through lives of prayer and ministry. Their ministry is both within the monastic community and to the world at large. Indeed, the Benedictine motto is

Ora et labora: prayer and work. These external ministries take many forms. Some sisters are teachers, some are health-care professionals, and some, like Lynn, are lawyers.

Lynn Marie McKenzie, a self-described "cradle Catholic," was born on June 20, 1958, in Mobile, Alabama—one of the eight children and the third of four daughters of Tom and Charlotte McKenzie. The family moved to Gadsden, Alabama, when she was ten years old. Lynn attended the University of Alabama, graduating a semester early with a degree in political science, and started law school there the following fall. Before enrolling in law school, she visited convents in different parts of the country. She had always thought about becoming a nun, but not many of her friends knew of her interest. Lynn attended law school for one semester and then left to follow her religious calling.

Sister Lynn thought she had left the law behind, until her fellow sisters asked whether she would like to return to law school. In January of 1983, she reenrolled at the University of Alabama and graduated two years later. Her law practice at the Knight & Griffith law firm in Cullman focused on working with children and the disabled. She did a lot of work in juvenile court with kids who had gotten into trouble. She also served as *guardian ad litem*—a person appointed by the court to represent the best interests of a ward—for abused and neglected children. In Lynn's view, "There is no more important work than the life of a child."

Lynn was very idealistic about law practice. She wanted to rescue the lost and lift up the downtrodden, be a voice for the voiceless, and advocate for those who had been treated unjustly. Mostly, though, she was a workaday lawyer doing the best she could. Lynn's office reflected her dual callings. In addition to the law books on the shelves and a diploma and various certificates on the walls, there was a framed cross-stitch in a bookcase that read: "Sister-in-law." It was complemented by a wood carving across the room: "Nun Better."

Lynn's days were structured around both of her vocations. A typical day began with morning prayers at 6:30 a.m. followed by communal breakfast in the monastery's dining room. She was usually in her office by 8:00 a.m. to meet with clients, do research, and confer with fellow lawyers. Sometimes she got back to the convent for the 11:30 a.m.

Mass, but not always. Evening prayers were at 5:15 p.m. Afterward, she frequently ran back to the law office to stay on top of a heavy case load.

To save expense and have the most time I could with Lynn when I traveled to Alabama, I thankfully accepted room and board from the sisters at Sacred Heart Monastery. I slept in Gusmus Hall, a small guest house for overnight visitors built by Will Gusmus, whose sister was Sacred Heart's own Sister Mary Paul. I would occasionally join the sisters for worship, which provided the treat of hearing Lynn's angelic singing voice. Lynn would note that Saint Augustine is credited with saying, "When you sing, you pray twice."

I confess that initially I was perplexed by the Sisters of Sacred Heart. Why would women today elect to confine themselves in a patriarchal, hierarchical faith like the Roman Catholic Church? Wasn't monastic life a form of segregating oneself from the realities of the world? Was sisterhood a form of naivete?

But as I spent time with them, it became clear that these women are neither naive nor sheltered. They are strong, socially aware, and dedicated to their work. To become a sister is not to place a restriction upon oneself. In some ways it is freeing, opening for them a world of possibility. Their vows are their manner of embracing the world, not rejecting it. Being a sister offers them opportunities to make both the Church and the world better. They see themselves as a bridge between what is and what could be. Constantly ministering to the suffering and oppressed can be exhausting and heartbreaking. It takes a person of courage to live such an atypical life. While those of us in law firms catering to corporations were doing well in life, Lynn and her sisters were truly doing good.

Lynn was just thirty years old and had only been out of law school for about four years when she received a call from the Alabama Prison Project, at the behest of the ABA Death Penalty Representation Project, asking whether she would be willing to assist an attorney from Chicago on the Tommy Hamilton death penalty case. Though she had never worked on a capital case, Lynn was passionately opposed to the death penalty. She believed that society did not need to be in the business of killing people to demonstrate that it is wrong to kill people. She was willing and able, and Cullman was only thirty-six miles from the courthouse in Moulton, where we would need to begin Tommy's legal proceedings. Lynn McKenzie was also fearless—the local Sheriff's office had bestowed upon her the nickname "Ninja-nun," apparently based on her toughness in pursuing justice for her criminal defendants.

In many ways, we were an unlikely pair. A married suburban father of two young children who was accustomed to litigating for Fortune 500 companies in the third-largest metropolitan area in the nation, combining with a single woman committed to monastic life, whose legal work was largely devoted to the problems that surfaced in a rural community. But on the fundamental issues of justice and mercy, we were identically committed. I embraced Lynn as a colleague; she quickly became a dear friend.

Post-conviction death penalty legal proceedings are conducted before a single Judge without a jury. They are civil, rather than criminal, in nature, and are proceedings in which a condemned prisoner claims impermissible incarceration by the state. Such claims are defended by the state's Attorney General—who, in October of 1988, was Don Siegelman. Born and raised in Mobile, Alabama, Siegelman earned his bachelor's degree from the University of Alabama, got his law degree at Georgetown, and studied international law for one year at the University of Oxford. He previously had been elected and served as the Secretary of State of Alabama.

Death penalty law is almost singularly complicated and unsettled. There are at least four applicable bodies of law, each of which requires the lawyer to analyze legal principles and precedents that are voluminous, complex, and constantly evolving. The four areas are: 1) general substantive criminal law and criminal procedure; 2) the operation and constitutional overlay of the state's death penalty statute; 3) the rules of "procedural default" that preclude consideration of valid constitutional claims on procedural grounds, the ways to get around them, and the ways to stop lawyers from getting around them; and 4) the doctrine of "abuse of the writ." The doctrine of procedural default alone has been compared to a "great labyrinth which houses a deadly sanction within its procedural passageways." Some have suggested that it is no more reasonable to expect a volunteer commercial lawyer to quickly command these areas of the law than it would be to expect a dermatologist to promptly become an expert in obstetrics.

In addition to involving the law's most extreme sanction, death litigation often presents significant time pressures as states attempt to
enforce death warrants. As one lawyer has put it: "When I lose or make
a mistake in my commercial practice, no one dies. They just write a
check."

Given this complexity, an entire section of the Alabama Attorney
General's Office is devoted exclusively to defending post-conviction
death penalty claims. It is staffed by attorneys who are very bright,
specialize in these cases, and know the governing law inside and out.
And when you serve the Attorney General of a state with one of the
highest number of convicts on death row in the country, you gain a lot
of experience defending post-conviction claims.

The attorneys representing the state of Alabama in Tommy
Hamilton's case were led by Ed Earl Carnes. Ed Carnes was born on
June 3, 1950, and received his bachelor of science degree from the
University of Alabama in 1972. Upon getting his undergraduate degree,
Carnes immediately enrolled in Harvard Law School—the same year
that the United States Supreme Court held the death penalty uncon-
stitutional as then applied. In 1975, when Carnes received his juris
doctor degree, the Alabama legislature adopted a new death penalty
statute that it believed would solve the constitutional infirmities of the
old regime. Immediately after law school, Carnes became an Assistant
Attorney General for the state of Alabama. In 1980, he defended the
constitutionality of Alabama's 1975 death penalty law before the United
States Supreme Court. In the case of *Beck v. Alabama*, the Supreme
Court struck down the revised statute. Thereafter, Carnes helped the
Alabama legislature draft a new law that established the bifurcated
proceeding in which a penalty-phase jury recommends a sentence,
but the sentencing Judge retains ultimate sentencing authority based
on weighing aggravating factors against mitigating factors. It was this
statute under which Tommy had been sentenced.

In 1981, Carnes became Chief of the Capital Punishment and Post-
Conviction Litigation Division of the Alabama Attorney General's
Office. As the *National Law Journal* stated, Carnes was now the "pre-
mier death penalty advocate" in America and one of the most preva-
lent advisors for capital punishment. Not only had Carnes authored
Alabama's death penalty statute; by the time I took on Tommy's

case, he had defended the state in death penalty litigation before the Supreme Court of the United States on two more occasions following *Beck v. Alabama*: first, *Hopper v. Evans*, in which the Supreme Court cleared the way for Evans to became the first Alabama inmate to be electrocuted since 1965; and then *Baldwin v. Alabama*, in which the Court cleared the way for Evans's accomplice, Wayne Ritter, to be executed. Although Associate Justice John Paul Stevens dissented from the Court's decision in *Baldwin*, he thanked Carnes during oral argument for his "very helpful brief." Wayne Ritter was executed in 1987.

Day-to-day work on Tommy Hamilton's case was handled by Deputy Attorney General Kenneth Sloan Nunnelley. Ken Nunnelley got his undergraduate degree from Auburn University and graduated from the Cumberland School of Law at Samford University in 1985. His entire legal career had been spent with the Attorney General's Office, in particular with Carnes's capital litigation section. Ken was humorless. To a battle of wits, he came unarmed.

Ken, of course, knew that I was from Chicago. One day, attempting to break the ice, I asked Ken if he had heard the story told about when Abraham Lincoln was a lawyer in Chicago. Ken said he had not. I informed Ken that one morning, Lincoln appeared in court and made eloquent arguments as to why his client should win the case. The Judge ultimately agreed and ruled in Lincoln's favor. That afternoon, Lincoln appeared in court representing a different client before the same Judge. The legal issue in the afternoon case was identical to the one that Lincoln had argued earlier that morning. In the afternoon, however, Lincoln argued in favor of the opposite result.

Before making his ruling, the Judge said to Lincoln: "Mr. Lincoln, this morning you were arguing the exact opposite of the proposition for which you are arguing this afternoon. How do you reconcile your conflicting positions?"

Lincoln responded: "Your Honor, this morning I was wrong."

Ken was not amused. He always bore a lemon-faced expression and seemed to resent our presence. He had a self-righteous and military demeanor. Despite our differences, I respected that Ken was as devoted to his client as I was to mine. He was experienced and tenacious in representing his client's interests. I have always found it easier to litigate against a lawyer who knows what he or she is doing, and in the case of Tommy Hamilton, I got what I wanted.

The first order of business for our side was to defer setting a date for Tommy's execution. In 1987, Alabama adopted a new post-conviction remedy procedure as set out in Rule 20 of the Temporary Alabama Rules of Criminal Procedure. We quickly informed the Attorney General's Office that we were representing Tommy Hamilton and intended to file a petition for post-conviction relief pursuant to Temporary Rule 20. We asked for a reasonable amount of time to do so and that the setting of an execution date await our filing. The Attorney General's Office agreed to give us a few months.

A Temporary Rule 20 petition had to be filed in the court in which the petitioner was convicted and sentenced to death. It was heard and decided by the presiding Judge of that court. For Tommy's case, that meant filing our petition in the Circuit Court of Lawrence County in Moulton, Alabama. Claims of innocence, especially those based upon newly discovered evidence, may be raised in a post-convic-tion proceeding; still, in many cases it is the judicial system—not the convict—that is put on trial. Most issues raised post-conviction will be assertions that an error of constitutional magnitude occurred during the original trial, an error sufficient to overturn a capital conviction and/or sentence of death.

It is hardly surprising that the very same Judge who presided over the original trial will be reluctant to find that such an egregious error occurred on her or his watch, especially after the state appellate court, state supreme court, and United States Supreme Court had declined, up to that point, to find such an error. It is also notable that the trial Judge is elected to the bench by the voters of the county in which that Judge presides. But in this regard, we had some early luck. After twenty years of service, the Honorable Judge Billy C. Burney retired as Judge of the Lawrence County Circuit Court. That meant our claims would not be heard by the Judge who had presided over Tommy's conviction by a Lawrence County jury—the Judge who had sentenced him to be executed.

The newly elected Presiding Circuit Judge for Lawrence County was the Honorable A. Philip Reich II. We quickly researched Judge's Reich's background. His family had been in the hotel business for three generations. Originally from Gadsden, Alabama, he spent his high school years in Chattanooga, Tennessee. He received an undergraduate degree in marketing from the University of Alabama in 1970; after working for a year, he graduated from its law school in 1974. Tommy's prosecutor, Timothy Littrell, was in that same law school class. Upon graduating, Reich had immediately joined his father-in-law, Harold Speake, at a small law firm in Moulton, where he focused his practice on litigation. We further discovered that the firm he was affiliated with had handled the probate estate of Tommy's victim, Lehman Wood. With no prior judicial experience, Reich was elected to the position in November of 1988 and took office in January of 1989.

We decided to move to disqualify Judge Reich from hearing Tommy's post-conviction case on two grounds related to his firm's representation of Lehman Wood's estate. At least, there was an appearance of impropriety; at worst, there was an actual conflict of interest.

To put it mildly, this was an aggressive first move for us to take. Because Judge Reich had been a litigator, we had no basis for believing that he personally had worked on Mr. Wood's estate; rather, he had simply worked at a law firm where that work was performed by other attorneys. Judges do not like to be told that they are biased to such a degree that they cannot preside impartially over a case, and it would be Judge Reich himself who would be ruling on our motion to disqualify him from the proceedings. We risked losing our very first argument and, at the same time, alienating the Judge who would decide all future arguments made on behalf of our client. As an attorney from out of state questioning the work of Alabama lawyers and Judges, I was already at risk of being viewed as an interloper at best and a carpetbagger at worst.

But it was a *calculated* risk. The only thing less likely than an experienced trial Judge acknowledging that an egregious constitutional error had occurred on his watch was the possibility that his neophyte judicial successor would second-guess his predecessor's judgments and make such a finding. Anything that might improve our odds was worthy of serious consideration. Moreover, there was only one Judge for the Circuit Court of Lawrence County. If we succeeded in removing Judge Reich from the case, a new Judge would have to be assigned from another county in Alabama—a Judge who was divorced from the electorate of Lawrence County. Even if we lost the motion to disqualify and Judge Reich ruled against us on future issues, not only could we argue on appeal that his adverse rulings were wrong, but we could also argue that he never should have made such rulings in the first place. We also thought that Judge Reich might welcome a respectable exit from these proceedings. He had been a Judge for only a few days, and the prospect of starting his judicial career by presiding over a controversial, time-consuming, and challenging effort to overturn a capital conviction and death sentence may have struck him as somewhat daunting.

As added weight to our argument, we could point to what happened when defense counsel was appointed to represent Tommy at his original trial (since he was indigent and unable to afford a lawyer of his own choosing). Judge Burney had determined that every lawyer in Moulton knew the victim, prominent citizen Lehman Wood; therefore, Tommy would need a lawyer from outside the county. Accordingly, Judge Burney appointed Wesley Miles Lavender of Decatur, in neighboring Morgan County, to serve as trial attorney at Tommy's arraignment on October 24, 1984. (Less than a month before Tommy's trial was to begin, attorney Lavender decided that he needed help. On August 1, 1985, in response to a request by Mr. Lavender and in recognition of "the seriousness of the offense" with which Tommy Hamilton had been charged, Judge Burney appointed Barnes F. Lovelace, Jr., also from Morgan County, as additional counsel.) In making our motion to recuse, we could offer Judge Reich some political cover by arguing that we were only asking him to apply the same standard here that was used in appointing Tommy's defense attorneys at trial.

Our strategy succeeded. On March 8, 1989, Judge Reich granted our motion and recused himself from Tommy's case. Tommy's post-conviction proceedings were referred to the Alabama Supreme Court for reassignment to a new Circuit Court Judge. On March 22, 1989, the case was assigned to the Honorable Ned Michael Suttle of neighboring Lauderdale County.

Ned Michael Suttle grew up in the Memphis, Tennessee, area. Born in 1951, he learned the value of hard work early in life. As a janitor, laborer, salesclerk, and letter carrier, "Mike" Suttle worked his way through college and law school. He received his undergraduate degree from the University of Memphis, and in 1976 he graduated with highest honors from the Indiana University School of Law. After working in Knoxville as a lawyer for the Tennessee Valley Authority, he moved to Florence, Alabama, in 1979 and joined the law firm of Potts, Young & Blasingame. He was a trial lawyer in cases involving personal injuries, wrongful deaths, contract disputes, and criminal charges. Judge Suttle was named a Circuit Judge in 1984 by then Governor George C. Wallace. It was a new judgeship created to reduce the workload on the other two Circuit Judges in that county.

Florence, Alabama, was incorporated in 1826 and named after the capital city of the Tuscany region of Italy. By 1989, Florence—a city of just over thirty-five thousand people, located next to bodies of water created by dams on the Tennessee River—was considered northwest Alabama's primary economic hub, and its median family income was forty thousand dollars. Florence was perhaps best known for being the birthplace and home of W. C. Handy, the "Father of the Blues," and it was still home to Sam Phillips, the record producer who had discovered Elvis Presley.

I greeted the appointment of Judge Suttle to our case as a blessing. We now had an experienced, smart Judge with no prior knowledge of, let alone intimate involvement with, Tommy Hamilton's original trial. Our Judge had life experiences beyond the state of Alabama, and he was not beholden to the voters of Lawrence County. We had won our first argument and established ourselves as zealous and aggressive advocates.

It was time to get to work. The transcript of Tommy's trial needed to be reviewed, as well as all the briefs and proceedings before the appellate courts. We had countless witnesses to track down and interview. Sensitive decisions about if, and when, we should contact Lehman Wood's family and the jurors from Tommy's trial needed to be considered. And Ed Carnes and Judge Suttle would only give us so much time to get our initial pleading on file.

CHAPTER FIVE

The Investigation

On my first trip to Alabama, I drove my rental car directly from Birmingham Airport to the scene of the shooting in Bankhead National Forest, at the intersection of Highway 33 and Ridge Road. My goal was to become familiar with the location before I interviewed any witnesses.

The deep verdant forest was dense; from the road, I could see just a few feet into its interior. The thickets of live oak trees and loblolly pine, with their dark green needles up to ten inches long and columnar trunks with plates of reddish-brown bark, would easily conceal a bootlegger's still or camouflage a hunter stalking prey. A pickup truck with a gun rack passed me as I walked the area taking pictures. Few times have I felt more out of place than when standing on the side of that red clay road in my three-piece suit.

From the scene of the shooting, I proceeded to the home of Tommy's mother, Lucille Hamilton, on County Road 217 in Hillsboro—a thirty-minute drive and a quarter-century trip back in time. Ruts in the grassy front yard served as a driveway to the ranch-style house. There were few trees, bushes, or plants to soften the setting. The building's outward appearance starkly proclaimed its sole purpose of providing shelter from the elements.

Lucille must have been waiting at the window for me to arrive, as she soon appeared at her front door. Born on February 16, 1935, Lucille Looney Hamilton was a heavyset woman with limited mobility and black hair worn bouffant-style atop her head. As I emerged from the car, she greeted me warmly and beckoned for me to come inside.

The inside of the home was sparsely furnished. Framed pictures of family members filled shelves on the walls. A television with rabbit ear antennas had a prominent place in the living area. The kitchen was clean but cluttered with dishes and glasses.

Lucille extended Southern hospitality by offering me some lemonade. I accepted and sat down on the cloth-covered couch. Almost immediately, Lucille began to talk about Tommy. It rapidly became clear that Tommy, as her youngest child, occupied a favored place in Lucille's heart. It also became clear that an emotional schism between Lucille and her daughter Janice ran wide and deep.

I asked Lucille to recall for me what had happened on the day Tommy was arrested. She offered few details other than confessing that she had known ahead of time that law enforcement was coming to her home to conduct a search, and that she had scattered aspirin, Pepto-Bismol tablets, and whatever else she could find in her medicine cabinet in a misguided effort to support an under-the-influence alibi for whatever Tommy had done to get himself arrested.

Over and over, Lucille gave thanks for my willingness to represent Tommy. Her greatest fear was that he would be executed. Lucille had already suffered more than her share of loss, losing two sons at birth: on May 10, 1955, and on April 16, 1956. Lucille made it clear to me that her sole objective now was to see that Tommy, her "baby," did not die. Lucille never cried in my presence. Given the life she had lived with her husband J. W., the deaths of her first two children in childbirth, and now Tommy being sentenced to die, maybe she had no tears left.

After my interview with Lucille, I went to see Tommy's wife, Debbie, and his sister Janice. I found both of them incarcerated in Tutwiler Prison.

The Julia Tutwiler Prison for Women opened in December of 1942 in Wetumpka, Alabama. The facility is named in honor of the "Angel of the Stockades," Julia Strudwick Tutwiler (1841–1916). A noted Alabama educator and crusader for educating inmates and improving prison conditions, she also wrote the lyrics to Alabama's state song ("Alabama, Alabama, we will aye be true to thee!") and was enshrined in Alabama's Women's Hall of Fame in 1971.

The Tutwiler facility serves as the receiving unit for all female inmates entering the state prison system. It holds over nine hundred women and includes a death row unit. The original building was designed for no more than four hundred prisoners. The main entrance is at the gable end of a rectangular building. Its exterior walls are whitewashed. Two windows covered with thick metal bars frame the single doorway that leads into the prison. The roof line is strung with razor wire. Inside, almost all furnishings are metal. Metal-framed bunk beds, arranged dormitory style, serve as sleeping quarters for most of the inmates. Metal tables with round metal stools welded to the table serve as gathering spots. As Alabama's only state prison for women, Tutwiler has no meaningful way to classify inmates for assignment to appropriate dorms. Women battling severe mental illness or emotional problems are grouped with other women, making dorm life chaotic and stressful.

For a female prisoner, there are few places worse than Tutwiler. Corrections officers have raped, beaten, and otherwise harassed women inside the aging prison for decades. More than a third of the employees have had sex with prisoners, which is sometimes the only currency for basics such as toilet paper, tampons, and clean uniforms. With only three security cameras in the entire facility, there are multiple blind spots for sexual encounters between prisoners and guards that would leave little evidence. The toxic, sexualized environment had been met with deliberate indifference from prison officials who were aware of the conditions for years but failed to address them. Women who reported sexual misconduct were punished and humiliated, placed in segregation, stripped of property, and denied contact with their families.

When I met Debbie at Tutwiler Prison for Women, she looked awful. Dressed in white prison-issue pants and a white buttoned-down shirt with "Alabama Dept. of Corrections" printed in black block letters on the back, she was gaunt, with deep, dark circles under her eyes.

She appeared broken—physically and spiritually. I could only imagine what the past three years in prison had done to her. She sat down in front of me and placed the interlocked fingers of her hands on the table in front of us. The letters L-O-V-E had been tattooed on the middle phalanges of each hand using prison-made ink and needles.

While only a decade into my legal career, I had interviewed a lot of witnesses by the time I sat with Debbie Hamilton. And I had played a fair share of hold 'em poker. My assessment of Debbie was that she was about to tell me the kind of truth that someone shares when everything else has been taken away from them and they have nothing else to give.

Debbie's account of the day of the murder was eye-opening. She told me that, at approximately 7:30 a.m. on July 11, 1984, Janice had cashed a check for eighty dollars. With the proceeds, Tommy, Debbie, and Janice—whose son Jason was in the back seat of the car—purchased half of a case of beer. At Janice's suggestion, they then drove to the Mallard Creek area of Lawrence County and surreptitiously entered the home of Loyle Chaffin—stealing two guns, including the weapon used during the robbery and murder of Lehman Wood. They continued drinking and driving around in Janice's car.

At this point in her narrative, Debbie told me that Lehman Wood, whom she described as Janice's sugar daddy, had "dumped" Janice a week earlier and that she expressed to Debbie her desire for revenge. Janice suggested to the group that they kill Lehman Wood and rob him. Janice and Tommy proceeded to arrange an ambush whereby Tommy would hide in the woods and shoot Wood with the stolen rifle.

Janice called Wood. Professing that she had car trouble and needed help, she made the request that he come to the forest more alluring by suggesting that she would go skinny-dipping with him after the car was fixed.

When Wood pulled up in his truck, Tommy shot him in the neck. Janice and Debbie dragged the body across the road since he had fallen in front of Janice's car. Debbie removed money from the victim's pocket, giving some to both Janice and Tommy. Afraid that Wood was not dead, Janice had Tommy shoot him again. The group washed the car at a car wash and hid the guns at Lucille Hamilton's house. As the group was leaving, Janice proclaimed: "We got away with it."

After Debbie testified at Janice's trial, and on the very day that Janice was convicted, Debbie wrote Tommy a letter. She told him, in part: "Tommy I'm sorry I went states [testifying for the prosecution] but I thought it was the best thing I could do. . . . They didn't have shit on Janice but they had a lot on you and me, you said you shot him and they got all that money off of me so I had to make sure I would get out of prison someday!"

I had arranged to see Janice—also incarcerated at Tutwiler—after my interview with Debbie. The contrast could not have been starker. Janice appeared for our meeting with her hair perfectly done and with precisely applied, albeit overdone, makeup. She had unbuttoned the top of her prison shirt, and her sleeves were rolled up over her elbows to reveal even more skin. She had thick black eyelashes, blush liberally applied to her prominent cheeks, and dark liner around her ruddy lips. Observing Janice's demure smile as she sat down, I could only wonder at what manipulation she must have engaged in to manage her appearance before me. Sex is an important commodity at Tutwiler. The inmates use it to get better treatment and secure contraband items such as makeup and perfume. To me, Janice's appearance and demeanor betrayed a poisonous core and completed the "Eve's Apple" posture she was projecting.

From what I had gathered from those I'd spoken to thus far, Janice had a complex relationship with men. When she was only a senior in high school, an announcement by her parents of her engagement and a planned June 1 wedding to twenty-five-year-old Quinten Michael Harper appeared in the May 19, 1974 edition of the *Decatur Daily* newspaper. Apparently, the wedding never happened. On February 14, 1975, seventeen-year-old Janice and twenty-five-year-old Duwayne Lee Glasco took out a marriage license. Those wedding plans also were deferred. One year later, on February 24, 1976, Janice and Duwayne again procured a marriage license. Apparently, Janice was two months pregnant with her son, Jason Earl Glasco, who was born on September 24, 1976.

Janice also had a storied history of manipulation. As Debbie had told me, before Janice enticed Lehman Wood to come and see her in the national forest, and while in the car with her brother and his newlywed wife, Janice had—apparently solely for entertainment—proceeded to spark an argument between Debbie and Tommy by telling her brother that Debbie had been prostituting herself and cuckolding Tommy by sleeping with a different fellow, who was coincidently known in town as "Big Tommy" Hamilton. Tommy reacted by proclaiming that he was going to kill his wife's alleged paramour.

After Janice had stoked Tommy into a jealous rage, they traveled to Lentz Grocery, where Janice purchased a box of rifle shells from Mamie Lentz. Someone in the group then called "Big Tommy" and asked him to meet them at Chickenfoot, a wildlife sanctuary off Highway 33 in Moulton. The group went there to wait for "Big Tommy," with Tommy hiding in the woods with the rifle. "Big Tommy" never arrived, but Tommy continued to simmer.

When I asked her about the murder, Janice told me the same unbelievable story that she testified to at her trial: She admitted she was present at the scene but denied that she encouraged Tommy to kill Lehman Wood or participated in any way. She told me she had been sleeping in her car just prior to the time that Wood drove up. She said that petite fifteen-year-old Debbie Hamilton was able to drag Wood's body across the road without assistance. Janice swore to me, as she had told the press at the time of her conviction, that she was romantically involved with Wood and "cared for him a lot." She purred and implored me to represent her in post-conviction proceedings, anything to get her out of jail as soon as possible. Given what I had been told by both Lucille and Debbie, my encounter with Janice went just as I expected.

After meeting all of the women in Tommy's life, it was time to meet the client himself.

The West Jefferson Correctional Facility, which opened in 1982 in Bessemer, Alabama, is set on 290 acres of land just outside of Birmingham. It was, and remains, some of the most dangerous real estate in Alabama. (It was later renamed the William E. Donaldson Correctional Facility in honor of a corrections officer who was stabbed to death by an inmate.) The prison had capacity for seven thousand inmates in dormitory housing. It specialized in handling repeat or multiple violent offenders who were behaviorally difficult to manage and were serving lengthy sentences. It had the largest solitary confinement unit in Alabama. Hundreds of its inmates were serving sentences of life without parole. In addition, it had a death row unit with a capacity of twenty-four inmates.

Condemned prisoners on death row were housed in a windowless building that was hot and uncomfortable. Each death row inmate was placed in a five-by-eight-foot cell with a metal door, a toilet, and a steel bunk. Most death row prisoners got few visits and even fewer privileges.

The prison grounds were surrounded by chain-link fence topped with shimmering loops of razor wire in an unequal-sided octagon. Signs warn against trespass; armed guards in watchtowers oversee points of ingress and egress. To enter the prison, Luke DeGrand and I had to navigate a series of checkpoints. The first was a general admission waiting area outside the perimeter of the prison grounds. It was here that we announced our presence for a legal visit. We signed the lawyers' book, which was separate and apart from the book used to log in family, friends, and others who came to visit prisoners.

A corridor of chain-link fence, also topped with razor wire, led to the next area. The main entry to the prison had sliding glass doors. The American and Alabama flags were painted on the white exterior wall, along with the words PROTECT and SERVE in ten-foot-tall, capitalized block letters.

We were directed to a small room, the walls of which were largely glass—allowing those on the outside to observe what transpired within. Soon Tommy Hamilton shuffled into the room, accompanied by watchful guards. Tommy looked like a young Elvis Presley. He stood six feet tall and weighed a lean 180 pounds. His hair had turned jet black. He was dressed in prison-issue white pants and a white buttoned-down shirt; his ankles were chained together with just enough slack to allow modest steps to be taken; and his wrists were bound behind his back. After the guards undid his handcuffs, we sat down with Tommy at the table in the center of the room for our first meeting as lawyers and client.

Among inmates, two emotions predominate in a prison such as "West Jeff": anger and fear. Tommy reflected the latter. Immediately, he made a plea. His speech was halting, at times almost lapsing into a stutter.

Tommy feared an incarcerated life more than the electric chair. As limited as his intellect was, he realized that even a reduced life sentence without the possibility of parole was—like electrocution—a death-in-prison sentence. And he was aware that life on death row (with its relatively small population and heavy security) was significantly safer for him than it would be in the overcrowded and understaffed general population areas of the prison where he would have to serve a life sentence. Tommy wanted us to get him out of prison. If we were unable to do that, he professed a willingness to be executed.

We told Tommy what every lawyer tells a client when they first take on representation: we were his advocates; in general terms, whatever we communicated to him and what he communicated to us was confidential; and in order to help him, we needed him to be truthful with us. We then asked Tommy to tell us what had happened on July 11, 1984.

In his halting manner, Tommy recounted his trial testimony almost verbatim. He admitted to shooting Lehman Wood, but he argued that it was in self-defense based on Wood's threat to kill Tommy and his reaching for what Tommy thought was a gun in his pocket. He denied that he robbed Wood, the fundamental element of the killing that converted it into a capital crime punishable solely by death or incarceration for life without possibility of parole. He could not recall a second shot being fired. He asserted that he was not only drunk on beer, but out of his mind on hallucinogenic pills he kept at his mother's home. In my mind, he lied to us about almost every aspect of the events of that day.

I was livid. I immediately stood up and got right in Tommy's face. I told Tommy that there was no time for him to come to trust me. And there certainly was no time for me to investigate fiction. Luke, Lynn, and I were the only people in a position to do anything to help him. No one else had volunteered to be his lawyers, and none were likely to do so. I was not about to repeatedly travel over six hundred miles between Chicago and Birmingham and work hundreds of hours for a client who would not tell me the truth. He had a decision to make—and he had to make it now. Either he would tell me the truth, or the second motion I would be filing in his case would be a motion to withdraw as his attorney.

Contrite and scared, Tommy pledged to be truthful. He proceeded to tell us everything he knew. Some of it we had suspected; little of it was a surprise. It increasingly became clear that Janice was the central figure in this tragedy.

I told Tommy he had to stop writing letters about what happened to anyone, including Debbie and Lucille. Letters other than to his lawyers would be read by correctional officers for security reasons and could be used as evidence against Tommy in the evidentiary hearing before Judge Suttle. I would see Tommy regularly, and he could communicate with me face to face. We left, and Tommy returned to Death Row.

As we continued our initial investigation, we hoped to talk to Tommy's trial lawyers. Unfortunately, Tommy's lead trial lawyer, Wes Lavender, would not meet with us. Wesley Miles Lavender was born on July 27, 1948, in Morgan County, Alabama. He graduated from the University of Alabama in 1970 and got his law degree at the Cumberland School of Law in 1973. More experienced than his co-counsel, Barnes Flournoy Lovelace, Jr., Lavender certainly understood our mission: namely, to revisit everything he had done (or failed to do) during Tommy's trial and appeals, searching for any errors or omissions to support a finding that Lavender's ineffective representation deprived Tommy of his constitutional right to counsel. He may also have hoped that we would not discover, or that he would not have to address, the poorly kept secret that he had a problem with alcohol to such an extent that it affected his performance as a lawyer.

Barney Lovelace did talk with us. He graduated from the University of Alabama in 1978 and received his law degree from the Cumberland School of Law at Samford University in 1983. His sister, Sharon, was an Assistant United States Attorney in the Northern District of Alabama, and his father was a longtime practicing attorney in Escambia County and a former member of the Alabama legislature. Lovelace told us that, while he and Lavender had divided up the representation of Tommy rather evenly, he had assumed an outsize responsibility for dealing with the sentencing phase.

Next we began reviewing the trial record to spot issues for further investigation. Often, what was not raised in the state court by the trial or appellate lawyers turns out to be even more important than what was raised. Therefore, reviewing the trial transcript was one of the most important things we had to do. We began that task in earnest.

A welcome surprise was that Judge Burney agreed to meet with us. Like Attorney Lavender, Judge Burney surely knew that we would evaluate every ruling he'd made during Tommy's trial, seeking a flawed rationale. And this we did. Since Judge Burney had presided not only over Tommy's trial, but also Janice's trial and the plea bargain entered in connection with the charges filed against Debbie, we reviewed their cases with him as well.

When we suggested a significant disparity between the outcomes of the cases, Judge Burney rightfully noted that it was Tommy who had fired the rifle not once, but twice, killing Lehman Wood. And he casually made the unsurprising observation that instead of treating Tommy more leniently, perhaps Janice should have been treated more harshly.

Indeed, an opening emerged when Judge Burney spoke to us about Janice's trial. He acknowledged that Janice had supplied the motivation and emotional fuel for Tommy's actions that day. He credited Janice with more intelligence and maturity than anyone else in the group. And he was disgusted that Janice had brought her seven-year-old son along for all the criminal activity, including the killing.

Disparity in sentencing was one of the touchstones for Supreme Court review of death penalty cases, and it was now a codified criterion for appellate review in Alabama's death penalty regimen. If Judge Burney would opine that, in retrospect, Tommy's death sentence was disproportionately severe compared to the sentences given to Debbie and Janice, it would provide a strong foundation for our post-conviction pleas before Judge Suttle.

As excited as we were about this possibility, we knew it would be asking a lot of Judge Burney to state such an opinion. We did not push him. We asked if we could continue to talk with him as our investigation proceeded. We embarked on nurturing a professional relationship with an eye toward seeing that justice was done.

We examined the physical evidence: the rifle; Lehman Wood's bloody clothes. I was taken aback at how casually this evidence was maintained. It was merely thrown together in a closet in the courthouse.

Next, we tried to talk to the jurors. Since Tommy's death sentence had been recommended by the bare minimum number of jurors required to sustain it, we hoped to find even one juror who might say that the presentation of certain evidence would have changed their mind and they would not have recommended the death sentence to Judge Burney. Running a gauntlet of barking dogs outside of trailer homes where some of the jurors lived proved unavailing. No juror other than the foreperson agreed to talk with us. And the foreperson stood us up at the appointed time and place for the interview.

While we were determined to leave no stone unturned, it was a difficult decision to contact Lehman Wood's daughter, Charlotte Wood Parker, to see if she would provide testimony that might be favorable to Tommy. Charlotte was born on October 10, 1946, and grew up in Moulton, Alabama. She graduated from the Lawrence County High School. She now lived with her mother in Naperville, Illinois, a suburb of Chicago not far from where I lived. When we contacted her, Charlotte said she wanted to consult with the prosecutor first, but that she was open to a discussion.

In retrospect, that Charlotte even responded to us amazes me. My brother, Tom, died unexpectedly during the time I was writing this book. Like Lehman Wood, he was only fifty-nine years old when he passed. It is only now, after my brother's passing, that I more fully realize the enormity of my request of Lehman Wood's daughter, Charlotte Parker. True, it had been years since her father's murder; still, death is not the lingering antagonist when you lose a family member too soon. Rather, the principal nemesis is grief—and it is not a fair or a predictable opponent. Actions that cause you to revisit the death of a family member can lead to waves of sorrow. At any moment you can be thrust back into a period of mourning. After consulting with prosecutor Littrell, Charlotte declined to engage with us further. However, her initial willingness to talk to me about Tommy and her father's murder was one of the most generous acts I have ever experienced.

CHAPTER SIX

The Petition

Continuing our investigation, we tried to arrange a complete psychiatric evaluation of Tommy. This would include a brain scan to search for damage or any sign of mental defect. Tommy was relatively calm living on death row after being sentenced to die in the electric chair; paradoxically, he was afraid of being confined in a tube for the brain scan or having electroencephalographic sensors attached to his body. In a sealed motion given only to Judge Suttle and not to the Alabama Attorney General's Office, so that our work product and litigation plans would not be disclosed, we asked for an order allocating funds so that we could retain a forensic psychiatrist from Boston to evaluate Tommy.

However, the Attorney General's Office and Judge Suttle were pressing for a filing from us. The clock was ticking. We could not buy any more time for further investigation before making at least our preliminary set of claims known. On March 1, 1989, we filed our Petition for Relief from Conviction and Sentence of Death with the Circuit Court of Lawrence County, Alabama. It was a written summary of the issues that we intended to present to the court in support of our contention that Tommy's conviction and sentence were unlawful.

———

Rather than again putting Tommy on trial, we put the criminal proceedings in Lawrence County, Alabama, on trial. Our first argument was that Tommy had not received the legal representation that was guaranteed to him under Alabama law.

Alabama law requires that counsel appointed to represent a defendant charged with a capital offense have at least five years of experience in the active practice of criminal law. Specifically, Section 13A-5-54 of the Alabama Code provides:

> Each person indicted for an offense punishable under the provisions of this article who is not able to afford legal counsel must be provided with court appointed counsel having no less than five years prior experience in the active practice of criminal law.

Notwithstanding, and in violation of, this statutory provision, Judge Burney had appointed Barnes Lovelace as one of Tommy's trial counsel and allowed him to undertake unsupervised responsibility for substantial portions of Tommy's representation. At that time, Mr. Lovelace had been a law school graduate with a general practice for less than two years. He lacked the experience required by the state both in terms of years and the scope of his practice. Indeed, our review of the transcript of Janice's criminal proceedings found that Judge Burney had admitted in a colloquy that Lovelace was not qualified for appointment as Tommy's trial counsel under the terms of the Alabama statute.

Even though he was statutorily unqualified to conduct Tommy's defense, Lovelace had been allowed to assume total responsibility for, and conduct some of the most important aspects of, Tommy's trial. For example, he gave the opening statement to the jury on Tommy's behalf; cross-examined thirteen of the prosecution's witnesses; presented Tommy's motion for acquittal at the close of the state's case; conducted the direct examination of half of the witnesses called to testify by the defense; presented the all-important first half of the closing argument on Tommy's behalf; and made the presentation to the jury in support of a recommended sentence of life imprisonment.

Lovelace had also been given primary responsibility for investigating, preparing, and submitting evidence in what arguably was the most important phase of Tommy's trial: the sentencing hearing. We asserted that, given his lack of qualification to do so, it was not surprising that Tommy's representation at the sentencing phase of his trial was woefully inadequate. The entire case presented on Tommy's behalf at the sentencing phase of his trial, after the jury had found him guilty of capital murder, consisted of a mere four witnesses: Tommy's mother, brother, sister-in-law, and a family friend. The transcript of that portion of the case ran to fewer than twenty pages.

I always like to introduce myself to a Judge by making a strong and winning argument. I thought we had done just that in our first substantive filing before Judge Suttle. The statute was unambiguous: an indigent capital defendant must be provided with court-appointed counsel having no less than five years' prior experience in the active practice of law. Barney Lovelace had been out of law school for only two years. While I feared the Attorney General's Office or Judge Suttle might discover and point out in response that I did not have five years of prior experience in the active practice of criminal law, the issue was that Alabama required a certain level of experience for counsel of capital defendants at the time of their trial—and this had not been provided to Tommy.

Tommy's mental capacity certainly should have been the subject of mitigation arguments during his sentencing; we had hopes that it might yet provide the basis for precluding imposition of the death penalty. On January 11, 1989, less than two months before we filed our petition for post-conviction relief, the United States Supreme Court heard oral argument in a case that raised the question of whether it was constitutionally permissible to execute someone with a mental disability. In *Penry v. Lynaugh*, Johnny Paul Penry, a Texas man who had suffered brain damage at birth and whose adult IQ was about sixty, had been found guilty of capital murder and sentenced to death by a Texas state court. Most mental health professionals define the intellectually disabled as those with an IQ of seventy or below. A psychologist testified that Penry was mildly to moderately intellectually disabled and functioned at a mental age of barely seven years. The issue before the Supreme Court was whether it was constitutionally permissible to execute someone with Penry's mental defects.

In anticipation of the decision in *Penry*, we argued in our petition that evolving standards of decency and the prohibition against cruel and unusual punishment under state and federal constitutional provisions precluded application of the death penalty and execution of a person like Tommy, whose intellectual functioning fell within the borderline range of intellect.

Tommy's sentencing hearing before Judge Burney had been a rushed affair, so we cried foul about this too. We asserted that Tommy was deprived of a fair sentencing hearing and denied effective assistance of counsel by Judge Burney's failure to grant a necessary continuance—which forced the defense to proceed when the only available lawyer was not prepared to do so. Consistent with the responsibilities he had assumed during the trial and sentencing hearing before the jury, Barnes Lovelace shouldered the burden of representing Tommy at the sentencing hearing before Judge Burney. But on the morning of that hearing, his wife went into labor and he attended to her during the birth of their child. Wes Lavender, Tommy's co-counsel, advised Judge Burney of this unforeseen circumstance and asked the court for a continuance so that Tommy could be adequately represented at this important phase of his trial. Judge Burney denied the request, forced the sentencing hearing to proceed, and promptly sentenced Tommy to death. The trial court's rush to impose its sentence with neither meaningful preparation time nor adequate representation deprived Tommy of a fair sentencing hearing and effective assistance of counsel.

We further argued that not only had Tommy's death sentence not been arrived at fairly, but it was also disproportionately severe when compared to the sentences of his alleged accomplices and the sentences imposed for other crimes. Both of Tommy's alleged accomplices, Janice Glasco and Debbie Gatlin Hamilton, were eligible for parole. Indeed, Janice received only a ten-year sentence for the crime of manslaughter and would be eligible for parole just months after we filed Tommy's petition for relief. Even assuming the state's evidence was sufficient to establish Tommy's commission of capital murder, the facts of his case were not sufficiently egregious to warrant imposition of the death penalty when compared to other capital offenses for which a lesser sentence was imposed. We argued that putting Tommy to death under these circumstances constituted cruel and unusual punishment and a violation of due process of law.

Our filing with Judge Suttle also put him on notice that we would argue that the prosecutor had made improper arguments and engaged in misconduct at trial. These actions had impermissibly infringed on Tommy's rights under the Fifth, Sixth, Eighth, and Fourteenth Amendments to the Constitution. For example, during the trial, the prosecutor repeatedly introduced Lehman Wood's daughter to the jury, unduly emphasizing her presence in court solely for the purpose of injecting passion and prejudice into the proceedings. To bolster the credibility of one of the state's witnesses, the prosecutor deceptively had an arresting officer testify while wearing a police uniform—even though the witness was no longer employed as a police officer. During the sentencing hearing, the prosecutor, under the guise of cross-examination, implied that Tommy had at one time engaged in violent and unlawful activity involving the discharge of a shotgun in a home. While no competent evidence was ever presented to substantiate what was merely innuendo and speculation, Judge Burney subsequently admitted taking this purported incident into consideration when sentencing Tommy to death. Similarly, during the sentencing hearing before the jury, the prosecutor impermissibly argued that the jury should recommend that Tommy be sentenced to death to deter others from committing crimes, including crimes for which Tommy had never been arrested, indicted, or convicted, and for which the death penalty could never be imposed.

To add color to our claims of prosecutorial overreach, and as an independent basis for challenging Tommy's conviction and sentence, we argued that Tommy had been deprived of his constitutional right to a fair trial because the jury was transported to and from the Lawrence County Courthouse in Lawrence County's Rescue Squad Vehicle. Why was that problematic? Because everyone in Lawrence County knew that Tommy's victim, Lehman Wood, had been instrumental in the acquisition of that vehicle.

We also argued that District Attorney Tim Littrell had failed to disclose exculpatory evidence—that is, evidence that is favorable to the defendant with respect to either a determination of guilt or the appropriate sentence. Tim Littrell was a longtime resident of Lawrence County. He graduated from the local high school in 1967. He obtained an undergraduate degree from the University of Alabama in 1971 and got his law degree from that university's law school in 1974. Immediately after graduating from law school, he ran for and was elected the town solicitor for the city of Moulton, taking office on January 20, 1975. When then District Attorney Don Parker became ill, Littrell filled in as prosecutor; and when Parker's illness prevented him from completing his term, Governor George Wallace appointed Tim Littrell to fill the term on February 16, 1976.

We asserted that Littrell's investigative staff and law enforcement investigators were specifically instructed to avoid creating a written record of evidence that might tend to exculpate the defendant or impeach evidence that the state intended to offer at trial. This practice amounted to a willful and transparent attempt by the state to avoid its obligation, under the Alabama Constitution and the Fourteenth Amendment to the United States Constitution, to disclose such exculpatory or impeaching evidence. This violated Tommy's rights to a fair trial and due process of law.

Beyond prosecutorial misconduct, we thought Tommy's youth at the time of the killing was a mitigating factor, and we wanted to tee up this issue for further consideration. We argued that because the trial court failed to conduct an independent, contemporaneous investigation and hearing, its summary denial of Tommy's request for Youthful Offender status violated his right to due process. Tommy was born on May 24, 1964. He was only twenty years old at the time of the offense for which he was arrested and indicted. Alabama law provides that a defendant who is twenty-one years of age or younger when committing an offense punishable by a term of more than one year in the penitentiary may apply for Youthful Offender status. Upon receiving such an application, the trial court is obligated to investigate and make an informed determination as to whether Youthful Offender status should be granted. The death penalty cannot be imposed upon a defendant who is granted this status. Tommy's attorneys had made timely application for him to be treated as a youthful offender, yet Judge Burney did not conduct the investigation required under Alabama law. On October 24, 1984, relying on a previous youthful offender investigation conducted in connection with a prior petty offense brought against Tommy, the Judge summarily denied Tommy's application in the Lehman Wood murder case.

We also argued that the trial court's refusal to grant Tommy a change of venue deprived him of his rights to a fair trial and due process of law. Tommy's motion requesting that he be tried somewhere other than Lawrence County was based upon the substantial pretrial publicity surrounding the killing of Lehman Wood, a citizen so revered that the county named its headquarters building, located at the corner of Walnut and Main Streets in downtown Moulton, after him. Statements made by prospective jurors during questioning acknowledged pretrial publicity indicating Tommy's guilt and strongly suggested that several of them already believed he was guilty. In addition, numerous members of the jury pool were personal friends or acquaintances of the victim, Lehman Wood.

Lastly, in making our first substantive filing in Tommy's case, and the first filing that would be considered by Judge Suttle, I felt we could not ignore three significant pieces of trial evidence: Tommy's directive to his wife to be silent as they were being arrested; the testimony of Janice's son, Jason Glasco, regarding whether the killing of Lehman Wood was self-defense or part of a planned robbery; and the recitation by Jimmy Dale Owens of Tommy's alleged jailhouse confession.

As to the first of the three points, during the presentation of the state's case against Tommy, District Attorney Tim Littrell repeatedly elicited testimony that Tommy had told Debbie to be silent. In fact, this comment was apparently so important to the prosecutor that he pointedly drew the jury's attention to it during his closing argument—which, we argued in a bit of a stretch, violated Tommy's right to remain silent and free from self-incrimination as guaranteed by the Fifth and Fourteenth Amendments to the Constitution. We argued that Tommy's decision to exercise his constitutional right to remain silent upon being arrested had been impermissibly circumvented, abrogated, and prejudicially exploited by the prosecutor during the trial.

With respect to the second of the three points, Tommy's seven-year-old nephew, Jason Glasco, had been present when Tommy, Debbie, and Janice were arrested on the day of the murder. The prosecution called Jason to testify at Tommy's trial, and we argued that Judge Burney had impermissibly allowed prosecutor Littrell to challenge the veracity of his own witness.

Jason was the only person who was present during the killing of Lehman Wood to be called by the prosecution to testify at Tommy's trial. Initially, Jason testified that Tommy had killed Lehman Wood during an argument and in response to a death threat. Prior to trial, Jason had been interviewed multiple times by law enforcement about the killing. According to Investigator Ed Weatherford, during his first two interviews, Jason indicated that Tommy had ambushed Wood. However, during a third interview, Jason had changed his story and indicated that Tommy and Wood had gotten into an argument and that Tommy, fearing for his life, had killed Wood. Thus, Littrell was certainly aware that prior to trial, Jason had told investigators at least once that Tommy shot Wood in self-defense. Nevertheless, when Jason testified to that effect at trial, Littrell claimed "surprise" and was permitted by Judge Burney to attempt to discredit Jason's testimony using the conflicting pretrial statements that Wood's death occurred during a robbery.

In general, a lawyer is not allowed to discredit his own witness unless the testimony comes as a surprise. Even then, the surprised lawyer may attack the credibility of the witness only by confronting the witness with previous contradictory statements—in which case, those contradictory statements may only be admitted for the limited purpose of evaluating the witness's credibility. They may not be considered as substantive evidence of alternative facts.

Judge Burney's error was compounded three more times: when he called Jason to the stand as a "court witness," thereby freeing the prosecutor to cross-examine Jason; when he failed to instruct the jury that it could only consider the contradictory statements as they might bear on Jason's credibility; and when he failed to instruct the jury that the statements could not be considered as substantive evidence of Tommy's guilt of a capital crime. The admission of this testimony in this manner, particularly given the critical nature of the evidence to the state's case, violated Tommy's rights. The only basis upon which a capital conviction could be sustained and, in turn, a death sentence imposed upon Tommy, was if the prosecution proved beyond a reasonable doubt and to a moral certainty that Lehman Wood was killed by Tommy during the course of a robbery. If, as Tommy contended at trial, Lehman Wood was killed during an argument and in self-defense, and not as part of a robbery, Tommy could not receive a capital conviction or death sentence.

As to the third of the three points, we needed to cast doubt on the testimony of Tommy's jailhouse cellmate, Jimmy Dale Owens. Before testifying at Tommy's trial, Owens had been tried in Lawrence County for certain crimes and found not guilty by reason of insanity. Based on this, Tommy's defense team raised timely challenges to the competence of Owens to testify. Because Judge Burney overruled the defense objections and admitted the testimony, we argued that the failure at trial to investigate and establish the competence of Owens to testify denied Tommy his right to a fair trial and due process of law.

———

On March 29, 1989, the state of Alabama filed an answer to our petition, denying all of our allegations. The state also argued that most of our challenges were legally barred from being considered—either because they had not previously been raised at trial or on appeal; or because the allegations *had* previously been raised and addressed at trial or on appeal.

As if we needed to be reminded of what was at stake, around this time Alabama began to carry out executions of Tommy's fellow death row prisoners at an unprecedented pace.

On May 26, 1989, less than three months after we filed our petition for post-conviction relief, Michael Lindsey, twenty-eight years old, became the fourth person to be executed in Alabama since the 1976 Supreme Court ruling that allowed states to resume capital punishment. He was also the first person to be executed even though his jury had recommended a sentence of life imprisonment without parole instead of the death penalty. The Judge, as permitted under Alabama law, had overridden the jury's determination and imposed the death sentence on his own. The United States Supreme Court rejected Lindsey's last-minute appeal. Governor Guy Hunt made it abundantly clear that death row inmates were unlikely to receive a reprieve at his hands. In denying Lindsey's appeal for clemency, the Governor's assistant press secretary said that the "Governor declines to alter the decision of the jury and the courts"—even though the jury's decision had been altered by the Judge. The Governor's legal advisor, Bill Wasden, said that clemency could be granted only if there were "evidence that was not presented at the trial that was so overwhelming as to preclude every other possibility but innocence."

Then on August 18, 1989, Herbert Lee Richardson, forty-three years old, was executed. Richardson was a Vietnam War veteran who suffered from post-traumatic stress disorder so severe that he was hospitalized in a veterans' hospital in New York City. Richardson met a nurse there, a woman from Dothan, Alabama. When she moved back to her home in Alabama, Richardson followed her. The two dated briefly, but Richardson's possessiveness led her to terminate the relationship.

Richardson came up with a deluded idea to win back his former girlfriend. He reasoned that if she felt threatened, she might come to him to seek protection. He constructed a small bomb and placed it on her front porch. He planned to detonate the bomb and then run to her aid, following which he was certain they would live happily ever after.

Richardson completed his assembly of the bomb and placed it on the porch. However, the former girlfriend's young niece found the device, picked it up, and shook it—triggering an explosion that killed her while Richardson watched from across the street.

Richardson was sentenced to die for the 1977 pipe-bomb slaying of ten-year-old Rena Mae Callins. Margie Callins, Rena Mae's mother, had said she could not rest "until he gets the chair."

Richardson never saw the execution chamber. He had requested to be blindfolded from the time he left the adjacent holding cell. In disposing of his personal effects, Richardson wrote a detailed list of items to be left to "my beloved wife," whom he had married in a prison ceremony not ten days earlier, and to fellow death row inmate Earl Jerome McGahee, who occupied the next cell over. Richardson had met his wife, Katie, a member of El Bethel Primitive Baptist Church, three years before he was executed, after writing to inform the church that he listened to its radio broadcasts. Among the items Richardson bequeathed to his wife were a nineteen-inch color television, thirteen packs of cigarettes, fifty-five matchbooks, legal transcripts from his trial, a broken hairbrush, $4.42 from his prison account, and a Bible. "I have no ill feeling and hold nothing against anyone," Richardson said in a final statement after the death warrant was read. Pronounced dead six minutes after about a two-thousand-volt charge of electricity had been administered, he was buried on the Holman Prison grounds. "When the body is not claimed by family, that's the procedure," said State Prison Commissioner Morris Thigpen. "She [Mrs. Richardson] had indicated that she did not have the means to take care of a private funeral."

Richardson's case is one of two types that test my resolute opposition to the death penalty. Like Thomas Jefferson, I believe treason is an existential threat to the rule of law and ordered liberty; capital punishment is appropriate for those convicted of such a crime. And I admit that crimes against children move me to seek retribution against such evildoers. I acknowledge some logical inconsistency in taking the first position, and yet it is what I believe. And I admit that human emotion drives my reactions to crimes against children, and yet it is what I feel.

On November 17, 1989, the state of Alabama electrocuted Arthur James Julius, who was forty-three years old. While serving a life sentence for a 1972 murder, Julius was given an eight-hour pass from a work-release center in Montgomery, borrowed a relative's car, and then beat and strangled his cousin to death after subjecting her to "grotesque sexual abuse." Pinned to the white sweat suit that he wore into the death chamber was the purple ribbon worn by inmates on death row to protest the death penalty.

The United States Supreme Court signaled how fragile our arguments might prove to be when it decided the *Penry* case on June 26, 1989—not even four months after the filing of our petition for post-conviction relief. Four Justices voted to uphold Penry's death sentence, finding neither a broad constitutional violation in executing the mentally disabled nor specific constitutional errors in his case. Four other Justices wanted to rule that the Eighth Amendment never permits a state to execute a mentally disabled person.

Justice Sandra Day O'Connor crafted a majority opinion from these two opposing camps. She agreed with Justices William J. Brennan, Thurgood Marshall, Harry A. Blackmun, and John Paul Stevens that Penry's death sentence had been imposed in error, because Texas law kept the jury from adequately considering his intellectual deficit. Consequently, the death sentence was set aside. But Justice O'Connor agreed with Chief Justice William H. Rehnquist and Associate Justices Antonin Scalia, Anthony Kennedy, and Byron R. White that execution of the intellectually disabled is not "categorically prohibited" by the Constitution. Consequently, Penry might be sentenced to death again in a new proceeding.

Justice O'Connor's opinion was premised on her finding that there was not yet a national consensus that it was cruel and unusual to execute a murderer who had severe mental deficits. Alabama quickly made it clear that it was not inclined to help form such a consensus.

On July 14, 1989, Horace Franklin Dunkins, Jr., was executed at Holman Prison in Atmore, Alabama. Dunkins and an accomplice were convicted of the rape and murder of a twenty-six-year-old mother of four. She was raped and then stabbed sixty-six times while tied to a tree. The accomplice was given a life sentence. "If you're going to have a death penalty, if you don't have it for a crime like this, what do you have it for?" Alabama Assistant Attorney General Ed Carnes asked rhetorically in statements to the press. But Dunkins's lawyer argued that the pertinent question was not the brutality of the crime, but whether his client had received a fair trial. Dunkins suffered from intellectual disabilities; Alabama officials argued that the jury had heard enough evidence about them to form an understanding of his mental impairments. They said an IQ of sixty-nine, at the borderline of intellectual disability, did not absolve him of responsibility for his actions.

Like John Louis Evans III before him, the electrocution of Dunkins was botched by correctional officials who plugged electrodes into the chair incorrectly, so that the first throw of the switch delivered only a partial charge of electricity that failed to kill him. Dunkins, his face covered by a black veil, sat strapped to the electric chair—apparently unconscious—while officials reconnected the cables. Waiting several minutes "for the body to cool," they threw the switch a second time; ten minutes later, Dunkins was declared dead.

Neither the Supreme Court's decision in *Penry*, issued after we filed our first petition on Tommy's behalf, nor the state's position in the Dunkins case, boded well for our argument that Tommy's intellectual functioning within the borderline range of intellectual disability should preclude his death sentence.

We presented many arguments in our petition for post-conviction relief from Tommy's capital conviction and death sentence, a total of twenty-nine in all, knowing that a failure to timely raise an issue would invite the court to find that we had abandoned it. We alleged that Tommy Hamilton had been unfairly tried, wrongly convicted, and illegally sentenced.

We attempted to reserve our right to amend the petition to raise additional matters and to grant our client the following relief:

- A stay of execution of his death sentence during the pendency of the proceedings;
- An opportunity to conduct necessary discovery, and an evidentiary hearing at which Tommy was present to enable him to prove the facts as alleged in the petition;
- The funds needed to present witnesses, experts, and other evidence in support of the petition's allegations;
- The opportunity to submit post-hearing briefs and argument;
- After a full hearing and complete briefing, an order that Tommy be relieved of his unconstitutional conviction and sentence of death; and
- Such other, further, and alternative relief as the court might find just, equitable, and proper.

Judge Suttle gave us a year to further investigate Tommy's case, and he tentatively scheduled an evidentiary hearing for April of 1990.

CHAPTER SEVEN

The Perjury

The filing of our petition for post-conviction relief did not complete our work. We continued to investigate and prepare for the evidentiary hearing that would follow.

Luke and I sought to develop mitigating evidence that had not been presented by Tommy's attorneys during the sentencing phase of his trial. Since mitigating evidence often involves family dysfunction, it is usually shameful to the client and his relatives and therefore difficult to obtain from them. But we pressed Lucille and everyone else who knew Tommy to be forthcoming.

We had Sister Lynn take the lead on this. Lynn would visit Lucille at her humble home. Lucille would proudly show Lynn the photos filling her shelves, relating the stories behind each one. Lynn engaged Lucille a good bit about those photos, even when it was not essential to our case, because Lynn was always about forming relationships with people. She was convinced that forging relationships makes it easier to get necessary work done—even difficult work like getting Lucille to talk about the awful things that she and her children had endured at the hands of her abusive husband.

We also met several times with Tommy, more to manage his expectations about the hearing, which he would attend and where we would present his case, than to garner any new information. Sister Lynn joined us for these prep sessions, providing the first opportunity for her to meet Tommy in person and to see inside the West Jefferson Prison. The three of us were in the meeting room when Tommy was led in. Luke and I shook Tommy's shackled hands as he entered. Lynn resisted her natural urge to hug Tommy, shaking his hand instead. Then we all sat on those uncomfortable steel stools that were locked in place by a bar connected to the steel table at which we sat.

Tommy was eager for the evidentiary hearing to begin, making proclamations about what he would say. I made it clear to Tommy that he would never testify while I was his lawyer. We had a litigation strategy and would not depart from it. That strategy was to put the prosecution on trial—not to give the Attorney General's Office an opportunity to refocus the hearing on Tommy's actions by letting him testify and then be cross-examined. Of course, the Supreme Court had made clear in the 1971 case of *Harris v. New York* that no matter what counsel thinks is best, a defendant has the right to insist on testifying in his own defense. While I didn't know whether that precedent would apply in a post-conviction proceeding, I did know that I would seek permission to withdraw as Tommy's attorney if he insisted on testifying.

Lynn thought I was cold toward Tommy during the meeting and told me so after he was taken back to his cell on death row. I dismissed her concern, telling her that we were there to be Tommy's lawyers, not his friends. While Sister Lynn agreed on an intellectual level, it was her natural inclination to want to encourage Tommy in order to help him feel better.

I suspect that some of the emotional barriers I erected between myself and Tommy were defensive in nature. I was bracing for the real possibility that, despite our best efforts, we would fail to obtain legal relief for Tommy, and the day would arrive when he was strapped into Alabama's electric chair. I knew that in pursuing every avenue on behalf of my client, I might find myself working right up to his last moment. I had read the excruciating accounts of lawyers who had gone before me as they lost these battles and ultimately witnessed the electrocution of their clients. While in most cases death was likely instantaneous, the psychological torment that accompanies the process leading up to an electrocution is almost beyond description. I could already imagine how things might proceed if worse came to worst.

Under Alabama law, the Commissioner of the Department of Corrections gives the green light for an execution to commence; but Charlie Jones, the Warden of Holman Correctional Facility in Atmore, Alabama—the home of "Yellow Mama," the state's electric chair—would push the button to send thousands of volts of electricity into Tommy's body. Born in Escambia County, Jones graduated from Atmore High School in 1966. He started to work at Holman Prison three years later. He advanced to the rank of Sergeant in 1972, became Deputy Warden by 1976, and was made Warden in 1988. A rotund man who wore cowboy boots, Jones was said to relish his responsibilities as an executioner.

The rest of the process is also heavily prescribed. Before the week of the execution, the Warden meets with the assigned execution team (its members may opt out of their roles, if they wish). The Warden also meets with the condemned prisoner to answer any questions they might have. An operational inspection of the electric chair is also conducted.

The week of the execution, the Warden and the execution team rehearse their roles. They also ensure that the telephone in the prison's viewing room, used to connect the Commissioner of the Alabama Department of Corrections to the offices of Alabama's Governor and Attorney General, is working. They then inspect the electric chair again and test it three times.

For security reasons, the Department of Corrections does not disclose how many hours or days before execution a prisoner is moved from death row to a cell where he or she is placed under constant observation, known as "death watch." No other staff or civilians, except for medical personnel, are allowed in the death watch area without the Warden's permission. While on death watch, the condemned has only a bed, necessary linens, and one change of clothes; all other personal belongings are kept outside the cell and provided as needed, including mail, a telephone, and medication. A television sits outside the cell. Under the death-watch protocol, the condemned may have a Bible and such other reading material as the Warden may approve. The prisoner's time with visitors—including their lawyers—is restricted to the visitation yard.

On the day of the execution, someone asks the condemned what they want for a final meal, which can be anything that the institutional kitchen is able to prepare from existing supplies. This ritual amounts to little more than advance notation of stomach contents for use in the autopsy report that must be prepared following the execution. Officers will inventory the prisoner's property and then designate the disposition of each item before signing the inventory in front of a notary. A medical evaluation of the prisoner is conducted, with the results recorded in a medical journal. The Warden gathers specific information about the funeral arrangements, to be shared with the Department of Forensic Sciences and the Coroner's office.

Before being led to the execution chamber, the condemned is given the opportunity to meet with a chaplain or religious counselor. Then it is time for the extraction team to enter the holding cell. The condemned kneels on the bunk facing the wall, and a body belt and leg irons are placed on them, with plastic zip ties used for handcuffs. Guards are present in force, in case the condemned refuses to go to the death chamber willingly. Thus restrained, and with no hope of escape, the condemned shuffles down the "last mile"—the path from the holding cell to the electric chair.

The space that holds the electric chair is more chamber than room. The door through which the inmate enters is painted robin's-egg blue. Three of the death chamber walls are solid brick; the bright-yellow chair faces the fourth wall, about four feet of brick rising from the floor and topped by clear glass looking into the viewing room. The entire area is about eight feet square.

Before the execution, the attorney for the condemned reviews the death warrant, which is delivered by a marshal to the Warden when the Alabama Supreme Court sets the date for execution. With the Warden's permission, the attorney is allowed to be in the witness room with a clear view of their client seated in the electric chair. Perhaps, in Tommy's case, I will be there, holding Lucille's hand.

The process of placing the chair's straps and belts around the body of the condemned is laborious. Electrodes are fastened to their left leg, with large wet sponges placed between the metal contacts and their skin to make sure that the electricity has as little resistance as possible. Guards sop up any excess water from the floor and put the soaked towels in a bucket. The sensation of wetness, leather, and a dozen hands on one's body while waiting for your inevitable demise must be maddening.

Finally, the guards fasten a metal headpiece on top of the condemned's skull. The water from its sponge runs down their face. The process complete, the Warden reads the death warrant and asks whether the condemned has any final words and whether they want a blindfold. Everyone except for two correctional officers then exits the death chamber.

The Warden proceeds to the room that houses the electrical power source. He throws a series of switches allowing the generator to distribute electrical power. The door between the death chamber and the power source has a single round window, much like a porthole in a ship. When the correctional officers are confident that all the connections between the electric chair and the condemned are secure, one of them holds up, to the window of the door leading to the room with the power source, a round yellow sign that says "ready."

The Warden, seeing this sign, checks with the Commissioner of the Department of Corrections to confirm that no last-minute stay of execution has been granted. It is then time for the final procedures to begin.

The soft whir of an exhaust fan is the only sound in the death chamber. The Warden pushes the button that delivers about two thousand volts of electricity through the condemned's body for twenty seconds, and then hundreds of volts for the one hundred seconds that follow.

Someone draws closed the curtains across the window before an official enters the death chamber to pronounce the condemned dead and declare the time of death. The lifeless corpse is wrestled into a body bag and taken to a van for transport to the Department of Forensic Sciences, where an autopsy is performed. There is only a "brief cleanup" of the execution chamber that night, but the prison staff will clean it more thoroughly the next day. The body is released to next of kin for internment at their expense; if they do not claim the body, the Department of Corrections will be responsible for burial.

Yes, it certainly was easier for me to picture myself representing legal principles rather than a condemned human being. I confess that I always remained one step removed from Tommy Hamilton; and, in self-defense, I plead the picture of his execution that was never far from my mind.

———

Throughout the year, Luke and I traveled to Alabama several times. We stayed in close contact with the Benedictine Sisters of Sacred Heart. I sent them frozen Chicago-style deep-dish pizzas as a token of my appreciation for the room and board they graciously offered me.

Over time, I became acquainted with certain Alabama idioms, at least some of the sayings that were often repeated in the parts of Alabama that I was frequenting. People would regularly introduce a topic of conversation by saying, "I'll tell you what." This translated to: "If you really want to know the truth of the matter, here it is." If you asked someone, "What's up?" the standard first reply was, "Nothing but the rent."

On one of my trips, we decided to dig deeper into the history surrounding the testimony of jailhouse informant Jimmy Dale Owens. Sister Lynn and I went to Moulton, where Owens's criminal court file was kept in the Clerk's office at the Lawrence County Courthouse Annex.

As Lynn and I approached the Clerk's desk, the woman behind the counter greeted me with a syrupy drawl and a smile from ear to ear. "How may I help you?" she asked. "I need to see the court's file on Jimmy Dale Owens, a criminal defendant who was tried in Lawrence County several years ago. Do you have those files stored here or elsewhere?" I replied brusquely. I could sense Lynn beginning to pace uneasily behind me.

"Why do you need them, darling?" the Clerk oozed.

"I represent Tommy Hamilton," I stated.

All the warmth drained from the Clerk's face. She became rigid. It quickly became obvious that she knew Tommy Hamilton was the convicted murderer of county icon Lehman Wood. "Well, bless your heart," she offered.

I was familiar enough with Southern culture by this point not to take her euphemism at face value, but I was pressed for time.

"Where can I get the files?" I asked curtly.

Sister Lynn pulled me out of the Clerk's office and upbraided me: "Don, you can't do that! You got to howdy with people."

Southern hospitality is a marvel, and Sister Lynn quickly schooled me on the subtle dance that is the Southern means of persuasion. I was appropriately chastened. My mistake was in treating the Clerk of Court for Lawrence County as if she were some patronage worker in Cook County, Illinois. The pressure I was feeling may have been an explanation, but it was no excuse for my behavior. If I could not remain disciplined with a court Clerk, I likely would be destructively vulnerable to the Attorney General's lawyers and the Judge.

When the Clerk finally brought us the files, the information contained within raised more questions than it provided answers. Jimmy Dale Owens was born on June 6, 1960. He grew up in Courtland, a small town of approximately five hundred people in Lawrence County. He quickly became familiar with law enforcement, and they became familiar with him.

At 7:30 a.m. on January 9, 1976, Owens, then only fifteen years old, escaped with three others from the Mount Meigs Campus of the Alabama Boys Industrial School, a juvenile correctional facility outside of Montgomery, in which he was incarcerated. He was recaptured by the end of the day.

On February 16, 1977, at the age of sixteen, Owens and three fellow inmates escaped from the Lawrence County Jail. Having advanced in his criminal exploits, Owens was behind bars for violating the terms of his parole from previous sentences and was awaiting trial on a second-degree burglary charge. Having opened their cell doors using a homemade key fashioned from a brass electrical switch plate, the jail-breakers went to a second-story window, sawed through its metal bars, and lowered themselves to the ground with a blanket rope. It was all for naught, though; Owens was recaptured a few days later.

On May 1, 1978, Owens shot up his hometown and himself. After bragging to companions that he was going "to shoot a couple of cops and then kill himself," he threw a garbage can through a hardware store window and stole a 12-gauge shotgun. He fired his first shot through the window of the Citizens Bank.

Owens then focused his attention on city hall. His second blast of deer slugs was aimed at the north door, ultimately passing through a wall, a bookcase, and two more walls before exhausting itself on a chair in the Clerk's office. His third and fourth shots shattered the window of the Mayor's office on the east side of the building, penetrating two walls before reaching the office of the Chief of Police. A fifth shot tore open the front door of city hall, which he entered and briefly trashed.

Leaving city hall, Owens then ran a block and hid in an abandoned boarding house. As police arrived, he shot out the rear window of a patrol car. After taking a few more shots at the police, he ran across the street into a grassy lot.

Police said they heard one more shot, and a few moments later they saw Owens crawling into the street, wounded. He had shot himself in the lower abdomen; a day later, he was still in critical condition. Jimmy Dale Owens was diagnosed as having "psychiatric illness with significant depressive component." He "does indeed have a psychiatric problem," the medical report stated. "It is felt he needs in-patient psychiatric examination and therapy, and he is to be transferred to the regional hospital for treatment." Six months later, in November of 1978, Owens "used a piece of metal coat hanger and penetrated the abdominal wall" in another attempt to kill himself. One month after that, he stuck an automobile antenna into his stomach. Not surprisingly, in May of 1979, he was found not guilty by reason of insanity of criminal charges brought against him for shooting up the town and himself.

We also discovered that in January of 1986, a mere five months after he testified against Tommy Hamilton, Jimmy Dale Owens was released from the Lawrence County Jail. His release was earlier than called for under the terms of his sentence. Moreover, upon his release, Owens was transferred to Georgia pursuant to an interstate compact for supervision of parolees and probationers.

Starting in 1937, agreements such as this one between the states of Alabama and Georgia were designed mostly to provide tracking and supervision of convicts who crossed state lines. Somewhat involuntary interstate transfers such as this one were unusual. The correctional theory behind sending and receiving felons between states appeared in part to be that removing them from the environment and the acquaintances that had led them to commit crimes might reduce the likelihood of future criminal activity. It appears to me that, any penal philosophy window dressing aside, in some cases the interstate compacts were used to conduct a bit of horse trading—a gamble that if I take your incorrigible in exchange for you taking my incorrigible, I might emerge better off in terms of future problems. In any event, for reasons not made clear in the court papers but which raised my suspicions, Lawrence County officials had taken action to get Jimmy Dale Owens out of Alabama shortly after he testified against Tommy. And I wanted to know why.

We needed to talk to Owens about his testimony at Tommy's trial and his subsequent release from jail. The court files revealed that he wound up back in the Lawrence County Jail after only a few months. Unfortunately for us—but perhaps conveniently for some—Jimmy Dale Owens was found hanged in the jail's drunk tank on November 2, 1986. An autopsy revealed a .14 blood-alcohol level and cocaine in his blood at the time of death, which was officially declared to be a suicide. So, Owens was not available to us as a witness.

We instead set out to locate his probation officer, hoping to get answers about how and why this had come to be. But the probation officer had little to offer. In our interview, we did not feel that he was hiding information from us; he just didn't have information to share. Early probation had been arranged without his participation; he did not know why, and he did not know how—which the officer acknowledged was unusual. He suggested we talk with the man who had been county Sheriff at the time, Daniel Ligon.

I was surprised that Sheriff Dan "Snooks" Ligon agreed to meet with us. Don Parker (Tim Littrell's immediate predecessor as District Attorney) had described the Lawrence County Sheriff's Department as "one of the most corrupt law enforcement organizations in the history of Lawrence County," apparently because of the free reign Parker felt Ligon had afforded bootleggers. Snooks Ligon was known to say, "Son, bootlegging is like country music—it's here to stay."

O'Neal Terry, a former investigator for the county, testified in 1989 that the Sheriff ran a "revolving door" jail where inmates guzzled beer from the evidence room and the Sheriff smoked marijuana in the lockup.

Ligon was shockingly cooperative. This probably was because either prosecutor Tim Littrell, the Attorney General's Office, or both wanted to know what issues we might be pursuing. A tall man partial to felt cowboy hats and western-cut suits, the Sheriff was one of those men who tried to loom large over you in conversations, invading your personal space. He told us straightforwardly that his investigator, James Ferris, and the District Attorney's investigator, Ed Weatherford, had interviewed Jimmy Dale Owens outside the Sheriff's house where, as a trusty, Owens was doing menial yard work. Ligon had publicly acknowledged that he and Owens's father "were friends."

James Ferris confirmed Ligon's account.

It turned out that the Judge at Tommy's trial, Judge Burney, had also entered the order granting the early parole—so, we went to ask him for his recollection. Judge Burney simply said that Ligon and Ferris showed up in his courtroom one day with Jimmy Dale Owens to make a request for early release. Judge Burney acknowledged that the parole officer had not been present at the hearing, which he agreed was unusual. Given the facts as presented to him, though, Judge Burney had released Owens and sent him off to Georgia.

Something was *definitely* more than unusual.

We wanted to know who else had been incarcerated in the Lawrence County Jail when Tommy supposedly confessed to Jimmy Dale Owens. We were able to locate one such inmate, William "Eddie" Oliver, who was now driving long-haul trucks. Oliver was more than reluctant when we sought to interview him. His criminal history dated to the early 1960s, with at least eight felony convictions prior to 1981. Two of those convictions were for grand larceny and for buying, receiving, and concealing stolen property. His most recent conviction had been for forgery and escape. Though he'd been sentenced to life imprisonment as a habitual offender, he was now on parole and told us that he feared reprisal from law enforcement if he told us what he knew and testified in court. When Oliver refused to set foot in the state of Alabama for anything remotely related to a legal proceeding—including meeting with us—Luke and Sister Lynn arranged to meet him just across Alabama's northern border in Tennessee.

At about nine o'clock one evening, Luke and Lynn drove about three hours to the designated rendezvous point at a truck stop in Pulaski, Tennessee. They were two fish out of water who had no business being at a truck stop dressed in lawyer uniforms, especially at midnight. Oliver had not provided a description of the truck he would be driving, and the truck stop was filled with semitrailer cabs and trucks. Unless Oliver reached out to them as they wandered around the truck stop, Lynn and Luke would be left to guess which of the parked trucks might contain the reluctant witness.

As time passed and impatience grew, they started knocking on the doors of parked trucks, which could have gotten them shot. Since locating Eddie Oliver that evening had turned into a lost cause, Lynn and Luke made the three-hour drive back to Sacred Heart Monastery.

They continued their hunt for Oliver the next day. Because his information about Jimmy Dale Owens could be important— and his ability to decline a meeting over the phone was too easy— extraordinary efforts were made once again to see him in person. Lynn and Luke drove to Anniston, Alabama, where we thought Oliver either owned a home, or at least lived, when he was not on the road. But Oliver, apparently still out on a trucking run, was not there.

Lynn and Luke had no remaining option except to call Eddie Oliver on the phone. He offered some lame excuse for why he had not met them at the truck stop in Tennessee. Frankly, he was just skittish about meeting with anyone associated with the legal system, let alone a lawyer from Chicago and a Benedictine nun. Nonetheless, Lynn and Luke persuaded him to meet at a Captain D's restaurant off Highway 65 in the northern end of Jefferson County, outside of Birmingham.

It was at this fast-food fish shack that Oliver made his blockbuster revelation: he said that after testifying at Tommy's trial, Jimmy Dale Owens had bragged to Oliver and other jail inmates that law enforcement had promised to release him from jail months before he completed his term of incarceration—in exchange for sworn testimony about Tommy's "confession" to remorselessly murdering Lehman Wood for money. Oliver, however, continued to be fearful of reprisals

by law enforcement. While he was willing to tell Lynn and Luke what
he knew, he was beyond reluctant when it came to telling others.

Documenting a witness's testimony is always important—
especially with a witness like Oliver. One, he had little motivation to
cooperate. Two, he had already proved to be slippery with us. Three,
we might never see him again. It was imperative to get Oliver's story
in writing.

Lynn went to a pay phone and called me to relate what Oliver had
told her and Luke. She also advised me that Oliver strongly resisted
the idea of telling anyone else. We hit on the idea of having Oliver sign
an affidavit as "John Doe." The most important thing was to record the
substance of Oliver's testimony; for now, his identity was less important. While we would have to disclose John Doe's identity to Judge
Suttle, we could promise Oliver that we would not disclose his identity
to the Attorney General or anyone else until the last possible moment.

Oliver found enough comfort in this proposal to agree to it.
Possessing the most legible handwriting among them, Lynn scrawled
a handwritten summary of what Oliver had shared on sheets of a lined
yellow legal pad. To make it clear that this was Oliver's testimony,
and not words that were being put into his mouth, she intentionally
included an innocuous, but factual, error. I believe it was Oliver's date
of birth. When Oliver read what Lynn had written, she had him cross
out the erroneous date, insert the accurate fact, and place the initials
"JD" beside the correction. Lynn then had Oliver sign the document
"John Doe." She brandished her notary stamp and notarized this
important piece of evidence.

We knew the importance of what Oliver had told us. We had to get
Oliver's story before Judge Suttle, in as persuasive a fashion as possible.
We were rightfully concerned that the affidavit would be insufficient,
that Ken Nunnelley and the Attorney General's Office would seek to
bar or at least diminish the evidence unless they could cross-examine
Oliver—who was adamant that he would not appear in any Alabama
court.

I don't know how she did it, but Sister Lynn found a way to "howdy"
Oliver into cooperating. With the affidavit as support, I asked Judge
Suttle to enter orders allowing "John Doe" to present testimony via
a videotaped deposition. Ordinarily, Oliver's proposed testimony

about what another person (Owens) had told him outside the court-room would be barred as hearsay. In this case, though, I argued that the proffered testimony fell under an exception to the hearsay rule, in part because it had been against Owens's interest for him to con-fess to another person that he had committed perjury. Judge Suttle entered the orders on November 28, 1989, over howls of protest from Ken Nunnelley.

I am not certain why local law enforcement purchased perjured testimony. But I believe Tommy's trial was the first capital murder trial for District Attorney Tim Littrell and the first such trial conducted in Lawrence County since 1976, when the death penalty was reinstated in Alabama. And the victim was a prominent citizen in that county. The pressures to secure a conviction and the maximum sentence possible must have been enormous.

Meanwhile, I was subject to pressures of my own. The McDermott law firm reflected the emerging changes in the legal profession that had prompted the failed merger at Isham, Lincoln & Beale. At large law firms at least, the law was becoming more of a business than a pro-fession. Work that used to be more intellectual than commercial was declining. Compensation increased dramatically, not because of price inflation but because law firms were caught in a market trap of their own making. In return for very high compensation, young lawyers were expected to work extremely long hours—not just when clients had emergencies, but to generate revenue. This Faustian bargain left these attorneys with little time for anything else. Family and personal lives often suffered, as did opportunities to contribute to the commu-nity and the profession. The sides of this "advancement pyramid" grew increasingly steep, and most associates were forced to realize that they would never become partners. As specialization increased, the abil-ity to engage in a general practice at a large law firm was vanishing. Personal relationships within large firms also became attenuated as lawyers competed not just against rivals at other firms, but also against their fellow associates for clients and billings. The notion of a partner-ship had devolved into a glorified office-sharing arrangement, and the metric for success became "what have you done for the firm today?"

While my compensation was exceedingly generous, I decided that it amounted to golden handcuffs. Everything required of me to succeed at McDermott, Will & Emery was just what I would need to find success at a law office of my own; but at my own firm, I could be free of the office politics over which I, as a "lateral hire," had little influence, let alone control. In other words, if I did not leave soon, the compensation I was being paid would be used to finance a lifestyle from which it would be difficult to disengage. I knew law partners who used equity lines of credit to pay their estimated quarterly income tax payments, because they spent their entire salary on lavish lifestyles. It was time to leave the nest.

I asked Luke to be my partner, and together we established the litigation boutique of Clark & DeGrand. Our law offices were modest. We had just two rooms and a reception area located in the LaSalle Bank Building at 135 South LaSalle Street in Chicago.

On August 31, 1990, we amended our petition for post-conviction relief to include the claims arising from the perjury and prosecutorial misconduct we had discovered. We itemized each of the reasons why Tommy's conviction and sentence of death were unlawfully and unconstitutionally obtained. The state of Alabama denied our claims in its answer to the amended petition, filed on September 14, 1990, and repeated its mantra that the claims had been brought too late. The evidentiary hearing in which it would be our burden to prove facts supporting our claims was scheduled to begin in five weeks.

CHAPTER EIGHT

The Hearing

The post-conviction evidentiary hearing in Tommy's case began on Monday, October 22, 1990, in the Lauderdale County Courthouse in Florence, Alabama. The third courthouse to serve the justice needs of the community, it was built in 1965 in what was then considered to be a modern style. Topped with a cornice that identifies the structure with tall serif letters, the brick facades of its five boxy stories are broken-up by white columns of trim, spaced about twenty feet apart, that rise from ground level to the roof.

Judge Suttle's courtroom was even blander than the building in which it was located. As in most courtrooms, His Honor's black leather chair was elevated, located behind a white marble desk that was positioned in front of a wall of white marble flanked by dark and faded wood paneling. A large Great Seal of the State of Alabama was centered on the wall behind the Judge's bench. An American flag was displayed to the Judge's right, where the witness stand was located; while the state flag was displayed to his left, where the court Clerk was seated and a jury box was located. A podium for attorneys and others speaking to the court was centered facing the Judge's bench, immediately in front of long, rectangular wood tables for the attorneys. A series of benches served as seating for the public. A dropped ceiling with florescent light panels completed the spartan but functional courtroom.

We arrived early and eager at the courthouse on the morning of the hearing. As outsiders, we were not part of Alabama's bar or culture. I thought we should own that; the more we presented as unusual and extraordinary, the more it played to the thrust of our argument that Tommy Hamilton's case was a departure from legal norms, that he had been unfairly tried and improperly sentenced. We dressed in three-piece suits, white shirts, and muted ties. Sister Lynn wore a prominent cross. With Tommy in the courtroom, there was a significant law enforcement presence. Entrances and exits were guarded by uniformed officers.

I addressed Judge Suttle directly in my opening statement:

> May it please the court, on July 11 of 1984, twenty-year-old Tommy Hamilton, his sixteen-year-old wife, Debbie Hamilton, and his older sister, Janice Glasco, were arrested in connection with the shooting death of Mr. Lehman Wood.
>
> Impoverished and unable to hire an attorney, Tommy Hamilton was appointed two attorneys to represent him in a trial for his life.
>
> Mr. Wes Lavender had yet to seek help for his drinking problem. Mr. Barney Lovelace had been out of law school for less than two years. In August of 1985, Tommy Hamilton was tried and found guilty of capital murder.
>
> The jury voted 10-2 to recommend

that Tommy Hamilton be sentenced
to die in the electric chair.
Under Alabama law, the jury's vote
represented the minimum necessary to
sustain a recommendation for a death
sentence.

On the minimum recommendation,
Judge Billy Burney sentenced Tommy
Hamilton to the maximum penalty.
Although Debbie Hamilton and Janice
Glasco were also indicted for the
capital murder of Mr. Wood, each was
treated differently and prosecuted
separately.

Pursuant to an agreement with the
state, Debbie Hamilton was sentenced
to life in prison with possibility of
parole. On October 26 of 1985, after
trial by jury, Janice Glasco was found
guilty of manslaughter and sentenced
to ten years in jail.

This court now has before it
Tommy Hamilton's petition for post-
conviction relief from his conviction
and sentence of death. Tommy
Hamilton's petition is not a plea for
mercy.

It is a plea for justice. As the
United States Supreme Court has said
repeatedly, "Death, the ultimate
penalty imposed by America's criminal
justice system, is different. It must

be meted out with meticulous fairness
and care."

In the Supreme Court's words,
"The qualitative difference of death
from all other punishments requires
a correspondingly greater degree of
scrutiny of the capital sentencing
determination."

When the record in this case is
subjected to the scrutiny it deserves,
it becomes readily apparent that the
ends of justice have not been met.
Errors of constitutional magnitude
have been made.

As set forth in our petition, many
of the errors that resulted in Tommy
Hamilton's conviction and sentence are
apparent from the evidence that is
already before this court.

Any one of these errors warrants
the granting of certain relief. At
this stage of these proceedings, we
will not address each of these errors,
because they do not involve additional
evidence.

This does not diminish their
importance. Rather, it simply means
that the issues can be presented to
this court during the briefing and
oral argument that will follow this
hearing.

As to the other issues, at this

hearing we will present evidence that
has never before been considered
by any court in deciding the fate
of Tommy Hamilton, never before
considered, largely because these
facts were either purposely concealed
or negligently omitted.

Again, the issues are quite
numerous, and they are set forth in
our petition, which I'm sure that Your
Honor has read. And therefore, I am
not going to mention each and every
one of them at this time.

My failure to mention a particular
issue, however, is not to diminish
its importance. I do, however, want
to briefly address some of the issues
that you will be hearing testimony on
and the testimony you will hear during
this hearing.

The evidence presented at this
hearing will show that among other
things, Tommy Hamilton did not receive
effective assistance of counsel in
violation of his rights guaranteed by
the law and constitution of Alabama,
and the Sixth, Eighth, and Fourteenth
Amendments to the Constitution of the
United States.

Not only were the most significant
portions, if not a majority of the
entire defense, entrusted to and

performed by a statutorily unqualified
attorney, but the representation given
by both of Tommy Hamilton's court-
appointed attorneys failed to meet the
standard which is constitutionally
mandated.

Now as Your Honor is well aware,
claims of ineffective assistance are
often made in death penalty cases. We
do not raise this issue, however, as
a matter of routine, or because we
particularly enjoy dissecting the work
of a fellow lawyer.

We raise this issue because the
evidence in this case compels the
conclusion that the constitutional
guarantees have not been fulfilled.

For example, despite the trial
Judge's offer to provide state funds
to enable defense counsel to secure
the assistance of mental health
experts, to support and present
evidence of Tommy Hamilton's mental
health problems, defense counsel never
sought the assistance of any mental
health experts.

Specifically, Your Honor will hear
from Dr. Merikangas, a board-certified
neurologist and psychiatrist, an
Assistant Clinical Professor at Yale.

Your Honor will also hear from Dr.
Beidleman, who has a doctorate with a

major in clinical psychology and is an
Associate Professor at the University
of Alabama at Birmingham.

The evidence will show that not
only are these gentlemen's opinions
substantiated by the tests that
they conducted on Tommy Hamilton,
but that an electroencephalogram
independently administered to Tommy
by the University of Alabama Hospital
proved to be abnormal and indicative
of neurological dysfunction in Tommy
Hamilton.

In addition, Your Honor will hear
testimony from over ten witnesses who
were never contacted, let alone called
to testify by Tommy's trial lawyers.

These witnesses, including
schoolteachers, coworkers, and
relatives, had important testimony to
tell the jury that heard Tommy's case.

Your Honor will hear Mr. Lavender
and Mr. Lovelace tell you how they
represented Tommy. They are not bad
men or, in general, bad lawyers.
Rather, each, due to his own personal
limitations at the time, could not
afford Tommy what he was entitled to,
that we all are entitled to under the
Constitution.

Your Honor will hear testimony from
Don Holt, a lawyer practicing in this

community and an expert in defending
capital cases. And you will hear his
opinions on what must always be done
in defending such cases, but what was
not done in Tommy Hamilton's case.

And Your Honor will hear the
testimony of Lucille Hamilton, Tommy's
mother, as we believe it should have
been presented to the jury and the
Judge that heard Tommy's case.

Your Honor will also hear testimony
concerning what we believe to be the
most troubling aspect of this case.
The evidence presented at this hearing
will show that Tommy Hamilton's
conviction and sentence were obtained
on the basis of perjured testimony
given by a convicted felon in exchange
for promises by Lawrence County law
enforcement officers that the perjurer
would be, and was in fact, released
early from jail.

This is a serious allegation, and
we don't make it lightly. But Your
Honor will see videotaped testimony
by a witness to whom this plan was
revealed.

The evidence that proves this
miscarriage of justice will also
be supported by the testimony of
another witness, a witness discovered
by the Alabama Attorney General's

investigation of this issue, and only
recently disclosed to us.

As one appellate court has recently
observed, there is substantial danger
that our society, concerned with the
growth of crime, will retreat from
the safeguards and rights accorded to
the accused by the Constitution.

The need to combat crime should
never be utilized to justify an
erosion of our fundamental guarantees.
Indeed, the growing volume of criminal
cases should make us even more
vigilant.

The greater the quantity, the
greater the risk to the quality of
justice. At the conclusion of these
proceedings and after you have heard
all of the evidence, we will ask you
to affirm these fundamental guarantees,
ensure the quality of justice in
our system, and thereby grant Tommy
Hamilton the justice that he deserves.

Thank you.

When I finished, Ken Nunnelley advised Judge Suttle that he would
reserve his opening statement until he presented the state's evidence
following the conclusion of our presentation. We thus proceeded to
call our witnesses and present our evidence.

Since Jimmy Dale Owens's perjured testimony was key to our case,
we first presented Eddie Oliver's videotaped deposition, in which he
answered our questions and those of the Attorney General's Office
as if he were on the witness stand. It was admitted into evidence and

played for the court. He stated that Ed Weatherford, an investigator for the District Attorney's Office, and James Ferris, an investigator for the Lawrence County Sheriff's Office, frequently came to the Lawrence County Jail. Ferris would ask Jimmy Dale Owens—like Oliver, a trusty at the jail—to attempt to get incriminating information from Tommy Hamilton, who was locked up in a cell awaiting trial for the murder of Lehman Wood.

> Oliver: They were always kidding [Owens]
> when he would come in. They would say,
> "Go up there and pick Tommy and see
> what you can find out and help us out
> here."
>
> . . .
>
> Mr. DeGrand: Okay. What did Owens say
> when Ferris would say that to him, if
> you recall?
> A: He would just pop something back, you
> know, like he was kidding with him.
> Q: Did he ever say, "Yes, I'll do that?"
> A: I never heard him say. On one occasion
> he said, "If you'll turn me loose I
> will."
> Q: And when was that?
> A: That was just a few days before
> that they approached him out at the
> Sheriff's house.

Oliver testified that a few weeks before Tommy's trial, he and Owens were working outside the home of Sheriff Dan Ligon. Oliver was mowing grass. Weatherford and Ferris approached the two prisoners, stating that they needed to speak with Owens. Then they accompanied Owens to a secluded area behind the Sheriff's garage, near a fishpond.

When, at the conclusion of their conversation, Weatherford and Ferris left the Sheriff's home, Owens rejoined Oliver.

```
Question: Now what exactly, the best you
    can recall, did Owens tell you when he
    came back from his conversation with
    Ferris and Weatherford?
Answer: Well, first he kind of smiled.
    He said, "After the trial I'll be a
    free man. I'm going to Georgia," or
    something to that effect. And I said,
    "What do you mean?" He said, "I'm
    going to testify for them."
    . . .
Q: Okay. Do you know why he did that? Did
    he explain to you why he did that?
A: Where he could get out of jail.
Assistant Attorney General interrupting:
    I didn't hear your answer. I'm sorry.
A: Where he could get out of jail. They
    told him that they would help him get
    out early.
Q: Mr. Weatherford and Mr. Ferris told
    Mr. Owens that they would help him
    get out of jail early if he gave his
    testimony?
A: Right.
```

Oliver recounted that prior to Tommy's trial, Owens confessed that he planned to give false testimony at Tommy's trial.

```
Answer: He [Owens] said that, uh,
    he had told them [law enforcement
```

authorities] that he would testify
that Tommy told him that he would
shoot the son of a bitch anyway.
Pardon my language.

Question: Referring to Lehman Wood?

A: Yeah. And, uh, he wasn't sorry he done
   it. And I asked him did Tommy tell him
   that. He said, "No, but that's what
   we're going to say."

. . .

A: And, uh, he said, "I'm going to say
   that Tommy said that he shot the
   son of a bitch, and he deserved to
   die, and he would shoot him again or
   something to that effect."

. . .

Q: Did Mr. Owens ever make any statement
   to you regarding whether that
   testimony was true or false?

A: Yes.

Q: What did he tell you?

A: He said he made it up. He said the
   more—the better he could make it
   sound, they would help him more.

Q: How many times did he make that
   statement to you that his testimony
   against Tommy Hamilton was false?

A: Well, after the trial is mostly
   when he did it. Because he was real
   nervous and upset, you know. And he
   was scared. He said, "I did the wrong
   thing. I did the wrong thing." And,

uh, he kept asking me what he should
do. I said, "You're the one that's got
to live with it now." He said, "Even
after I did that they've lied to me."

Q: Did he tell you on more than one
occasion that the testimony he gave at
the trial of Tommy Hamilton was false?

A: Yes.

Q: Did he tell you as many as five times?

A: I don't recall, but I do know more
than once because one time he even
cried about it.

. . .

Q: Do you remember anything else that
Owens said?

A: Then later he told me that he wished
he hadn't have told him that because
Tommy hadn't told him that.

Oliver stated that after testifying against Tommy, Owens repeatedly pressed law enforcement authorities to honor the deal they had
made with him.

Answer: Not—well, after—you know, a few
weeks after the trial and every day he
would ask him, "When are you going to
turn me loose?" And they were telling
him it was too early now and, uh,
because it would look funny.

. . .

A: Well, he asked Weatherford on one
occasion. And Weatherford told him,

```
said, "I didn't make the deal with
you. You'll have to talk to Ferris."
```

. . .

```
Q: Okay, uh, and as I understand your
   testimony, Owens every time he would
   see Ferris he would just go up to him
   and ask him when am I getting out of
   jail?
A: Yes.
Q: Would he say what about our deal or
   anything like that?
A: Yeah.
Q: So he—
A: He would say, "I did my part now y'all
   do y'all's part."
```

In court before Judge Suttle, we moved on to a slate of witnesses who could support certain facts in Oliver's testimony. We questioned Sheriff Ligon, Investigator Ed Weatherford, and Investigator James Ferris about the testimony given by Jimmy Dale Owens at Tommy's trial. Weatherford and Ferris admitted to speaking with Owens at the Sheriff's home before Tommy's trial. Weatherford acknowledged that another inmate from the Lawrence County Jail was working there that day, while Sheriff Ligon acknowledged that there had indeed been occasions when Oliver and Owens were together at his home. Weatherford confirmed Oliver's estimate that the conversation between Owens, Ferris, and Weatherford lasted approximately ten minutes.

We questioned Sheriff Ligon about the unusual nature of interviewing a material witness in a murder investigation in the Sheriff's yard.

```
Question: I just want to ask you about
   what your customary practice was at
   the time. And let me ask you again,
```

```
        would it have been customary practice
        at the time for interviews of jail
        inmates or potential witnesses to have
        occurred at your home?
Answer: No, sir.
Q: And in fact, would it have been
        unusual for jail inmates or potential
        witnesses to have been interviewed at
        your home?
A: Yes, sir.
```

Indeed, Sheriff Ligon repeatedly acknowledged that the interview of Jimmy Dale Owens at his home was unprecedented.

Sheriff Ligon testified that he instructed all his investigators, as a matter of policy, to make notes of witness interviews. Weatherford confirmed that notes of an interview with an important witness would be made:

```
Question to Weatherford: Would it be
        your practice and policy to keep
        notes or records, or some kind of
        written documentation with respect to
        interviews when the information the
        witness had to give was of importance
        to a case you were investigating?
Answer: Yes, sir.
```

Similarly, Ferris admitted that it was his custom to make sure that someone was recording important interviews, adding that he personally took notes unless someone else was recording the interview. Weatherford considered the information provided by Owens to be productive with regard to his investigation into the murder of Lehman Wood. Inexplicably, however, neither Weatherford nor Ferris took notes during this extraordinary interview.

We questioned Sheriff Ligon about the circumstances of Owens's release and the arrangements that were made for Owens to leave Alabama and go to Georgia.

> Question: Now do you recall if the
> release of Jimmy Dale Owens at that
> time was an early release for him?
> Had he completed the sentence he was
> supposed to serve when you sought the
> release for him?
>
> Answer: No, sir, I don't believe he had.
> I believe he lacked eight or nine
> months maybe.
>
> Q: Okay, now when you say that you
> initiated the request with Judge
> Burney that he be released early,
> there were no court proceedings or
> anything—you just went and talked to
> Judge Burney?
>
> A: No sir. Private conversation with
> Judge Burney and I.
>
> . . .
>
> Q: Did you initiate the conversation with
> Judge Burney?
>
> A: Yes, sir. I went and talked to him.
>
> Q: Now to the best of your recollection,
> Mr. Ligon, were special arrangements
> made for Jimmy Dale Owens to leave the
> state of Alabama early on probation?
>
> A: Yes, I believe that's right.

The early release of Jimmy Dale Owens on probation was unusual
to say the least. His probation officer at the time was Willis Bynum.
Mr. Bynum testified as follows:

> Question: And it was part of your duties
> and responsibilities, as being Jimmy
> Dale Owens's probation officer, to be
> fully informed and abreast of any
> efforts that were being made with
> respect to him getting probation, was
> it not?
>
> Answer: Yes, sir. In general terms, I
> would have been involved in developing
> a program or checking out a program.
>
> Q: Okay. You weren't involved in
> developing a program that Jimmy Dale
> Owens pursued, were you?
>
> A: No, sir, I wasn't.
>
> Q: And in fact, isn't it the normal
> practice for when a person's put on
> probation, for there to be court
> proceedings in which that probation is
> granted by a Judge in open court?
>
> A: No, sir. On occasion, that's true.
>
> Q: And in Jimmy Dale Owens's case, there
> were no court proceedings with respect
> to his probation, were there?
>
> A: I don't recall any.
>
> Q: And you never attended any court
> proceedings in the case of Jimmy Dale
> Owens's probation, did you?
>
> A: Not after his original hearing.

Q: And you certainly didn't attend any
   court proceedings in January of 1986
   when Jimmy Dale Owens was granted
   probation, correct?

A: I don't believe so.

Q: And Sheriff Ligon never talked to you
   about Jimmy Dale Owens getting early
   release on his probation, did he?

A: Yes sir. He did not talk to me. He
   dropped a letter off at the office that
   had been sent to him by Jimmy Dale's
   sister. He gave the letter giving the
   employment and the address, which
   I put in the form of an Interstate
   Compact Request for Supervision in the
   State of Georgia. At that point, that
   was the contact I had with Sheriff
   Ligon about this.

Q: So it was Sheriff Ligon that initiated
   your involvement in Jimmy Dale Owens's
   probation, correct?

A: He advised me of that program, yes, sir.

Q: But he never discussed with you the
   appropriateness of probation for Jimmy
   Dale Owens, did he?

A: No, sir.

Jimmy Dale Owens's absence from Lawrence County lasted only a
few months. As stated by Sheriff Ligon:

Question: And Jimmy Dale Owens ended
   up back in the Lawrence County Jail
   before the end of 1986, didn't he?

Answer: Yes, sir.

Q: In fact, Jimmy Dale Owens died in the
   Lawrence County Jail on November of
   1986, didn't he?

A: I believe that's right.

Q: He was found hung inside his jail cell
   there at that time?

A: Yes, sir.

Q: Mr. Ligon, in a civil lawsuit filed
   in federal court, you were recently
   found personally liable for the death
   of Jimmy Dale Owens in the Lawrence
   County Jail, weren't you?

A: Yes, sir.

In spite of all the irregularities on which we shone a spotlight at the hearing, Weatherford and Ferris vehemently denied that they had solicited testimony from Owens in exchange for a promise of lenient treatment.

After we discovered evidence of the offer of lenient treatment that led Owens to commit perjury, we had amended our petition for relief to include this claim—which, in turn, prompted the Alabama Attorney General's Office to conduct its own independent investigation of this issue. On or about September 6, 1990, investigator Hollis Gandy sought to locate other individuals who had been incarcerated at the Lawrence County Jail at the time of Tommy Hamilton's trial. Among the individuals Gandy managed to locate and interview was Anthony Winchester, an ex-felon who had been convicted in June of 1980 of both theft of property in the second degree and escape, of escape again in October of 1981, and of burglary in 1986.

The Attorney General was aware of his responsibilities under both the Constitution and Judge Suttle's order of May 17, 1990, granting our motion requiring him to disclose such exculpatory information. Accordingly, by letter dated September 25, 1990—less than thirty days before the date set for the evidentiary hearing—he advised us of certain statements made by Winchester to Investigator Gandy. In response to our request for production of all records connected with the Gandy investigation, we received interview notes but with the state's redactions. Only after the evidentiary hearing began, when we pressed in court for enforcement of Judge Suttle's disclosure order, were we provided with unredacted copies.

When we put Gandy on the stand, his testimony authenticated the notes of his September 6, 1990 interview of Anthony Winchester. The notes, now admitted into evidence at our request, revealed that three weeks after Jimmy Dale Owens testified at Tommy's trial, Winchester heard Owens say, "They ain't done what they were going to do for me." Gandy's notes also stated: "Charlie [Garrison] heard it too," and, importantly, "'they told me they would cut me loose if I testified for them against Tommy,' Jimmy Dale Owens said."

Anthony Winchester was called to testify.

> Question: Now in August of 1985 and prior
>   to Tommy Hamilton's trial for the
>   death of Mr. Wood, did you have any
>   conversations with Jimmy Dale Owens
>   about Mr. Owens possibly testifying at
>   Tommy Hamilton's trial?
> Answer: Yes, sir.
> Q: Do you recall what Mr. Owens said to
>   you during this conversation?
> A: Yes, sir.
> Q: What did he say to you?
> A: He told me, he says, uh, "I went over
>   there," he says, "the DA," he said,
>   "offered me a deal." And he said, "I
>   went over there and testified against
>   Tommy." And he come back, about a
>   couple weeks after that. He said,
>   "Well, I don't believe they're keeping

their end of the bargain." But a few
weeks after that, Jimmy Dale Owens did
get out. Now I don't know whether the
DA give him a deal or not. But he said
they offered him a deal.

Q: Okay, and he told you that they made
the offer before he went to testify at
Tommy's trial?

A: Yes, sir.

Q: And then after the trial and after Mr.
Owens had testified, what did he tell
you about this deal?

A: After he testified, he says, uh, "I
don't know," he says, "I don't believe
the DA gonna keep their bargain up."
He said, "They offered me probation
and leave the state." And then a few
weeks after the trial, Jimmy Dale
Owens got out.

Q: Okay, now it was sometime after the
trial that he actually got out of
jail, wasn't it?

A: Yes, sir.

Q: You don't recall exactly how long a
period of time?

A: No, sir, I sure don't.

We had Judge Burney testify as to the disproportionate nature of
Tommy's sentence when compared to that received by his sister Janice.

Question: Okay, I'll be happy to rephrase
it, restate it. Tommy Hamilton's death

```
sentence is disproportionately severe,
is it not, Judge?
Answer: When compared to the sentence
     that Janice received, in my mind so.
     .  .  .

Q: But my question is, then, if Tommy had
     been tried and sentenced after Janice
     had received ten years from you, would
     his sentence be the same?
A: I can't believe that I would have
     sentenced him to death.
Q: And Judge, that would be true, even
     if the jury had recommended that you
     sentence him to death?
A: Yes sir.
```

He made it clear that this was because of his assessment that Janice bore responsibility for the crime.

```
Answer: And in fact, my own opinion, I
     felt like she (Janice) was more of
     an active factor. Had Janice never
     participated, I don't believe Tommy
     would have ever been involved.
```

Judge Burney also testified that he invited Tommy's trial attorneys to petition for funds to secure expert witnesses. Meaningfully, he added that had Tommy's attorneys requested funds to pay for mental health experts who could have evaluated Tommy and then testified in court to their findings, he would have granted that request.

```
Question: Judge Burney, do you recall
     offering Tommy Hamilton's trial
```

> lawyers an opportunity to petition
> the court for the appointment of
> psychiatric assistance at state
> expense?
>
> Answer: Yes, sir.
>
> Q: And if they had made such a petition
> to the court, and followed up in your
> invitation in that regard, would you
> have granted such a petition?
>
> A: Yes.

We were off to a strong start.

We suspected that mental illness ran in Tommy's family. For example, we had reason to believe that his sister Joyce suffered from schizophrenia so severe and untreated that she was housebound in a small home next to Lucille's. We therefore had Dr. James Ray Merikangas, a forensic psychiatrist, perform tests on Tommy and prepare an assessment.

Dr. Merikangas is a neuropsychiatrist—that is, a medical doctor who specializes in diseases of the brain, with an emphasis on their relationship to human behavior, mental illness, and what are generally called psychiatric conditions. He obtained his undergraduate degree from Villanova University in 1960 and graduated from Johns Hopkins University School of Medicine in 1969. He interned at the Washington Hospital Center and completed residencies in both psychiatry and neurology, including a term in 1973 as chief resident in neurology at Yale University's School of Medicine. Dr. Merikangas, who was certified as a specialist in psychiatry in 1974 and in neurology in 1978 by the American Board of Psychiatry and Neurology, was one of only eighty-five doctors in the United States to have been board certified in both psychiatry and neurology in the last twenty-five years.

On August 29, 1987, Sister Lynn escorted our expert to the prison to examine Tommy. The psychiatrist was experienced in dealing with the requirements of a prison. He carefully and calmly explained to prison staff the purpose and use of each of the instruments that he needed to bring inside in order to conduct a thorough exam, including a sharp-pointed rolling instrument used to check reflexes. Lynn accompanied the doctor into the chilly examination room and witnessed the forensic evaluation. She suppressed both her desire to ask numerous questions and a natural inclination to pat Tommy on the back and tell him everything would be okay.

In addition to a complete physical examination, the psychiatrist requested that an Alabama hospital independently perform an electroencephalogram, or EEG. Doctors routinely use a device called an electroencephalograph to record brain waves on tracings called electroencephalograms (or EEGs). (In courtroom testimony, sometimes the abbreviation EEG is used interchangeably for both the device and the test.) An EEG can detect brain and neurological dysfunctions, including epilepsy and other seizure disorders. The EEG performed on Tommy showed an irregularity in brain-wave function after twenty-one minutes of assessment. The Alabama hospital's report concluded that Tommy's brain-wave activities were "abnormal."

Based upon the results of these examinations and tests, the interviews he conducted, and all other available information upon which specialists customarily rely to formulate their opinions, Dr. Merikangas concluded to a reasonable degree of medical, neurological, and psychiatric certainty that, in the summer of 1984 when Tommy shot Lehman Wood, Tommy 1) was under extreme emotional and mental disturbance; 2) acted under extreme duress and without the capacity to appreciate the criminality of his conduct or to conform his conduct to the requirements of the law; and 3) was substantially impaired by his mental illness. Specifically, Dr. Merikangas testified that Tommy is a brain-damaged individual suffering from a mild intellectual disability and impulse control disorder problems with a neurological basis. Each of the expert's three opinions are recognized under Alabama law as mitigating circumstances.

We also asked a psychologist, Dr. William B. Beidleman, to evaluate Tommy. Dr. Beidleman obtained his undergraduate degree from Emory University in 1974, where he majored in sociology and minored in criminology. He obtained a master's degree from Georgia State University in the assessment and treatment of criminal offenders and a doctorate in clinical psychology from the University of Alabama. Dr. Beidleman is certified by the state of Alabama as a forensic examiner;

was one of the five members of the Alabama State Ethics Board in Psychology (the body that regulates the ethical practice of psychology in the state of Alabama); and was an Associate Professor of psychiatry and an Associate Professor of medical psychology at the University of Alabama in Birmingham.

On June 28, 1989, and again on October 27, 1989, Dr. Beidleman interviewed and examined Tommy Hamilton in prison, conducting a clinical interview and administering numerous tests. Based upon the results of these examinations, Dr. Beidleman concurred to a reasonable degree of psychological certainty that, in the summer of 1984 when Tommy shot Lehman Wood, Tommy 1) was under the influence of extreme emotional distress; 2) acted under extreme duress and without the capacity to appreciate the criminality of his conduct or to conform his conduct to the requirements of law; and 3) was substantially impaired by psychological problems. In short, Dr. Beidleman agreed completely with Dr. Merikangas's assessment. He also testified that Tommy had a very severe substance abuse problem at the time he killed Lehman Wood.

Next, we turned to the issue of inadequate representation of counsel: namely, lead attorney Wesley Miles Lavender and the co-counsel he chose to assist him, Barnes F. Lovelace. For starters, we presented evidence in support of our claim that Barney Lovelace was statutorily unqualified to represent Tommy. Lovelace himself admitted that he fell short of the standard:

```
Question: And at the time that you were
    appointed to represent Tommy Hamilton,
    did you have five years of prior
    experience in the practice of
    criminal law?
Answer: No.
```

Wes Lavender made it clear that Lovelace was no mere assistant, but in fact acted entirely on his own—acknowledging that he had fully delegated certain aspects of Tommy's defense to Lovelace.

Answer: Well, that's why I said that
about lead. The way we handled this
case, the way we handle all cases when
people are appointed with me, or we
are retained together, is generally we
decide what has to be done and assign,
"You do this, and I'll do that."

. . .

Question: Then with respect to both the
trial level and the appellate level
of Tommy's representation, it's fair
to say that you both did portions of
each?

A: I would say so, yes.

Q: And you delegated some
responsibilities to be handled by Mr.
Lovelace at the trial level?

A: Yes.

Among the responsibilities Lavender delegated to Lovelace was responsibility for the gathering of evidence to mitigate a jury recommendation or judicial sentence of death, if Tommy was convicted of capital murder. We established that Lavender did nothing in this regard; rather, it was solely left to Lovelace, as Lavender himself testified.

Question: During the time between October
24 of 1984, when you were appointed
to represent Tommy Hamilton, and
August 1, 1985, when Mr. Lovelace was
appointed to represent Mr. Hamilton,
did you do anything in an attempt
to obtain, investigate and obtain

```
evidence for presentation at the
sentencing hearing?
Answer: No, probably not.
```

Lavender's failure to attempt to mitigate a recommendation or sentence of death got even worse. In entering Tommy's plea of not guilty, he had advised Judge Burney that there were "reasonable grounds to believe that the said Tommy Hamilton may be presently insane or otherwise mentally incompetent, and as such, may be unable to assist in his own defense." In spite of that, he chose not to seek mental health expertise to assist in Tommy's defense. We got Lavender to acknowledge he had no tactical reason for that choice, and we attacked him for his failures in preparing Tommy's defense in general and the presentation of mitigating evidence at the sentencing hearings in particular.

```
Question: Now you mentioned the Southern
    Poverty Law Center, that you sought
    out their assistance. Do you consider
    them as a source of authoritative and
    reliable information on how to defend
    capital cases?
Answer: Yes.
Q: And did you in fact make use of and
    rely on some of the materials and look
    to those materials for guidance and
    assistance in defending Tommy?
A: Yes.

    .  .  .

Q: Now in the manual prepared by the
    Southern Poverty Law Center that you
    requested and considered authoritative
    and relied upon, they address the
    issue of whether or not psychological,
    psychiatric, or mental health
```

professionals ought to be consulted in
defending a capital case, don't they?

A: I believe so, yes.

Q: Okay, and specifically, on page 3 of
that manual, they address that issue.
And I'd like to know if you could read
for the court that particular portion
of the manual that you relied on.

A: (Reading from the document)

"In order to be able to give the jury
a reason not to kill, you must
conduct the most extensive background
investigation imaginable. You should
look at every aspect of your client's
life, from birth to the present, talk
to everyone that you can find that
has ever had any contact with the
defendant.

"Somewhere in the course of the
investigation, you will always be able
to discover important facts. In most
every situation, it will be useful
to have your client evaluated by a
competent, private psychiatrist or
psychologist.

"That evaluation can usually provide
important mitigating evidence. A good
background investigation can enable
you to make a giant step forward in
finding that all-important reason which
will make the jury spare your client's
life.

"Failure to make that background
investigation will seal your client's
fate."

Q: And the same topic is also addressed
on page 10 of that manual that you
relied on. And I'll ask you if you
would read that to the Court, that
particular section of the manual.

A: (Reading from the document)

"Almost every state death penalty
statute has statutory mitigating
circumstances which deal with the
defendant's mental state. Typically,
they allow a jury to consider whether
the capacity of the defendant to
appreciate the criminality of his
conduct, or to conform their conduct
to the requirements of the law,
was substantially impaired; or to
determine whether the capital felony
was committed while the defendant was
under the influence of extreme mental
or emotional disturbance.

"These circumstances clearly contemplate
a situation wherein the defendant
suffers under a mental health problem
which is serious but does not fall
within the legal parameters of
insanity.

"In addition, the law permits extensive
presentation of such nonstatutory
mitigating circumstances as alcoholism

and drug addiction or usage. It is
virtually impossible to successfully
present this kind of evidence without
professionals such as psychologists
and psychiatrists.

"These kinds of witnesses can explain
the defendant's behavior in meaningful
terms to the jury, and help them
understand that a particularly
horrible homicide may not solely be
the product of the defendant's evil,
but may be directly related to a
mental disease or other condition such
as alcoholism or drug addiction or
usage.

"Psychiatrists and psychologists can
provide the all-important reason which
a jury must have in order to vote for
life over death. If your client cannot
afford the professional services such
as a psychologist or psychiatrist,
then petition the court and request
funds for their employment."

Q: Did you ever have occasion to review
the Taylor Hardin report that was
prepared on Tommy before making your
decision whether or not to pursue
independent psychiatric or mental
health assistance?

A: Yes.

Q: What was your reaction or opinion to
the fact that the report indicated

that Tommy Hamilton was borderline
intellectual functioning?

A: My observations of Tommy, I was
surprised by—well, let me put it this
way. I had read that report before I
met Tommy, And I was surprised by that
report after I met Tommy, because I
would not have suspected that myself.

Q: So apparently the mental health
professionals at Taylor Hardin were
able to spot something in Tommy that
you didn't see, is that right?

Assistant Attorney General: Objection.
Leading, Your Honor.

The Court: Overruled.

A: I guess you could put it that way.

. . .

Q: So was there any possible disadvantage
that you could think of to asking
the court for the funds to ask a
psychologist/psychiatrist or other
mental health professional to give you
an oral opinion or the benefit of oral
consultation with respect to Tommy
Hamilton before you went to trial?

A: If it was not discoverable by the
state, probably not.

Q: Do you know of any rule, statute or
case law in Alabama that would have
required you to disclose to the state
such a consultation prior to trial,

```
    if you decided not to present such
    testimony in evidence at the trial?
A:  We have pretty limited discovery in
    criminal cases. I'm not sure that
    there were any at that time.
```

The decision by Lavender and Lovelace not to seek state-funded mental health evaluations and assistance becomes even harder to explain given Lavender's testimony that the state of Alabama had paid for an independent psychologist in the death penalty case he had most recently handled prior to taking on Tommy's defense.

We fortified our attack on Lavender's representation of his client through the testimony of Don Holt, an Alabama criminal defense attorney with extensive experience in trying capital murder cases in that region of the state. Holt had graduated from the University of Alabama School of Law in 1962 and practiced law in Alabama for over twenty-eight years. He had tried over two hundred homicide cases, at least one hundred of them involving the charge of murder—dozens of which were tried to verdict. He had represented defendants in well over twenty capital murder trials. Holt had represented Janice at her trial.

Generally, attorneys are poor witnesses. And trial lawyers, who are frequently frustrated thespians, are particularly incorrigible. But Don Holt was the most respected criminal defense attorney in northwest Alabama. We needed an expert to establish the standard for providing effective assistance of counsel to capital defendants in that part of the country and opine that the standard had not been met by Tommy's trial attorneys. We also needed to blunt any notion that this case was about Chicago lawyers unfairly critiquing the Alabama attorneys. So, Luke persevered in getting Don Holt to deliver the goods.

```
Question: In your opinion, is it
    necessary in order for a lawyer
    representing a defendant charged with
    a capital offense, to render adequate
    and effective legal representation, to
    retain and consult with an independent
```

psychologist or psychiatrist, even
where the defendant has been evaluated
for competency and sanity at the
Taylor Hardin Secure Medical Facility?

Answer: In my opinion, it is necessary.

Q: And on what do you base that opinion?

A: Well, my primary basis for that
opinion is that I have had, over the
twenty-eight years that I've practiced
law, I've had several defendants who
were evaluated at Bryce (a mental
health hospital in Tuscaloosa) or at
Taylor Hardin.

I've had some of those clients privately
evaluated. I have had clients that got
a very distinctly different evaluation
from private practitioners than they
received from the staff at Bryce.

I have also had defendants acquitted
on the pleas of insanity where Bryce
reps came up and testified that their
evaluations showed them to be sane,
when the private employed psychologist
and/or psychiatrist said that, in
their professional opinion, they were
insane by the standards at that time,
the legal standards at the time of the
alleged offense was committed.

I had two separate murder clients that
Bryce sent back, said they were okay,
that local people said were insane,
and juries acquitted.

. . .

Q: Mr. Holt, at our request, you have
   reviewed the trial transcript of the
   capital murder trial of Tommy
   Hamilton for the death of Lehman Wood,
   haven't you?

A: Yes, I have.

Q: And have you formulated certain
   opinions based upon that review?

A: Well, I'm sure I have formed lots of
   opinions. I don't know specifically
   what you are inquiring about.

Q: Have you formulated an opinion as
   to whether Tommy received inadequate
   representation because his trial
   lawyers failed to retain or consult
   with a psychiatrist or a psychologist
   regarding his mental status?

A: Well, you know, I hate to get on the
   witness stand and be critical of a
   fellow lawyer. But I'll say if I had
   represented Tommy Hamilton, or if I'd
   represented any other person under the
   same or similar circumstances, I would
   have deemed it extremely necessary
   and very advisable to secure an
   evaluation.

Assistant Attorney General: Your Honor,
   I object, and ask that the answer
   be struck, that it's nonresponsive.
   The witness was asked whether it was
   effective assistance, or not.

```
The Court: Your objection is volunteering
    information, but it's overruled.
A: Well, I'll answer it the way he
    wants it answered then. In my
    opinion, in order for adequate
    representation to have been provided
    Tommy Hamilton, he should have—the
    lawyer representing him should have
    secured a psychological or psychiatric
    evaluation, or both.
Q: And that's independent of Taylor
    Hardin?
A: Absolutely.
```

At that point, I whispered to myself, "Thank you, Mr. Assistant Attorney General."

Lovelace's ineffectiveness could be attributed in large part to the fact that he was only two years out of law school—and had participated in the trial of only two felony cases—before being entrusted with the defense in a capital murder case. Lavender's ineffectiveness and lack of judgment, on the other hand, may be attributed to the fact that he abused and was dependent upon alcohol.

Lavender declined to fully acknowledge this problem to the court.

```
Question: Mr. Lavender, at the time of
    Tommy's trial, you were an alcoholic,
    weren't you?
Answer: I am now.
Q: You were at the time of Tommy's trial?
A: I drank a lot of whiskey. I don't know
    if I was an alcoholic then or not. I
    never hid it. Everybody knew it.
```

```
Q: When did you seek treatment for that?
A: November of 1987.
```

The scope and extent of Mr. Lavender's addiction was vividly described by those who knew him best.

Harvey Pride was the Vice President of manufacturing for Lakeland Industries. He was "very close friends" with Lavender for fifteen years, seeing him "at least four or five times a week, sometimes more" from July 1984 (when Tommy was arrested) through all of 1987 (when Tommy's last direct appeal was completed). Pride saw Lavender sometimes at lunch and quite a bit at night at the Freeway Night Club in Southland Plaza in Decatur, Alabama.

James Roger Lowery owns the Freeway Night Club. He first met Lavender when the club opened in April of 1985, seeing him "every day or two" from the time the club opened for business through Tommy's direct appeal to the Alabama Supreme Court in 1987.

Between July of 1984 (when Tommy was arrested) up to August of 1985 (when Tommy's trial began), Lavender drank heavily, as described by Harvey Pride:

```
Question: Now I'd like to focus on the
    time period between July of 1984 to
    the beginning of August 1985 for a
    moment. How many times a week did you
    see Mr. Lavender drinking during that
    particular time period?
Answer: Probably 80 percent.
Mr. Nunnelley: Objection. Nonresponsive.
The Court: Overruled. I take it it was 80
    percent of the time that you saw him.
A: Eighty percent, yes.
Q: And on each of these occasions,
    approximately how much alcohol did Mr.
    Lavender drink?
```

A: Wesley would have ten doubles, which
   is probably close to a bottle.

Q: Now from what you could observe, what
   effect did this amount of alcohol have
   on Mr. Lavender?

A: He'd get pretty drunk. Matter of fact,
   real drunk.

Q: From what you could observe, was his
   ability to drive a car impaired?

A: Yes.

Q: From what you could observe, was his
   ability to walk impaired?

A: He would wobble. He would not be
   straight.

Q: From what you could observe, was his
   ability to talk impaired?

A: Very much so.

These observations were confirmed by James Roger Lowery:

Question: Mr. Lowery, I'd like to, for
   the moment, focus on the time frame
   from when the Freeway Club opened in
   April of '85, up until the beginning
   of August of '85, and ask you some
   questions about that particular time
   period.

How many times each week, during that
   time period, did you see Mr. Lavender
   drinking alcohol?

Answer: I would say daily to every
   other day.

```
Q: And on each of these occasions,
   approximately how much alcohol did Mr.
   Lavender drink?
A: A lot.
Q: Do you have any idea as to how much
   the quantity was in terms of number of
   drinks or however you might be able to
   measure it?
A: He drank a lot, a whole bottle.
Q: Now from what you could observe, what
   effect did this much alcohol have on
   Mr. Lavender?
A: He would be—he'd be intoxicated.
Q: From what you could observe, was his
   ability to drive a car impaired?
A: Definitely.
Q: From what you could observe, was his
   ability to walk impaired?
A: Yes.
Q: From what you could observe, was his
   ability to talk impaired?
A: Yes.
```

Harvey Pride testified that Lavender's intoxication continued at nights during Tommy's trial:

```
Question: I'd like to, for a moment,
   focus on the time period of August
   1985. How many times a week did you
   see Mr. Lavender drink alcohol during
   this time period?
Answer: At least every time I was with
   Wesley.
```

```
Q: And approximately how often were you
   with him during that time period?
A: Four to five times a week.
Q: Now on each of these occasions
   approximately how much alcohol would
   Mr. Lavender drink?
A: A lot. Close to a bottle.
Q: From what you could observe, what
   effect did this much alcohol have on
   Mr. Lavender?
A: He'd be very drunk.
   .  .  .
Q: What occasion did you have to count
   Wes's drinks, Mr. Pride?
A: It was very obvious he was drinking
   two to three to my one. And you could
   sit there and see the gentleman get
   extremely intoxicated. I couldn't keep
   up with him.
```

Pride's observations of Lavender's drinking during the time of Tommy's trial were confirmed by Lowery, who testified that "every other day or so," Lavender would come to the Freeway Club in the evenings "after 7:30, 8:00, 8:30, something like that" and leave the club at "closing or thereabouts," which was 2:00 a.m.

```
Question: Now from what you could
   observe, approximately how much
   alcohol did Mr. Lavender drink each
   time you saw him drink at this time of
   year?
Answer: It's just hard to say. He drank a
   lot. You know, it's just a lot. Looked
```

```
like, we are talking about—when I'm
talking about a bottle, I'm talking
about a bottle of scotch. He always
drank J&B Scotch. And I don't know how
they measure them in liters. It used
to be fifths and quarts, but I would
say it's the size of between a fifth
and a quart. You know, it was a lot of
whiskey.
```

Pride testified that Lavender's pattern of drinking continued after the jury found Tommy guilty and recommended a death sentence in August of 1985. In fact, it persisted even beyond the sentencing hearing that was held before Judge Burney in October of 1985 to the filing of briefs in Tommy's appeals to the Alabama Court of Criminal Appeals and the Alabama Supreme Court.

In November of 1987, Lavender and Lovelace filed their motion asking the Alabama Supreme Court to reconsider its affirmation of Tommy's capital conviction and sentence of death. At that same time, Lavender's friends took action with respect to his alcoholism, as stated by Pride:

```
Question: I'd like to focus on the time
    period of the fall and the winter of
    late 1987 for a moment.
Answer: Mm-hm.
Q: During that particular time, did you
    have occasion to do anything with
    respect to Mr. Lavender's drinking?
A: Yes. A group of friends and I had
    an intervention in my home with the
    help of counselors from Bradford
    Rehabilitation Center with Wesley. And
    we had the intervention at my home,
```

```
and carried Wesley immediately to the
rehab center, at which he spent thirty
days there to get himself straight.
```

As stated by Lowery, this intervention was not undertaken because Lavender's condition had deteriorated over time.

```
Question: Okay, Mr. Lowery, let me ask
    you this. Did Wes's drinking get worse
    over the time period from when you met
    him until y'all intervened?
Answer: No. He was the same, as far as
    I could tell, just about from the
    time I met him until the time he quit
    drinking.
```

On cross-examination, the Alabama Attorney General challenged the proposition that Tommy's lead attorney had been drinking during the trial, but Pride held firm:

```
Assistant Attorney General: And it's
    possible, isn't it Mr. Pride, that you
    are mistaken about whether or not you
    saw Wes during the time frame of this
    trial, isn't it?
Answer: No, sir. I saw him during the
    trial.
Q: That's your answer, that you definitely
    saw him during the trial?
A: Yes, I did.
```

To accentuate our claim that Lavender and Lovelace were ineffective counsel, we presented testimony from ten mitigation witnesses whom Tommy's trial attorneys never contacted. For example, Jeanette Borden is Tommy's aunt, the younger sister of Tommy's mother. She lived with Tommy's parents when she was fourteen years old. In later years, she would visit Tommy's childhood home once a month. Aunt Jeanette personally witnessed beatings that Tommy's father administered to his wife—beatings so severe that she had to be hospitalized. Jeanette also saw BBs embedded in Tommy's mother's arm from shots fired at her by her husband. In Jeanette's words, Tommy's father was "drunk more often than sober." Her testimony painted a grim picture of Tommy's home environment during childhood:

```
Question: What was—based on what you
    were able to observe, what was his
    [Tommy's] home life like?
Answer: Well, the home life of all the
    children. To me it was terrible.
    I mean, I did not—I would not want
    a home life like that. I mean, the
    violence, the fighting, the cursing. To
    me it was terrible.
```

Given her intimate knowledge of the Hamilton family and its children, I found her reaction to the killing of Lehman Wood to be telling:

```
Question: What was your reaction?
Answer: Well, I was shocked.
Q: Why were you shocked?
A: Well, I just—I never thought that
    they would do something like that.
    After I thought about it, you know—
    well, Janice was violent, but Tommy—it
    surprised me about Tommy.
Q: Why is that?
A: Because he was—he was—to me, I had
    never known of him being violent or,
    you know, like his dad or—you know,
```

> Janice I had seen, but Tommy was quiet
> and, you know, seemed like a bashful
> person. I just don't feel that Tommy
> would have done it on his own. I was
> surprised.

The evidence presented by Tommy's father's side of the family was perhaps even more compelling. Virginia Hamilton Washburn is also Tommy's aunt, the sister of Tommy's father. She was quite candid in describing her brother, Tommy's father.

> Question: Could you describe him
>   generally for the court?
> Answer: Well, J. W. was my brother. He
>   was an alcoholic. He was just as mean
>   as he could be. It did not make any
>   difference what it was, if he was
>   drinking, if he wanted to fight, he
>   would fight.
>
> . . .
>
> Q: How did Tommy behave around J. W. when
>   you observed them together?
> A: He was a good child.
> Q: Okay.
> A: He had to be. J. W. would have beat
>   him half to death.

In what became a haunting litany repeated by all the family witnesses who testified at the hearing, Mrs. Washburn continued:

> Question: Were you ever contacted by
>   either Mr. Wesley Lavender or Mr.
>   Barnes Lovelace with regard to the
>   possibility of your presenting

testimony at Tommy's trial in August
of 1985?

Answer: No, sir. Nobody never did
contact me.

Q: And if one of them had contacted you
and asked you to testify at Tommy's
trial, would you have done so?

A: I would have went.

Q: Were you available to testify on
August of 1985?

A: Yes, sir, I was.

Q: And had you testified, you would have
given the same testimony [as you have]
today?

A: I would, yes, sir.

We also presented testimony from Tommy's grade school principal, Ed Braidfoot (Tommy was courteous, respectful, and did not get into fights or do anything violent), seventh-grade biology teacher Glenda Terry (Tommy twice failed the class but was never a discipline problem; Tommy was a follower rather than a leader), eighth-grade English teacher Sheila Reeves (Tommy was not violent and was doing the best he could, given his home life), and the principal of the East Lawrence School when Tommy was there, Robert Bentley (Tommy was quiet and withdrawn; never a discipline problem).

A former employer, Bobby Smith, who was at the courthouse for Tommy's trial but was never called by Tommy's trial attorneys to testify, testified at the post-conviction hearing that Tommy had an exemplary work ethic, so much so that he recommended Tommy to another employer. Another employer, Willard Coffey, had similar praise.

Law enforcement officials and others familiar with Tommy's conduct while incarcerated testified that they were never contacted or called to testify by Tommy's trial attorneys. For example, Tom Ligon—a friend of Lehman Wood—was the Sheriff's brother and Chief

Jailer at the Lawrence County Jail while Tommy was incarcerated. He testified as follows:

> Question: Did you know Tommy Hamilton
>   when he was incarcerated at the
>   Lawrence County Jail?
> Answer: Yes, sir.
> Q: As an inmate, how did Tommy behave?
> A: Very good, the first year he was in
>   jail there.
> Q: Did you have any trouble with him?
> A: No, sir.
> Q: How did he behave toward you?
> A: Very good.
> Q: Was he respectful toward you?
> A: Yeah, he was real respectful.
> Q: Was he courteous?
> A: Polite, cooperative.
> Q: Was he ever made a trusty during that
>   year?
> A: Yeah. The best I remember, he was a
>   trusty about ten months of that year
>   he stayed in jail.
> Q: And how did he perform as a trusty for
>   the jail?
> A: Good.
>   . . .
> Q: Did he ever exhibit any violent
>   behavior that you can recall?
> A: Not as I remember.

The importance of Tommy's behavior while incarcerated, to a jury deliberating whether to recommend a sentence of life in prison or death, cannot be overemphasized.

Tommy's trial attorneys also failed to contact the Reverend R. C. Borden and ask him to testify on Tommy's behalf. He became pastor of the Sulphur Springs Baptist Church in July of 1977, and Tommy's mother became a member of the church in 1979 or 1980. Reverend Borden certainly would have testified at trial as he did at the post-conviction hearing: Tommy never disrupted services when he attended with his mother and was always courteous and polite.

We concluded our presentation with testimony from Tommy's mother, Lucille, about Tommy's upbringing and the horrors he and the rest of the family had suffered at the hands of Tommy's father, J. W. Hamilton. Sister Lynn had the delicate task of trying to elicit the saga from Lucille, who gave wrenching testimony about her son's very sad childhood.

> Question: Would you describe J. W.'s
>   relationship with Tommy?
> Answer: Well, it wasn't no father
>   relationship. He was always mean to
>   the kids. He was mean to me, and it
>   was just cruel torture. It wasn't a
>   life. It was just torture. He'd always
>   beat on them, knock them around.
>   . . .
> Q: Would you tell the Judge, is Tommy J.
>   W.'s biological son?
> A: Yes, he is. Definitely, he's
>   J. W.'s son.
> Q: And did J. W. claim him as his son?
> A: When he wasn't drinking, he never
>   mentioned, you know, that he didn't
>   think Tommy was his son. But when he'd

get drunk, he'd make his remarks and say that Tommy was Dwight Holiday's boy. And Dwight Holiday was just a kid, I'd say about fourteen years old at the most. He was a sick man.

Q: You're talking about J. W.?

A: J. W. was a sick man.

Q: Did J. W. ever say this in Tommy's presence. . . .

A: He'd well, he'd smart off when he'd get drunk. He wouldn't actually say Dwight was his daddy, but he'd say, "You're not my g.d. boy," and just say all kinds of things that a drunk says.

Q: When was the first time you remember J. W. saying that to Tommy?

A: Tommy was about five, three, or four years old. He was just a little boy, and he'd get mad at him. And then several times when he got on up a little older.

Lucille testified that her husband was an alcoholic. He would often stay drunk for days at a time. His abuse of alcohol was so extreme that he had to be hospitalized for months at Bryce Mental Health Hospital in Tuscaloosa, Alabama, for alcohol-induced disorders.

Lucille also testified that on at least one occasion her husband tried to hit Tommy in the head with a hammer and severely beat him with the branch of a tree. These assaults were so frequent and severe that Mrs. Hamilton and her children would often have to spend nights in a cotton field next to their house to escape physical abuse by J. W. She testified that J. W. fired a shotgun at her and their children on at least three different occasions. In turn, Lucille actually shot her husband once in self-defense.

Lucille testified that her husband tried to commit suicide in front of Tommy.

> Question: I want to ask you about J. W.
> and some suicide attempts. Tell us
> about those, and how old Tommy was.
> Just describe the event.
>
> Answer: Okay. Well, the first time that
> he tried to kill hisself, he cut both
> wrists. And I called the ambulance.
> And they took him to Moulton. And
> Tommy was there.
>
> Q: Tommy was there?
>
> A: Tommy was there in the living room,
> saw it all.
>
> Q: How old was Tommy at this time?
>
> A: He was about—Tommy was about four
> then, because he had never started to
> school when this incident happened.
> But the other kids were in school. But
> at this time, Tommy was just there.
> And then the next time he tried to
> kill hisself was several years later.
> And Tommy was already in school then.
> They was all at school. He took a
> straight razor, slit his throat from
> ear to ear.
>
> . . .
>
> A: Okay, I called the ambulance. Blood
> everywhere, all through the living
> room, on the couch, to the bathroom.
> Ambulance come, got him, took him to

        Decatur General Hospital. They kept
        him up there three or four days.
    Q: What did you do then?
    A: I followed that ambulance to the
        hospital. And then I come back home so
        I'd be there when the kids got there.
        But I didn't make it back. They had
        got in before I got there.
    Well, they all was setting there, just a
        crying their hearts out. And they said
        they thought their daddy killed me.
        They was setting right there where the
        blood was everywhere.

When J. W. Hamilton worked, it was with a traveling-carnival operation. As a result, he was frequently away from home for long periods of time. Occasionally, he would take Tommy with him. Tommy's father would get women to take Tommy to their campers to have sex. Tommy had sex at least ten to twelve times before the age of fifteen.

    Question: Now I'd like for you to tell
        the court, did Tommy have a pet dog
        when he was a young boy?
    Answer: He sure did. It was a big old red
        dog. Tommy knows what it was. I didn't
        know what kind of dog it was, I just
        know it was a big old dog.
    Q: Tell us about the incident with J. W.
        and Tommy, and this pet of his. How
        old was Tommy?
    A: Tommy was, I guess, about ten years
        old then. But Tommy, he loved that
        dog. And the dog would, you know, go

```
with him everywhere. And J. W. come
in one day. He was drinking. The dog
jumped up on him. And J. W. got the
ball bat and beat the dog to death.
And then he told Tommy to get the
gas and pour on the dog and drag him
across there and set it afire. Tommy
was just boo-hooing. He was crying his
heart out. But Tommy went along and
done what his daddy told him. He drag
it across the road, but he didn't set
it afire. J. W. set the dog afire.
```

Lucille concluded her testimony by telling the court that Tommy began using drugs at the age of twelve. He failed the seventh grade. The second time he took seventh-grade classes, he was absent from school fourteen days the first semester and forty-seven days the second semester. Tommy missed thirty-two days of school during the first semester of eighth grade and failed every class except for physical education. He dropped out of school at that time. All in all, Tommy obtained only a sixth-grade education.

During puberty and his adolescent years, Tommy's abuse of alcohol and drugs continued. He would black out from alcohol consumption. He smoked marijuana several times a week. As a teenager, he took amphetamines and speed. Sometimes, he would keep himself high for as many as six straight days. He took Valium and Mellaril—a drug used by his sister Joyce to treat her schizophrenia—and drank codeine.

Lucille also testified that Tommy had his own suicidal episodes.

```
Question: Did Tommy ever. To your
    knowledge—did Tommy ever try to commit
    suicide?
Answer: Yes, he did.
Q: Tell us about that and when that was.
```

A: Well, he come in, it was after he had served the year in jail.

Q: When was that?

A: It was about three months before—he got out of jail, and he was out of jail about three months before he got, got into this other trouble.

Q: With Lehman Wood?

A: Yes. But when he was home, he was setting there. And he was real depressed. And he went into the bedroom, got my .38. And he says, "I'm going to kill myself." And I started pleading with him. And he said he didn't have no reason to live. But I talked to him and I took the gun. And from then on, I kept it hid.

Q: How long was this before Mr. Wood was shot?

A: Couple months, because he was only out, I think three months. But then the other time that he tried to kill hisself, well, he didn't pull the trigger or he would have been gone.

To her embarrassment, Lynn deeply felt the force of Lucille's account of Tommy's travails—to the point that she was weeping as she posed the open-ended questions that gave Lucille the opportunity to detail the physical and mental abuse heaped upon her young son. While Lucille recounted the stories dry-eyed with her straightforward strength of character, the tender-hearted lawyer was crying. Sister Lynn had several photographs of the Hamilton family marked as exhibits and admitted into evidence, and then she proceeded to explore other important topics with Lucille:

```
Question: Tell us about Tommy's
    relationship with Janice. How much
    older was Janice than Tommy?
Answer: Seven. It was seven years.
Q: Tell us how they got along as they
    grew up.
A: Well, Tommy would go along with
    Janice, anything Janice would say for
    him to do. If Janice said, "Come on,
    let's go do this," or Janice, you
    know, wanted him to do something, he'd
    go right along with her.
```

Lucille Hamilton was not the best witness, but she effectively conveyed the very difficult childhood that Tommy had endured. The Attorney General's Office wisely did not cross-examine Lucille, which only would have drawn more attention to her sad story. We could not assess what impact Lucille's testimony had on Judge Suttle. As always, he was an enigma in the courtroom.

Evidentiary hearings, like jury trials, can be exhausting. I was living on the caffeine and sugar of Coca-Cola, my lifelong drug of choice. The direct examination of our witnesses had gone well. We tried to keep an eye on Judge Suttle's demeanor, but he betrayed nothing. I would not want to be across the table from him in a poker game.

We left the courtroom that Friday afternoon, exhausted but encouraged. After a drink at a local bar, I quickly climbed into bed in my motel room. I knew I had a difficult weekend ahead of me. I had been suffering from migraine headaches for some time. Helpfully, the onset of these debilitating, painful episodes came not at moments of psychological pressure, but rather after the stressful events had passed. They were let-down headaches, my body's method of punishing me for putting it through a period of stress, and its attempt to deter me from engaging in such stress-inducing behavior in the future. Standard migraine attacks could be managed with mild doses of codeine. Severe attacks could lead to temporary loss of vision in one eye and require a trip to a hospital emergency room for more potent pain-relieving medication. After five days of presenting our case for Tommy, I knew I was in for a massive migraine attack. My plan was to sleep much of the weekend, endure the pain, and replenish my energy before the state began to present its case on Monday morning.

Silly me.

CHAPTER NINE

The Escape

At six on Saturday morning, October 27, 1990, I woke to the ringing of the telephone in my motel room. Luke told me that Tommy Hamilton had escaped from the Lauderdale County Jail just a short while earlier. Another inmate in the jail had overpowered a guard during a transfer of prisoners from their cells to the cafeteria for breakfast. Devoid of any impulse control, and likely recalling the jailbreak he and Debbie had attempted while awaiting trial in the Lawrence County Jail, Tommy followed the leader and dashed out with his fellow prisoner. The two of them split up on the streets of Florence. Law enforcement chased both men, eventually surrounding Tommy on the roof of a building where he had taken refuge.

Tommy was lucky that law enforcement had not carried out his death sentence right then and there. No explanation would have been necessary. A convict, sentenced to death for murder, had escaped from jail and was loose on the streets of the city. The officers gunning him down likely would have been honored for saving the public from a notorious killer. Fortunately, they took him into custody peacefully—but his situation would change dramatically. Tommy had been a "guest" in their jail for purposes of the post-conviction proceedings, but now he had more than worn out his welcome. After his capture, Tommy was sent back to the Lawrence County Jail in Moulton.

When we drove to Moulton to see Tommy, the jailers turned us away—impermissibly (if somewhat understandably) refusing to let us see our client. Nonetheless, I was determined to see Tommy immediately. We rushed back to Florence in search of Judge Suttle, hoping to get an order directing the Lawrence County jailers to relent.

For security reasons, Judges do not list their home addresses or phone numbers in a telephone directory. We had no idea where His Honor lived. Florence was a city of over thirty-six thousand people; it was like looking for a needle in a haystack. We asked anyone we could find that Saturday morning whether they knew where to find Judge Suttle. A series of leads brought us to the appropriate neighborhood and, eventually, Judge Suttle's home.

His wife, Michele, answered our knock on the front door. After we explained who we were and that we needed to see the Judge, she went upstairs to get him. Dressed in a bathrobe, Judge Suttle descended the stairs. We briefly explained what had happened, why we were at his home on a Saturday morning, and why we sought his handwritten order directing the Sheriff and jailers to let us see Tommy. Judge Suttle said little in response. He simply signed the order we had drafted. Judge Suttle, already a mystery inside the courtroom, proved just as unreadable to me on the outside.

With Judge Suttle's order in hand, Tommy's guards had no choice but to admit us. The jail was medieval. Even though the windows in the brick exterior walls were covered with metal bars to prevent escapes, the jailers had also covered three quarters of each window with plywood, making it impossible to get any view of the world outside and shrouding the entire cell area in darkness. We found Tommy sitting on the concrete floor of a cell that had three walls of floor-to-ceiling bars. The jailers would not let us enter the cell, noting that our order said that we could see him, but it didn't say we could be with him. Given the cell's mostly open-air construction, there was no way to have a substantive discussion that would not be overheard. After we heard Tommy's pitiful relation of the escape, we had to limit ourselves to explaining that while he might not be allowed to attend the remainder of the hearing, still we would let him know what was happening as best we could.

Tommy's ill-conceived escape couldn't have come at a worse time. I needed to spend the weekend resting up and completing my prepa- rations for the cross-examination of the witnesses the state would call on Monday morning. Instead, thanks to Tommy's impulsive decision, I had to devote the remainder of my time to researching Alabama and United States Supreme Court precedent on whether an escape consti- tuted a waiver of one's right to post-conviction relief. Just seventeen months before, on March 8, 1993, the United States Supreme Court had revisited its application of the doctrine of "fugitive dismissal" in the case of *Ortega-Rodriguez v. United States*. The holding stated that appellate courts may dismiss an appeal if the criminal defendant's fugitive status has sufficient connection to the appellate process. The Court noted in part that "our cases consistently and unequivocally approve dismissal as an appropriate sanction when a prisoner is a fugi- tive during the ongoing appellate process." The Court stated that such a rule is amply supported because of the belief that flight disentitles the fugitive to relief; a desire to promote the efficient operation of the appellate process and protect the dignity of the appellate court; and the view that the threat of dismissal deters escapes. Given the circum- stances of Tommy's escape, the Court's opinion offered little room to maneuver, stating without qualification: "We have no reason here to question the proposition that an appellate court may employ dismissal as a sanction when a defendant's flight operates as an affront to the dignity of the court's proceedings."

I hurriedly cobbled together an argument that, because flight is punishable as a separate offense under Alabama's criminal code, Judge Suttle could impose a separate sentence that would adequately vin- dicate the public interest in deterring escape and safeguard the dig- nity of the court. Also, speculating that Judge Suttle might find the evidence we had presented at the previous week's hearing sufficient to merit vacating Tommy's death sentence, I weighed an argument that Tommy's loss of his right to obtain that remedy would result in a sentence that was erroneously imposed. Finally, under these circum- stances, a dismissal of Tommy's petition would be tantamount to the imposition of a death sentence as an additional punishment for the crime of escape—a disproportionate sanction that the Supreme Court would certainly not approve.

But I was constructing arguments on the fly, without firm precedent to support my contentions. Ken Nunnelley was sure to show up on Monday armed with pointed pronouncements from the United States Supreme Court that were less than two years old. He would argue that Tommy, who had escaped in the very midst of the hearing, had abandoned his post-conviction rights by exhibiting contemptuous disrespect for Judge Suttle and the judicial process. If the Judge agreed, then all our work would have been for naught. This could be a Humpty Dumpty moment, leaving me unable to put all the laboriously collected pieces warranting judicial relief back together again. There was one upside to the situation, though. With pressure building and adrenaline flowing, I remained blessedly migraine-free.

Monday morning came too soon. And it began as I had feared. The state of Alabama argued that Tommy's escape constituted grounds for the dismissal of his post-conviction petition. In support of his argument, Ken Nunnelley, over my objection, called Lauderdale County jailer Gary Risner to the stand. Judge Suttle allowed Nunnelley to present testimony from the jailer subject to a ruling on my pending objection.

Risner testified to what everyone knew already, admitting that he could provide few details beyond the fact that on October 27, 1990, Tommy and two others had somehow left the jail and made their way onto the streets of the city of Florence, with Tommy being apprehended fifteen minutes later.

With Risner's provisional testimony out of the way, I asked that Judge Suttle strike it from the record, and I proceeded to make the legal arguments I had prepared over the weekend. I also tried to make taking up the issue as distasteful as possible for Judge Suttle. I pointed out that the Attorney General's Office had presented no evidence as to why or how Tommy had followed other inmates out of the Lauderdale County Jail. Based on the record as it stood so far, we could only speculate as to whether Tommy knowingly engaged in a flight from custody; was coerced by others to join in such an endeavor; or—consistent with his known mental deficiencies and impulsivity—was ineptly and ineffectively acting out behaviorally when, as I put it, he was "briefly absent from custody." I told the Judge that if he admitted the state's evidence on this issue, we would need to conduct extensive discovery of the facts in order to present our rebuttal, an endeavor that might take some time and require depositions of numerous witnesses.

Judge Suttle was understandably prickly. Our quick agreement that Tommy could remain in the Lawrence County Jail rather than in the Judge's courtroom for the remainder of the proceedings did not soften his mood. While I was fairly certain he was disinclined to go down this rabbit hole, Judge Suttle probably wanted to put the fear of God in me and my client. He ruled that he would admit the testimony, while reserving his right in the future to strike it from the record.

With the issue of Tommy's "brief absence from custody" behind us, the state of Alabama put on its case in opposition to Tommy's petition for relief from his capital conviction and death sentence. Ken Nunnelley called few witnesses.

Barney Lovelace returned to the witness stand and testified that he never saw Wes Lavender drinking or inebriated at Tommy's trial, and that he and Lavender had done the best they could with what they had.

Dr. Harry McClaren, a psychologist, and Dr. Irwin Lewis, a neurologist, testified for the state that Tommy had no discernable neurological or psychological deficits. Given the importance of this point to our case, I cross-examined both men forcefully. Although Dr. Lewis was combative, it was imperative that his testimony and "expert" opinion that Tommy had no mitigating neurological deficits be challenged.

Perhaps the clearest evidence that Tommy is a brain-damaged individual can be found in the results of the objective scientific tests performed upon him by medical experts. My task was to get Dr. Lewis, the state's own expert, to convince Judge Suttle that such tests could be important evidence.

```
Question: Now since brain activity is
    accompanied by electrical signals,
    it's possible to measure changes in
    this neural activity by applying wires
    and electrodes to the surface of a
    person's skull, correct?
```

Answer: Correct.

Q: And when the electrical signals from
   these wires are amplified, they can be
   recorded as voltage versus time waves
   on a writing instrument, correct?

A: Right.

Q: And an electroencephalograph or
   EEG is an instrument that measures
   and records the brain's electrical
   activity in this fashion, correct?

A: Yes, sir.

Q: Now to conduct an EEG on a person,
   electrodes located in the standard
   positions are placed on a person's
   skull, correct?

A: Yes, they are.

Q: And the changing electrical activity
   in the person's neurons below each of
   the electrodes is recorded by the EEG
   and printed out as a series of waves.
   Correct?

A: Correct.

Q: Now evaluation of a person's EEG
   involves visual inspection of the
   waveforms, their amplitude and their
   frequency, correct?

A: Right.

Q: And evaluation of a person's EEG
   also involves visually inspecting the
   waveforms to see if there are any
   paroxysmal events, such as spikes or
   isolated bursts of activity, correct?

A: Correct.

As confirmed by Dr. Lewis, abnormal EEG waveforms are more likely to appear in a person who has brain damage than in a person who does not. Furthermore, as stated by Dr. Lewis:

Question: Now a person cannot fake or
    make himself look bad on an EEG, can
    they?
Answer: No.
Q: An EEG is an objective and accurate
    measure of the electrical activity
    in a person's brain during the time
    the EEG is recording that activity,
    isn't it?
A: Correct.

As evidence that Tommy has brain damage affecting his behavior, we admitted into evidence the results of the EEG performed on Tommy by the University of Alabama at Birmingham Hospital at the request of our neurological expert, Dr. Merikangas. We also submitted the independent analysis provided by Dr. Reuben Kuzniecki of that same hospital, who was neither affiliated with nor retained by either side. Kuzniecki concluded: "This record is abnormal. It shows evidence of epileptiform abnormality, which at times is generalized and multifocal."

Whereas our expert, Dr. Merikangas, had reviewed the results of the EEG performed by the University of Alabama at Birmingham Hospital and agreed with Dr. Kuzniecki's findings, Dr. Lewis dismissed the importance of the test results, stating that they "were of no clinical significance." I pressed him on this interpretation.

Question: Now while you characterize them
    as very minor, the fact of the matter
    is that the EEG performed on Tommy

Hamilton by the University of Alabama
did have evidence of irregularities,
correct?

Answer: Oh, yes.

Q: And you went through the EEG printout
and marked those irregularities that
you noticed on the document, correct?

A: I did.

. . .

Q: Now Dr. Kuzniecki and you both
graduated from the Montreal
Neurological Institute?

A: Yes, we did. That's sheer coincidence.

Q: And you are sure that Dr. Kuzniecki is
competent, correct?

A: I have never met him, but he does
a lot of seizure work, and running
the seizure program down at the
university. And I'm sure he's very
competent.

Q: In fact, you respect Dr. Kuzniecki's
opinion, don't you?

A: I would certainly respect his opinion.

Q: Now in fact, you were not calling
the EEG that was conducted by the
University of Alabama Hospital on
Tommy Hamilton a normal EEG?

A: Not at all. I'm calling it borderline.
There's a shade of gray between normal
and clearly abnormal. And it's a very,
very useful category.

To buttress his opinion that Tommy was without organic mental defects, Dr. Lewis had had another EEG conducted on Tommy at Brookwood Hospital on May 14, 1990. The tracing was not independently interpreted by Brookwood, as had been done at the University of Alabama at Birmingham Hospital by Dr. Kuzniecki for Dr. Merikangas; rather, it was interpreted by Dr. Lewis alone. His interpretation was that this subsequent EEG "was normal." This opinion, and the data that supported it, had to be attacked.

I got Dr. Lewis to admit that the University of Alabama Hospital had administered an EEG lasting twenty-seven minutes, with abnormalities beginning to appear after twenty-one minutes of recording. Importantly, the EEG administered by Dr. Lewis had recorded electrical activity in Tommy's brain for a total of just twenty minutes.

```
Question: Now the EEG only gives a
    picture of the electrical activity
    in a person's brain while the EEG is
    recording that activity, correct?
Answer: Very much so.
Q: And so an EEG that is normal for
    the period of time it is recording
    that activity does not mean that the
    electrical activity in a person's
    brain is normal either before the
    recording begins, or after the
    recording ends, correct?
A: Correct. For example, when the
    technologist is running the EEG, we
    tell the technologist, "As you change
    runs, as you change formats, do not
    turn the machine off because in that
    instant, you may get something."
Q: Okay.
```

A: Any decent EEG technologist would know
   that.

Q: And indeed, in your opinion, a single
   normal EEG never completely excludes a
   seizure disorder. Does it?

A: Very definitely. Very much so. That's
   correct.

Q: It very definitely does not exclude a
   seizure disorder?

A: Very definitely does not exclude a
   seizure disorder.

   . . .

Q: Now if you will bear with me a moment,
   doctor, but would you agree with me
   that the EEG you performed on Mr.
   Hamilton ran for just over twenty
   minutes, in fact, I think its twenty
   and a half minutes.

A: Twelve hundred some seconds, divided
   by sixty. So it would be something
   over twenty minutes, right.

Q: Just over twenty minutes?

A: Something over twenty minutes, yes.

Q: Now the EEG that was performed on
   Tommy Hamilton at the University of
   Alabama Hospital ran for longer than
   that; it ran for twenty-seven minutes
   approximately, didn't it?

A: Well, you know, I'll take your word
   for it. It may well have. They vary.
   The length of these EEGs varies, not

so much from lab to lab, but from
person to person.

. . .

And here again, I'm not sure that you
could make that much of the slight
difference in length. EEGs can be
very, very—they can be variable.

Q: Well, the point I want to make,
doctor, is that when you reviewed
this EEG that was performed by the
University of Alabama, and you marked
on it where you saw the abnormal
results—

A: Yes.

Q: —the first time when the abnormal
results occurred was at the
twenty-one-minute mark of that
EEG, wasn't it?

A: Well, I'll have to take your word for
it. I didn't measure that, that it was
at the twenty-one. But that's not of
any particular significance, because
these discharges can occur at any
time. There are times when you could
run an EEG for two hours on a patient
and pick up nothing, and a week later,
pick up discharges from page 2. It's
variable.

Q: And it's possible that if the EEG you
had conducted had run for a longer
period of time, it would have picked
up abnormalities in Tommy Hamilton?

```
A: Sheer speculation. It is possible. If
   we had run for another two or three
   hours, we may well have got something.
```

I felt the point was made. It allowed me to argue later that Dr. Lewis, like the jury that only took twenty-eight minutes to recommend that Tommy be sentenced to death, had engaged in a rush to judgment by relying on a too-brief encephalographic tracing.

I further got Dr. Lewis to acknowledge that seizure disorders occur when there is an excessive or abnormal electrical discharge from the neurons in a person's brain. It is, in effect, "an electrical storm in a person's brain." He also agreed that seizure disorders can frequently affect cognitive behavior, sensory and motor activity, as well as the emotional character of a person. I elicited testimony that would support Tommy's statement at trial that he felt threatened by Lehman Wood.

```
Question: Now, if a person is having a
   seizure or electrical storm in his
   brain, he can have a brain dysfunction
   that causes him to misperceive
   what a normal person would view as
   nonthreatening activity, and the
   person having this dysfunction might
   view it as threatening activity,
   correct?
Answer: Possibly.
```

In addition, Dr. Lewis conceded that, during such an episode, the capacity of a person to control his behavior is "very much" impaired.

Dr. Lewis continued to spar with me. But because the parties were required to disclose the opinions of their expert witnesses before the hearing began, we had been permitted to depose Dr. Lewis as to what his opinions were. Because I had gotten him to commit to a number of positions during his prehearing deposition, I was able to spank him during the hearing before Judge Suttle when he strayed from his previous testimony. And I got him to admit, begrudgingly, that Tommy suffered from several disorders at the time of Lehman Wood's death.

> Question: Dr. Lewis, it is your opinion,
>   to a reasonable degree of neurological
>   certainty, that Tommy Hamilton
>   suffered from psychoactive substance
>   use disorder at the time of Mr. Wood's
>   death, isn't it?
> Answer: I'm not sure that I used that
>   term exactly, but there's a very good
>   history of him being on many different
>   psychoactive substances. So I think
>   the answer would be yes.
> Q: I don't want there to be any doubt in
>   your mind about the terminology that
>   was used. Let me show you page 154 of
>   your deposition, beginning on line 12.
>   If you will read that question and
>   that answer.
> A: (Reading from the transcript)
> "Q: Have you formed any opinions to a
>   reasonable degree of neurological
>   certainty as to whether or not Tommy
>   Hamilton suffered from psychoactive
>   substance use disorder at the time of
>   Mr. Wood's death?"
> And I said my answer was, "A: I think
>   there was a very good possibility that
>   he suffered from that." And I would
>   have nothing to conflict really with
>   that answer.

Q: And in fact, it is your opinion, to
   a reasonable degree of neurological
   certainty, that Tommy Hamilton
   suffered from impulse control
   disorder at the time of Mr. Wood's
   death, isn't it?

A: Well, impulse control disorder
   perhaps triggered by his psychoactive
   substance abuse.

   . . .

Q: And I'll ask you again, doctor, it is
   your opinion, to a reasonable degree
   of neurological certainty, that Tommy
   Hamilton certainly was an individual
   with a very definite antisocial
   personality disorder, isn't it?

A: Yes, sir.

   . . .

Q: And in fact, in your opinion, Tommy
   exhibits traits of personality
   disorders other than antisocial
   personality disorder, and specifically,
   he exhibits traits of borderline
   personality disorder as well, correct?

A: That's why I diagnosed him as
   suffering from the personality
   disorder, not otherwise specified.

Q: People with borderline personality
   disorder traits are impulsive, aren't
   they?

A: Often, they are.

```
Q: And they are people who are full of
   rage, aren't they?
A: Often, they are.
Q: And they may react by being aggressive
   and defiant?
A: At times.
Q: And the mental or emotional
   disturbance that at times they might
   be suffering from because of their
   borderline personality disorder traits
   can influence their behavior?
A: Oh, absolutely.
Q: And borderline personality disorder
   traits can substantially impair a
   person's ability to control their
   conduct, can't they?
A: In the most extreme forms.
```

I also got Dr. Lewis to admit that Tommy's family background played a role in Tommy's behavior.

```
Question: Doctor, it is your opinion to
   a reasonable degree of neurological
   certainty that Tommy's family
   situation plays a very major role
   in the trouble he has with the law,
   isn't it?
Answer: Yes, it is.
```

With that foundation laid, it was time to make it clear to Judge Suttle that Dr. Lewis was *not* testifying that there were no mitigating circumstances, because Dr. Lewis had no opinions on that question.

Question: Now Dr. Lewis, at the time that
   you conducted your evaluation, tests,
   and formed opinions of Tommy Hamilton,
   you were not aware of those matters
   that are considered to constitute
   mitigating circumstances as a matter
   of Alabama law in a death sentence
   case, were you?

Answer: (Shakes head negatively)

Q: The answer?

A: The answer is no. I'm sorry.

Q: And in fact, Dr. Lewis, you have
   never before examined an individual to
   determine whether or not there is a
   link between their neurological makeup
   and a capital offense of which they
   have been accused, have you?

A: Correct. I've never been involved in a
   case such as this. That is, again, not
   what I do.

Q: Dr. Lewis, based on your work for the
   Alabama Attorney General in this case,
   you are not in a position to comment
   on and do not have an opinion as to
   Tommy Hamilton's mental status at the
   time of Lehman Wood's death?

A: No. I would have no opinion on that.

Q: And you have no opinion as to whether
   or not Tommy Hamilton was under
   the influence of extreme mental or
   emotional disturbance at the time of
   Mr. Wood's death?

A: I have no specific knowledge of that.

Q: And you have no opinion as to
   whether or not Tommy Hamilton acted
   under extreme duress or under the
   substantial domination of another
   person at the time of Mr. Wood's
   death?

A: I have no knowledge of that. I have no
   opinion on that.

Q: And you have no opinion as to whether
   or not Tommy Hamilton's capacity to
   appreciate the criminality of his
   conduct or to conform his conduct
   to the requirements of law was
   substantially impaired at the time of
   Mr. Wood's death?

A: I'm sorry, Mr. Clark. I may have
   missed part of that question. I have
   to get you to repeat it.

Q: You have no opinion, do you, as
   to whether or not Tommy Hamilton's
   capacity to appreciate the criminality
   of his conduct or to conform his
   conduct to the requirements of law,
   were substantially impaired at the
   time of Mr. Wood's death?

A: No. I'd have to say I have no
   knowledge of that, or no opinion on
   that.

Redirect examination—asking your witness additional questions after the witness has been cross-examined—is always risky. Rather than minimizing any damage done during the cross-examination, an attorney may inflict additional wounds. This is especially true when an attorney does not know in advance what the witness's answer to those questions will be. In spite of this risk, Ken Nunnelley chose to ask further questions of his witness after I had completed my cross-examination of Dr. Lewis.

> Mr. Nunnelley: Doctor, Mr. Clark asked
>   you whether you could rule out, as
>   I believe was the phrase he used,
>   seizure disorder based on one
>   electroencephalogram.
> Dr. Lewis: Yes, he did.
> Q: And I believe your answer was you
>   couldn't do it based on one EEG?
> A: (Nods head affirmatively)
> Q: But what would your answer be when
>   you have the borderline EEG that
>   was conducted at the UAB Hospital
>   and the normal EEG that was
>   conducted at Brookwood Hospital? Do
>   you feel that you could rule out
>   seizure disorder based on those two
>   electroencephalograms?
> A: I would say, based on those two, we
>   still can't 1,000 percent rule out
>   seizure disorder.

"Thank you, Ken," I said to myself.

The state's other medical witness, Dr. Harry McClaren, was one of the psychologists who had evaluated Tommy prior to his trial. His assessment was incorporated into the presentencing report that Judge Burney had relied upon in sentencing Tommy to death. Dr. McClaren's opinions and the test results that supported them needed to be attacked.

At the start of my cross-examination, I got Dr. McClaren to acknowledge that intellectual disability is significant subaverage general cognitive functioning that exists concurrently with deficits in adaptive behavior. Intellectual disability is a lifelong condition that gravely affects a person's ability to understand, communicate, remember, reason morally, and control one's behavior.

General intellectual functioning is measured, and thus defined, by intelligence tests—quantified in a score called the "intelligence quotient," or IQ. Dr. McClaren acknowledged, using the terminology of the time, that "someone with an IQ as high as seventy-five may be classified as mentally retarded, depending upon the person's adaptive behaviors," and that "testing the IQ with some flexibility permits inclusion in the mental retardation category of people with IQs somewhat higher than seventy, who exhibit significant deficits in adaptive behavior." He confirmed that Tommy has significantly subaverage general intellectual functioning.

> Question: Now in your opinion, Tommy
>   Hamilton has significantly subaverage
>   general intellectual functioning,
>   doesn't he?
> Answer: Yes. He's borderline intellect.

The Wechsler Adult Intelligence Scale—Revised (WAIS-R) is one of the tests used frequently to measure a person's intelligence and mental functioning. It consists of eleven different kinds of subtests, or tests within a test. Six of these subtests are verbal and five are performance tests. On the WAIS-R test administered to Tommy on March 1, 1985, at the Taylor Hardin Secure Medical Facility, Tommy's full-scale score, or IQ, was seventy-five—within the range of scores that can support a diagnosis of mild intellectual disability. On the WAIS-R test administered by our expert, Dr. Beidleman, on June 28, 1989, Tommy had a full-scale score of seventy-two, again within the range of scores that indicate mild intellectual disability. When Tommy was tested just six months later by Dr. McClaren, the Alabama Attorney General's psychologist reported that Tommy had achieved a full-scale score of seventy-seven. This was the first and only time Tommy's measured IQ fell outside the range of scores that are consistent with mild intellectual disability.

The questions asked or the tasks to be performed in a WAIS-R test are always the same, even if the test is administered to the same person time and time again. As a result, a person's score on a WAIS-R test readministered shortly after a prior test was given can be expected to rise by several points. This is recognized by experts as the "practice effect." We needed Judge Suttle to understand that, and to discount the test results submitted by Dr. McClaren. This could be done, in part, by getting Dr. McClaren to recognize other individuals as authorities on psychological testing and admitting into evidence excerpts from treatises and articles those individuals had written on the subject.

Question: All right. Now Dr. McClaren,
        you agree, don't you, with the
        following statement which appears
        on page 248 of the fifth edition
        of *Psychological Testing* by Anne
        Anastasie, that,
"Some data were obtained on the stability
        of WAIS-R scores over time."
And she goes on to talk about,
"This retest study revealed a tendency
        for IQs to rise on the second test.
        The mean gain in the two groups being
        six and seven points for full scale
        IQ. Such an expected practice effect,
        although slight, should be taken into
        account when retesting individuals
        after a short time interval."
Answer: Yes. I think that's generally
        true.

```
Q: So if a person takes a WAIS-R test,
   say within six months of when he took
   it before, his score may go higher on
   the basis of the practice effect that
   Anne Anastasie mentions in her book,
   correct?
A: Absolutely.
```

Moreover, the WAIS-R is not the only recognized and accepted test for measuring a person's IQ and, indeed, may reflect inaccurately inflated scores for individuals in the lower ranges of intellect. Dr. McClaren admitted that experts in the field have repeatedly found that below-average examinees score higher on the Wechsler IQ test than they do on other IQ measures.

```
Question. Now the WAIS-R is not the
   only recognized and accepted test for
   measuring a person's IQ, is it?
Answer. No. there are many others.
Q: And one other well-recognized and
   accepted exam is the Stanford-Binet
   test, correct?
A: That's right. Although it is more
   often used with children.
Q: In some circumstances, however,
   the Stanford-Binet test may be more
   reliable and valid as an IQ measure
   than the WAIS-R, correct?
A: Especially at the much lower levels of
   intelligence in adults, and as I said,
   in children.
Q: Okay. And indeed, then, you agree with
   Dr. Anne Anastasie when she states on
```

```
     page 247 of the fifth edition of her
     treatise:
"It has been repeatedly found that above
     average examinees tend to score higher
     on the Stanford-Binet than on the
     Wechsler scales, while below average
     examinees score higher on the Wechsler
     than on the Stanford-Binet," correct?
A:  I don't have much experience with
     the Stanford-Binet, so I can't
     independently agree or disagree. She's
     an authority. I would think that to be
     true.
```

This allowed me to argue later that all of the evidence suggested that every IQ test administered to Tommy Hamilton resulted in a score that, if correctly interpreted, was indicative of a person suffering from significant subaverage general intellectual functioning.

In determining whether a person has deficits in adaptive functioning for purposes of a diagnosis of intellectual disability, Dr. McClaren admitted that adaptive functioning refers to the person's effectiveness in areas such as social skills, communication, and daily-living skills, and how well the person meets the standards of personal independence and social responsibility expected of his or her age. Dr. McClaren admitted that Tommy had deficits in his adaptive functioning.

```
     Question: Now you stated in your opinion—
         or let me back up a minute. In your
         opinion, Tommy does have deficits in
         his adaptive behavior, doesn't he?
     Answer: He has some deficits.
```

Dr. McClaren also admitted that Tommy had traits of a mildly mentally disabled individual. He testified that people with mild intellectual disability "typically develop social and communication skills during the preschool years, age zero through five, have minimal impairment in sensory motor areas, and often are not distinguishable from normal children until a later stage," and that "by their late teens, they may acquire academic skills up to approximately sixth-grade level." Dr. McClaren admitted that Tommy, who dropped out of school after the first semester of eighth grade, fit these criteria.

> Question: Well, it is your understanding
>   that during this particular period
>   of his life, his achievement scores
>   indicated he was only able to perform
>   two grade levels below the grade he
>   was enrolled in, correct?
> Answer: That's my memory.
> Q: That's what the presentence report
>   said, correct?
> A: That's my memory. If you have it
>   there, I'd like to look at it.
> Q: Sure.
> A: In fact, if I could just follow along
>   with you, I'd feel more comfortable in
>   my answers.
> Q: Sure. Exhibit 8 is the presentence
>   report, and it has a section on
>   education in it. And I have turned to
>   the page and handed it to you.
> A: Thank you.
> Q: It in fact notes that Tommy's
>   achievement scores indicated he was
>   only able to perform two grade levels
>   below the grade he was enrolled in,
>   correct?

A: That's right.

. . .

Q: Well, in your opinion, doctor, given what you know of Tommy and his school records, he's got basically a sixth-grade education, correct?

A: That's right.

Dr. McClaren agreed that Tommy could be led astray.

Question: And your notes reflect, doctor, that when asked why Tommy took these drugs, Tommy told you that he, quote, "trusted the people who gave him drugs," and that he, quote, "thought he would be impressing people if he did what they told him to do," correct?

Answer: I clearly remember him talking about trusting people. The impressing, I don't have a clear recollection for. But that sounds right. I don't have it written down, so I can't be a hundred percent certain.

Q: Now why would these statements be so important in explaining Tommy's behavior in general?

A: Well, I think it gives credence to the idea that Tommy was far down the path of substance abuse and wasn't very discriminative in what he would use to alter his state of consciousness,

and apparently had selected a group of
friends who had similar ideas of what
was fun.

Q: Not only that, doctor, but isn't it
your opinion that those statements
reflect that Tommy didn't have a high
self-esteem, and it was very important
to him to have other people like him?

A: It might reflect that, yes.

Q: And that he would do what others told
or goaded him into doing to get their
approval?

A: It might mean that too.

I wanted Dr. McClaren to acknowledge that the intellectual disability Tommy suffered from, and over which he had no control, was mitigating because it had a bearing on his behavior.

Question: Now a person suffering
from mild mental retardation is
suffering from a mental or emotional
disturbance, isn't he?

Answer: I would say they certainly are.

Q: And the mental or emotional
disturbance associated with mild
mental retardation can influence that
person's behavior, can't it?

A: Yes. It would make them much, make
them have much more difficulty doing a
lot of things.

Q: Mild mental retardation can cause a
person extreme distress, can't it?

A: At times.

Q: And mild mental retardation can
   substantially impair a person's
   ability to control their behavior,
   can't it?

A: Especially in the lower levels. But by
   no means does a person who is mildly
   mentally retarded have no control over
   their behavior.

Q: That's not my question. My question
   is simply, mild mental retardation
   can substantially impair a person's
   ability to control his behavior,
   can't it?

A: It might in certain circumstances.

Q: Let's talk about some of those
   circumstances where it particularly
   might. Since alcohol reduces impulse
   control, the intoxicated mentally
   retarded person with innately
   lower impulse control will have
   substantially less control than the
   average intoxicated person, won't he?

A: They might.

When I pushed this line of questioning, Dr. McClaren came to admit that everything he knew about Tommy was consistent with the conclusion that Tommy had been under the influence of alcohol at the time of the shooting. Indeed, Dr. McClaren ultimately conceded that Tommy suffered from psychoactive substance abuse disorder at the time of Lehman Wood's death.

Question: Now the group of mental

disorders that's classified in the
DSM-III-R [*Diagnostic and Statistical
Manual of Mental Disorders*, Third
Edition, Revised—at that time, the
authoritative manual created to
assist psychologists in identifying
mental illnesses and disorders] is
psychoactive substance use disorder,
correct?

Answer: That's right.

Q: And do you agree with Dr. Graham [an
individual Dr. McClaren repeatedly
said he turns to for authoritative
opinions] when he says that,

"This diagnostic class deals with
symptoms and maladaptive behavioral
changes associated with more or less
regular use of psychoactive substances
that affect the central nervous
system"?

A: Yes.

Q: Do you agree with him when he says
that,

"The conditions are here conceptualized
as mental disorders, and are
therefore to be distinguished from
nonpathological psychoactive substance
use, such as moderate imbibing
of alcohol or the use of certain
substances for appropriate medical
purposes"?

A: That's right.

```
Q: Somebody who is diagnosed as suffering
   from a psychoactive substance use
   disorder is a person that has a mental
   health problem, correct?

A: Indubitably.

Q: Now Tommy was diagnosed as suffering
   from mixed substance abuse when he
   was sent to Taylor Hardin in December
   of 1984, shortly after the shooting,
   correct?

A: That's right.

   .  .  .

Q: Now since Tommy was diagnosed as
   suffering from this mental disorder by
   the Taylor Hardin folks in December of
   1984, is it your opinion that Tommy
   suffered from this mental disorder at
   the time of Mr. Wood's death?

A: Yes.
```

Dr. McClaren testified that a personality is defined as a "deeply ingrained pattern of behavior, which includes the way we relate to, perceive, and think about the environment and one's self," and that a personality trait is "a facet of personality that undergoes a very slow rate of change across time and situation." When a personality trait becomes inflexible or maladaptive, a person has a personality disorder. Dr. McClaren gave his opinion that Tommy "indubitably suffers from a personality disorder," stating: "In my view it was more appropriate to see features of both the borderline personality disorder and an antisocial personality disorder in this man." He recognized the significance of a personality disorder:

```
Question: Now a personality disorder can
   be very serious, can't it?
```

```
Answer: Yes.
Q: In fact, a personality disorder can be
   debilitating, can't it?
A: It can.
Q: In fact, by definition, a personality
   disorder causes either significant
   functional impairment or subjective
   distress in a person who has the
   disorder, doesn't it?
A: That's right.
```

During my cross-examination, Dr. McClaren also acknowledged that much mental illness has as its origin, or at least a contributing factor, family structure.

```
Question: And you personally think that
   the form of many mental disorders is
   definitely influenced by the family
   structure, don't you?
Answer: Yes, I do.
Q: Indeed, many psychological theorists
   point to the important role that the
   family plays on its members' mental
   health, don't they?
A: Sure.
Q: And mental illness is associated with
   family pathology, isn't it?
A: In many instances, it is. A child's
   relationship to his parents in
   general, and a son's relationship
   to his father, in particular, is
   especially important to the child's
   psychological well-being.
```

Q: And of what importance to a child's
   well-being is its relationship to his
   father?

A: If it is a male child, it is the
   source of the primary role model, if
   the father's present, teaching the
   child, the boy child, what a man is
   and how a man should act.

Q: So a son's relationship to his father
   is a particularly important factor
   in his psychological well-being,
   isn't it?

A: Theoretically, it certainly is.

Q: Well, it's more than theoretical. You
   believe that a son's relationship to
   his father is a very important factor
   in his psychological well-being,
   don't you?

A: In most cases, for certain.
   Tragically, there are many people that
   are not given that opportunity.

**A dysfunctional family can lead to low self-esteem for its children,
which in turn can lead to behavioral problems.**

Question: A dysfunctional family fails to
   teach its children how to communicate
   its feelings and deal with this anger,
   doesn't it?

Answer: In many cases, it does.

Q: And as a result, there's no
   appropriate outlet for the anger that
   is felt for the children, is there?

A: In many such families, the outlet
   tends to be through behavior rather
   than through verbal expression.

Q: Indeed, where assaultive behavior is
   part of family life, a child can learn
   that assaultive behavior is how one
   deals with one's problems, can't they?

A: The work of Albert Bandura abundantly
   illustrates the role of learning by
   modeling, so in a word, yes.

Furthermore, I got Dr. McClaren to acknowledge the detrimental impact of the intra-family assaults by Tommy's father.

Question: Now why is an event like that
   so psychologically harmful to a child?

Answer: Well, it gives the child the
   expectation of abuse. It may give a
   model of, "This is how men act." It
   may make the child fearful to express
   his feelings verbally out of fear of
   punishment.

Q: And instead express those feelings
   behaviorally, correct?

A: That's right.

Q: These incidents have an adverse effect
   on somebody's personality development,
   and may lead to personality disorders
   like borderline personality disorder,
   mightn't they?

A: They are thought to, yes.

Q: And you think that they do too,
   don't you?

A: Yes.

Dr. McClaren admitted that by forcing Tommy to have sex at a young age, J. W. Hamilton had sexually abused his son—causing resentment and anger.

> Question: It might also cause the person
>   to feel used and abused, mightn't it—
> Answer: It might.
> Q:—to have anger directed at others,
>   correct?
> A: I think a lot of things in Tommy
>   Hamilton's life had the potential to
>   make him feel angry.
> Q: Especially cause him to feel anger
>   toward people who actually had or were
>   perceived to have authority or control
>   over him, mightn't it?
> A: Well, I think Tommy Hamilton is a
>   person who has greater difficulty
>   dealing with authority, and has more
>   than his share of hostility. Given
>   the things that happened to him as a
>   child, you could certainly theorize a
>   causal connection.

I made sure to get Dr. McLaren on the record about the killing of Tommy's pet dog.

> Question: Well, but you consider, Doctor,
>   you personally consider that an
>   event like this provides a model for
>   violence and a disregard for life,

```
    don't you?
Answer: Yes, a bad thing.
Q: And that you personally, Doctor,
    consider that people exposed to
    violence like this more frequently
    or more easily engage in violence,
    don't you?
A: Probably so. My best bet is they do.
```

The Attorney General took two days to present the evidence in support of the state's position.

A total of thirty-one witnesses testified at the hearing on our petition for post-conviction relief, and sixty-five exhibits were admitted into evidence. At the conclusion of the hearing, Judge Suttle granted our request to submit briefs and present oral argument in support of the petition, based upon the evidence that had been admitted. It would be our last chance to make our case before Judge Suttle issued his ruling.

CHAPTER TEN

The Arguments

As we prepared to make our closing arguments, the issue of Tommy's escape during the evidentiary hearing still loomed. We needed to know where Judge Suttle stood on this issue, so we formally made a motion asking Judge Suttle to strike the testimony of the Lauderdale County jailer and all other references to the escape from the record of the post-conviction proceedings. Judge Suttle granted our motion on February 18, 1991.

On April 9, 1991, Tommy's sister Janice was granted parole after serving five years of her ten-year sentence. On April 22, she was released from custody and immediately left Alabama to live in Oklahoma City. That same day, we filed our brief in support of Tommy's petition for relief from his capital murder conviction and sentence of death.

We began by outlining what we alleged were foundational legal principles. As a matter of substantive constitutional law, the imposition of death as a criminal sanction is fundamentally and qualitatively different from every other punishment meted out by the state. It is different substantively from life in prison; it is also different substantively from life in prison without possibility of parole. Indeed, death, because of its severity and finality, occupies a constitutional classification that is unique unto itself. As the Supreme Court explained in *Woodson v. North Carolina* (1976), the Constitution requires a reliability in death penalty cases that has no parallel in other cases. We then articulated each of the grounds and the evidence supporting our petition for relief.

One lesson you learn as an attorney is: just because you have an argument you can make, that doesn't mean you should make it in that moment. But in a death penalty case, with few exceptions, if you do not make an argument at the earliest possible moment, you lose your right to make it in the future. For the most part, an argument not made in the lower state court cannot be considered later in the state appellate court or a federal court.

We raised a total of thirty arguments in our brief to Judge Suttle.

First and foremost, we argued that Tommy's conviction and sentence were obtained based on perjured testimony in violation of his rights under the Constitution of the United States and Alabama law.

We argued, a bit inaccurately, that the only difference between the evidence presented during Tommy's trial and Janice's trial was the testimony of Jimmy Dale Owens, and that the stark difference in the outcomes of those trials and sentences was telling. Left unspoken was the question of whether Owens's death inside the Lawrence County Jail months after Tommy's trial was a guilt-ridden and remorseful suicide—or a criminal cover-up.

We also argued that Tommy had been denied his constitutional right to due process of law.

More than thirty years earlier, the United States Supreme Court had decided the case of *Brady v. Maryland* (1963). During separate trials, juries found John Brady and Charles Boblit guilty of first-degree murder during a robbery. At his trial, Brady maintained that while he did indeed participate in the robbery, he had nothing to do with the killing. Prior to his trial, Brady's lawyer asked the prosecution for access to Boblit's extrajudicial statements. Several of these were provided to defense counsel, but one statement in which Boblit admitted to the actual killing, while still implicating Brady as an accomplice, was not provided. At sentencing, both men received the death penalty. Brady did not learn of the prosecutor's failure to disclose that statement until after the Maryland Court of Appeals had affirmed both his conviction and sentence of death.

On post-conviction review, the Supreme Court held that constitutional guarantees of due process set forth in the Fourteenth Amendment required that "material" exculpatory evidence, that is, evidence that "would tend to" exculpate the defendant or reduce the penalty, must, if requested, be turned over to the defense by the state. The Court also held that the good or bad faith of the prosecutor in failing to do so is irrelevant to finding a constitutional violation.

On July 2, 1985, however, the Supreme Court narrowed the application of the Warren Court's decision in *Brady v. Maryland*. In *United States v. Bagley*, Hughes Bagley was indicted for federal narcotics and firearms offenses. The government's principal witnesses were two private security guards, James O'Connor and Donald Mitchell, who were assisting with an undercover investigation of Bagley by the Bureau of Alcohol, Tobacco and Firearms (ATF). In response to a discovery request for any promises or inducements made to O'Connor and Mitchell, the government produced affidavits from both men stating that each had spoken without any threats or rewards being made or promised. Almost three years after his conviction on the narcotics charges, Bagley received responses to Freedom of Information Act requests he had filed, which revealed ATF form contracts promising O'Connor and Mitchell payments of three hundred dollars each as informers. Bagley then sought to overturn his conviction and sentence because of the government's failure to disclose evidence that would have permitted his defense attorney to impeach the government's witnesses during trial.

The Supreme Court held that the government's failure to disclose the contracts neither violated the Due Process Clause nor required automatic reversal of the conviction. A majority of the Court held that undisclosed exculpatory evidence is "material" only "if there is a reasonable probability that, had the evidence been disclosed to the defense, the result of the proceeding would have been different."

Accordingly, we presented our argument that the facts of this case fell under *Brady* as modified by *Bagley*. First, that Jimmy Dale Owens had been given early release in exchange for testimony at Tommy's trial. Second, that Tommy would neither have been convicted nor sentenced to death if that information had been revealed at trial. Third, the state had therefore been obligated to disclose the information to the defense, violating Tommy's constitutional rights by failing to do so.

Finally, while we denied that Tommy ever made the statements attributed to him by Owens, we argued that, should the court conclude that Owens's testimony was credible, the introduction of Tommy's alleged statements into evidence was constitutionally precluded because he had neither been represented by an attorney nor given additional *Miranda* warnings at the time.

The Sixth Amendment confers upon individuals the right to counsel. This right has been interpreted as including the right to counsel not only at trial, but also during the critical stages of the criminal justice process prior to trial. As stated by the Supreme Court in *Spano v. New York* (1959), "what use is a defendant's right to effective counsel at every stage of a criminal case if, while he is held awaiting trial, he can be questioned in the absence of counsel until he confesses?" For the right to counsel to be meaningful, the prosecutor and the police have an affirmative duty not to use tactics that dilute this right.

Thus, the Supreme Court held in *Massiah v. United States* (1964) that, "although the government may properly continue to gather evidence against a defendant after he has been indicted, it may not nullify the protection *Miranda* affords a defendant by using trickery to extract incriminating statements from him . . . [A]fter indictment and counsel has been retained, the Fifth Amendment prevents law enforcement authorities from deliberately eliciting incriminating statements from the defendant by the surreptitious methods used in this case." In *Massiah*, the defendant's confederate cooperated with the government in its investigation and allowed his automobile to be "bugged." The confederate subsequently had a conversation in the car with the defendant during which the defendant made incriminating statements. The confederate then testified about the defendant's statements at the defendant's trial. The Supreme Court held that the government had "denied [the defendant] basic protections of [the Sixth Amendment] when it used against him at trial evidence of his own incriminating words, which federal agents had deliberately elicited from him after he had been indicted and in the absence of his counsel."

In *United States v. Henry* (1980), the Supreme Court applied its ruling in *Massiah* to a situation involving a jailhouse informer. A paid informer for the FBI happened to be an inmate in the same jail in which defendant Henry was being held pending trial. An investigator instructed the informant to pay attention to statements made by the defendant, while admonishing the informer not to solicit information regarding the defendant's indictment for bank robbery. Nonetheless, the informer did so engage the defendant, and he subsequently testified against the defendant at trial based upon these conversations. The Supreme Court held that the informer had deliberately elicited incriminating statements by engaging the defendant in conversation about the bank robbery. It was held irrelevant under *Massiah* whether the informer had questioned the defendant about the crime or merely engaged in general conversation that led to the disclosure of incriminating statements. The government insisted that it should not be held responsible for the inmate's interrogation of the defendant in light of specific instructions to the contrary; but the Court held that employing a paid informer to converse with an unsuspecting inmate, while both are in custody, amounts to "intentionally creating a situation likely to induce [the defendant] to make incriminating statements without the assistance of counsel."

We argued that the testimony at the evidentiary hearing had established a *Massiah* violation in Tommy's case. From Eddie Oliver's videotaped testimony, it was clear that Ferris repeatedly encouraged Owens to "[g]o up there and pick Tommy and see what you can find out and help us out here." Jimmy Dale Owens certainly did much more than merely engage Tommy in general conversation or act as a passive listener.

We acknowledged that the courts had ruled that not every interrogation in violation of the rule set forth in *Massiah* mandates reversal of a conviction. But, citing the Supreme Court decision in *Chapman v. California* (1967), we argued that, to avoid reversal of a conviction, the state needed to prove beyond a reasonable doubt that the use at trial of incriminating statements in violation of Sixth Amendment rights did not contribute to the guilty verdict and, therefore, was harmless error. We argued that no such showing had been made in Tommy's case, nor could it be made.

We further argued that Tommy had been deprived of his constitutional right to effective assistance of defense counsel.

On May 14, 1984, the Supreme Court had decided the case of *Strickland v. Washington*, a death penalty case in which the defendant argued that his lawyer failed to investigate and present potentially mitigating evidence prior to and during his sentencing hearing. David Washington had pled guilty in a Florida State court to three capital murders. During his plea colloquy, he told the Judge that although he had committed a string of burglaries, he had no significant prior criminal record. At the time of his crime spree, he added, he was under extreme stress caused by an inability to provide for his family. At the sentencing, Washington's attorney did not seek out character witnesses or request a psychiatric evaluation, preferring to rely on the plea colloquy for evidence of his client's character and emotional state—thus preventing the state from cross-examining Washington or presenting psychiatric evidence of its own. Washington's attorney also decided not to request a presentence report, because it would have revealed Washington's past criminal history and thereby undermined his claim of no significant prior criminal history. During the plea colloquy, the Judge told Washington that he had "a great deal of respect for people who are willing to step forward and admit their responsibility." In sentencing Washington to death, however, the trial Judge cited numerous aggravating circumstances and found no mitigating circumstances.

On post-conviction review, the Supreme Court held that the Sixth Amendment accorded criminal defendants a right to legal counsel who renders "reasonably effective assistance given the totality of the circumstances." The Court stated that a criminal defendant complaining of ineffective assistance of counsel must show that the representation fell below an objective standard of reasonableness. Further, judicial scrutiny of counsel's performance must be highly deferential. Concerned that its standard for attorney error might result in numerous appeals and reversals of convictions, the Court held that convictions and capital sentences should remain undisturbed even when defendants could demonstrate that their counsel's performance fell below the bar of "reasonable competence"—unless those defendants could also show "prejudice" resulting from specific errors. The Court defined "prejudice" as "a reasonable probability that, but for counsel's unprofessional errors, the result of the proceeding would have been different," noting that "[a] reasonable probability is a probability sufficient to undermine confidence in the outcome." The Supreme Court found that the defense attorney's conduct in Washington's case was not unreasonable and that, even assuming it was, Washington had suffered insufficient prejudice to warrant setting aside his death sentence.

We argued that Tommy's defense counsel, under professional norms prevailing at the time of the trial, had an obligation to conduct a thorough investigation of his background. In a death penalty case, counsel has a duty to make reasonable investigations or must at least have a reasonable basis for concluding that a particular investigation is unnecessary.

In Tommy's case, his two trial attorneys, Barnes Lovelace and Wes Lavender, barely conducted any investigation into circumstances that might have mitigated against imposition of the death penalty. Although they nominally put on a case in mitigation by calling four witnesses to the stand, the record leaves no doubt that it was largely an empty exercise. The evidence was presented to the Judge by Wes Lavender, who had not prepared to present that portion of Tommy's case; the four mitigation witnesses he called to testify spent only a total of a few minutes on the stand. Lavender effectively abandoned a presentation on Tommy's background after providing the Judge with only the most rudimentary summary from a limited set of sources. On top of that, he ignored pertinent avenues for investigation—namely, Tommy's psychiatric and intelligence status—of which he should have been aware. This is particularly remarkable given that the original plea entered by defense counsel was one of insanity. There was no evidence that these oversights and lapses by defense counsel were tactical decisions; rather, they appeared to have been driven by the lack of financial resources devoted to the defense.

In addition, defense counsel did little to rebut the evidence of aggravation offered by the prosecution. The state's case in aggravation included an assertion that Tommy had wantonly fired a shotgun. There is no indication that defense counsel independently investigated this allegation, which, as we showed during the evidentiary hearing before Judge Suttle, was unsupported in fact. No counternarrative to the state's arguments was provided. By failing to conduct even a marginally adequate investigation, the defense not only compromised its opportunity to respond to the case in aggravation, it effectively conceded that case.

Together, these deficiencies amounted to an abnegation of prevailing professional norms, rising to the level of ineffective assistance of counsel.

We argued that this prejudiced Tommy, because Alabama law required at least ten of the twelve jurors to recommend a death sentence—and the vote in Tommy's case was exactly 10–2. Therefore, to demonstrate prejudice required only a reasonable probability that at least one juror would have struck a different balance, if all of the mitigating evidence presented during a competent representation had been considered.

We particularly highlighted Judge Burney's own acknowledgement that, in hindsight, he would not have sentenced Tommy to death if Janice had been tried first, given the disparity in outcomes of the two trials.

In all, our brief supporting Tommy's petition for relief was 391 pages long.

By contrast, the Alabama Attorney General did not submit a brief at all. Rather, on July 15, 1991, in a remarkable display of hubris, it tendered a sixty-six-page-long draft, "Opinion and Order," proposing findings of fact and conclusions of law that would reject our claims. There was no critical examination of the extensive facts and law that supported Tommy's claims for relief, although the assertion that Tommy's claims were waived or barred because his original attorneys did not raise them at trial or on appeal was renewed. It was the Attorney General's position that Judge Suttle need only sign the document as submitted and issue it as his own. Apparently, this display of overconfidence was born from the state's almost uniform record of success in defending against post-conviction death penalty proceedings; it was standard practice in the circuit courts of Alabama. By doing the Judge's work for him, in both substance and form, the Attorney General apparently sought to offer Judge Suttle an easy way out of wrestling with our claims.

On August 12, 1991, we filed a seventy-five-page reply brief castigating the form and substance of the Attorney General's response.

The integrity of the judicial process was at issue—and the petitioner's life was at stake. Under these circumstances, we argued that such a response to a well-documented claim for post-conviction relief was a universally condemned practice. Therefore, Judge Suttle must resist the temptation to adopt the proposed "Opinion and Order." We noted that the United States Supreme Court had denounced the verbatim adoption of prepared findings of fact, calling this practice "an abandonment of the duty and the trust that has been placed in the Judge." Moreover, the Alabama Court of Criminal Appeals had held that courts should be reluctant to adopt verbatim the findings of fact and conclusions of law prepared by a party to post-conviction proceedings. The Supreme Court opinion in *United States v. El Paso Natural Gas Company* (1964) stated our view more forcefully than we might have been willing to. We therefore quoted directly from it:

> [Litigants] in their zeal and advocacy and enthusiasm are going to state the case for their side in these findings as strongly as they possibly can. When these findings get to the courts of appeals they won't be worth the paper they are written on as far as assisting the court of appeals in determining why the Judge decided the case.

Once again, we argued that the claims raised here had not been waived nor were they otherwise barred from consideration. In fact, claims of ineffective assistance of counsel are never barred; the remainder of Tommy's claims were based upon newly discovered evidence that could not reasonably have been discovered at the time of trial or direct appeal.

We further pointed out that, in any event, Alabama courts would not allow fundamental miscarriages of justice to go unredressed. The Alabama Supreme Court's decision in *Ex parte Frazier* made this point:

> In cases like the present one, where the death penalty has been imposed, the "plain error" doctrine . . . requires the Court of Criminal Appeals to search the record and notice any prejudicial error committed by

the trial court and to take appropriate action, even though the defendant's counsel may have failed to preserve the error and raise it for appellate review. It follows therefore, that in death penalty cases, where perjured testimony is given and where there is a significant chance that the jury would have reached a different result had it heard the truth from the witness, attorney oversight or negligence in failing to challenge the testimony during trial cannot be a basis for denying a new trial.

The Alabama Attorney General's proposed opinion and order had urged Judge Suttle to give a higher priority to the goal of promoting the finality of judgments by barring claims that could have been, but were not, timely raised. While we conceded that the policy of promoting the finality of judgments is worthy of respect, we also insisted that it need not be blindly followed. We urged the Judge to carefully consider the Alabama Supreme Court's comments in *Ex parte Frazier*:

Perfection is not demanded of our judicial system, but we must aspire to that perfection. It would be perfidy for this Court not to use its power to require a new trial when perjury has permeated the testimony of a major witness for the State. We must strive to maintain the integrity of our judicial system by promoting the efficient administration of justice, but without impinging on the rights of the accused. In certain cases, such as the present one, fundamental fairness dictates the reversal of a conviction and sentence of death. Our organic law demands that an individual receive a fair trial before he can be put to death for his acts. If it did not, surely there could be no confidence in our judicial system. . . . Justice Cardozo wrote in *The Nature of the Judicial Process* that "the sordid controversies of the litigants are the stuff out of which great and shining truths will ultimately be shaped." The one "great and shining truth" that has been shaped from

this sordid controversy is that the courts of this state
shall strive always to ensure fair treatment to all those
who, because of their alleged criminal acts, stand to
lose their lives or liberty, regardless of who they may
be and regardless of what their alleged offenses may
be. Our Constitutions require, and we will insist on,
no less.

Oral arguments were heard by Judge Suttle on October 24, 1991,
with each side granted one hour to present its case. With the Judge's
permission, we elected to allocate fifty minutes of our time to arguing
our case while reserving ten minutes to rebut whatever the state might
present.

My focus was on three issues: purchased perjury; disproportional-
ity of sentences; and ineffective assistance of counsel. As most lawyers
would, I argued the strongest claims first and last, with the weaker of
the claims sandwiched in the middle:

> The first issue confronting this
> court was concisely framed by the
> Alabama Supreme Court in *Ex parte*
> *Frazier*.
>
> Can this court acquiesce in the
> execution of a man, knowing that the
> jury that convicted him of capital
> offenses had before it the perjured
> testimony of a material witness for
> the state?
>
> As in *Frazier*, the answer in this
> case is clearly no.

Anticipating that the state was likely to attack Eddie Oliver's testimony about Jimmy Dale Owens's confession, I tried to bolster Oliver's
credibility by pointing out his status as a parolee from a sentence of life
imprisonment:

> Mr. Oliver had nothing to gain and
> a great deal to lose by lying to this
> court on this matter.
>
> Specifically, Mr. Oliver is well
> aware that a conviction for lying to
> this court can result in him being
> imprisoned apart from his new wife and
> baby for the rest of his life.

I then explained to the court that the manner in which Owens's testimony was presented to the jury demonstrated how important that testimony was to Tommy's capital conviction:

> There is a significant chance that
> had the jury not heard the lies told
> by Jimmy Dale Owens, that they would
> have reached a different conclusion
> with respect to whether Tommy Hamilton
> was guilty of capital murder.
>
> . . .
>
> It must be recognized that in every
> trial, final impressions are often
> the most lasting impressions. It is
> therefore not unusual for lawyers
> to save their best for last. It is
> therefore not surprising that Jimmy
> Dale Owens was the last witness to
> give substantive testimony against
> Tommy at his trial.

In making our argument that Tommy's sentence was disproportionately severe when compared to those of his fellow defendants, we had to deal with the fact that Tommy alone fired the shots that killed

Lehman Wood. I did my best to fix the principal blame where it rightly belonged:

> In April of this year, Janice was granted parole. She is currently living in Oklahoma City.
>
> The Attorney General argues that the disproportionate sentence imposed upon Tommy is justified by the fact that he pulled the trigger of the gun that killed Mr. Wood. It is not surprising that Janice did not pull the trigger.
>
> The plotters and planners responsible for so much of the crime that plagues our society routinely seek to insulate themselves from accountability by soliciting and inciting those who are easily manipulated to do their bidding.
>
> Is the human mule that smuggles drugs across the border more responsible for the ruined lives of addicts and their crime victims than the drug lords that plan and finance those activities?
>
> Is the person that pulls the trigger more responsible for the death of another than the individual who contracts for such a killing? Of course not. No one contends that Tommy would have done this alone.

As stated by Judge Burney, had
Janice never participated, I don't
believe Tommy would have ever been
involved. Tommy would not have done
this alone. Tommy could not have done
this alone.

This crime only occurred because of
the mix of people involved and because
of Janice Glasco in particular.
To treat one member of the group
responsible so disproportionately from
the others is arbitrary.

To grant parole after five years
to the then twenty-seven-year-old
adult involved in this killing while
executing the then twenty-year-old who
has the intelligence of a child half
that age, is indefensible.

But the Attorney General argues
that it was the jury that determined
the sentences that could be imposed.
A jury found that Janice was only
guilty of manslaughter, a crime only
punishable by up to ten years in jail,
whereas a jury found that Tommy was
guilty of capital murder.

I suppose that if you honestly
believe that these disparate verdicts
were the result of an objective,
evenhanded weighing of the parties'
actions, you could make that argument.

If, however, you believe in

part, that Janice was found guilty of manslaughter because she was represented at trial by Don Holt, and Tommy was found guilty of capital murder because a predominant portion of his defense was presented by someone who was only two years out of law school, you cannot.

In this regard, Judge Burney, the jurist that presided at both trials, very candidly stated his view. When asked if Tommy's sentence would have been the same if Tommy had been tried and sentenced after Janice had received ten years, Judge Burney stated, "I can't believe I would have sentenced him to death."

. . .

Thus, Tommy awaits electrocution solely by virtue of having been the first of three defendants to have been tried. The arbitrary factor of timing should not be the most critical determinant in deciding the fate of an individual.

This is precisely why a review of the proportionality of sentences must be conducted and why in this case, Tommy Hamilton should be granted relief from his sentence of death.

I concluded my initial presentation by hammering Tommy's trial attorneys:

> Twenty-eight years ago, in *Gideon v. Wainwright*, the United States Supreme Court held that every poor person charged with a serious crime is constitutionally entitled to a lawyer provided by the state.
>
> The *Gideon* decision is a solid precedent, hailed by all branches of legal philosophy. The Supreme Court, even while at times finding it appropriate or necessary to review and reevaluate other rights of criminal defendants, has consistently described the right to counsel as fundamental.
>
> Shortly after it was decided, however, *Gideon*'s trumpet on behalf of justice became muted. In the real world, the promise of *Gideon* was not being fulfilled. Poor men and women in large numbers were going to trial in this country with lawyers who were so incompetent that the defendant's right to counsel had become meaningless at best and a detrimental hoax at worst.
>
> That appointed counsel's failures mattered was obvious. That these failures mattered most in death penalty cases was undeniable. In case after case, where the death penalty

had originally been imposed, judgments
were being overturned by higher
courts.

The defendants then got new lawyers
who presented facts and arguments
that had been overlooked or ignored.
As a result, life sentences were
being imposed, as opposed to death
sentences.

Believing the death penalty should
be imposed on an individual because
that individual is guilty of the most
heinous crime and not because that
individual has the most inexperienced
counsel, the Alabama legislature in
1975 passed a law to guarantee that
the promise of *Gideon* was kept in this
state.

Like the principle it sought
to defend, the law passed by the
legislature was simply stated:

"Each person indicted for an
offense punishable [by death] . . .
who is not able to afford legal
counsel must be provided with court
appointed counsel having no less than
five years prior experience in the
active practice of criminal law."

. . .

The reasons for this statutory
requirement are equally clear. The
consequences to a defendant in these

cases are too significant to entrust
the safeguarding of a defendant's
legal rights to an inexperienced
attorney, no matter how sincere, well-
intentioned, or willing to study,
learn, and work that attorney may be.

Thus, Alabama law provides that
a defendant such as Tommy must be
provided with court-appointed counsel
having no less than five years'
experience. Significantly, the statute
does not say that such defendants must
be provided with at least one court-
appointed counsel having the necessary
qualifications and, thereafter, any
number of unqualified attorneys may
also be appointed.

And no Alabama court has ever held
that this is permissible.

. . .

Tommy Hamilton was denied his right
to qualified legal representation. Mr.
Barnes Lovelace admittedly did not
have five years prior experience in the
active practice of criminal law.

Indeed, at the time of his
appointment as co-counsel for Tommy,
Mr. Lovelace had been practicing law
for less than two years. Mr. Lovelace
had never tried a death penalty case
before.

Indeed, from the period of time

from his graduation from law school to his appointment to represent Tommy in a trial for Tommy's life, Mr. Lovelace had tried a total of only two felony cases.

Even though he was statutorily unqualified to conduct Tommy's defense, Judge Burney did not place restrictions on the kind of work that Mr. Lovelace could perform in representing Tommy.

And as a result, Mr. Lavender assigned Mr. Lovelace significant responsibilities in connection with Tommy's defense. Indeed, but for Mr. Lavender's three-question cross-examination of one prosecution witness and a two-page epilogue after Mr. Lovelace's closing argument, Barnes Lovelace handled the entire sentencing phase of Tommy Hamilton's trial before the jury.

Mr. Lovelace's fundamental role in Tommy Hamilton's representation continued during appeals to both the Alabama Court of Appeals and Alabama Supreme Court.

The appointment of Mr. Lovelace violated Alabama law and requires that Tommy be granted a new trial, at which he may be represented as the Alabama

legislature assured him he would be
before being sentenced to die.

Laudably, Alabama has sought
to provide indigent defendants
with qualified counsel to avoid
the accusation that only those
with "capital" don't get capital
punishment.

The lawyers provided to Tommy
Hamilton, however, were either not
statutorily qualified or otherwise
ineffective in their representation
of him.

. . .

Death is an absolute punishment,
and an absolute punishment is not
proper for an individual who is not
absolutely responsible. Clearly, Tommy
is not absolutely responsible for the
unfortunate death of Mr. Wood.

Mitigating circumstances are not
excuses for a crime. An individual
guilty of capital murder will be
severely punished by death or a
life sentence. But there are reasons
which the law recognizes as valid for
imposing life sentences rather than
death.

In Tommy's case, many of these
reasons were either ignored or never
considered due to the ineffectiveness
of his unqualified and misguided trial

counsel. They failed to articulate
for the jury the nature of mitigating
evidence and the difference between
the sentencing decisions the jury and
Judge were called upon to make.

They failed to convey the message
that while life in prison may not
at the moment strike the public's
imagination as forcibly as would
death by electrocution, that to the
offender, the prolonged suffering
of years in confinement may well be
the more severe sentence and form of
retribution and expiation.

Indeed, a life sentence without
possibility of parole represents a
kind of civil death penalty, the death
of one's civil life. It is both a
profound punishment and compassionate.

They failed to present evidence
and tell the jury that Tommy Hamilton
wasn't born evil, he wasn't born a
monster. If anyone had intervened when
he had been a child, he would not be
on death row today.

Luke concluded our initial presentation.

Judge, in preparing my remarks for
this afternoon, I sat down and tried
to think what was the single most
important piece of the jigsaw puzzle

we have laid at your doorstep. If you
told me that out of all the testimony,
the days of testimony, the dozens of
witnesses, the thousands of pages
of exhibits and documents, and the
hundreds of pages of legal memoranda,
I had to come up with a single piece
of evidence for you to take with you
when you decide this case and issue
your opinion, what would it be?

For me, the answer presented
itself immediately. There was one
truly impartial witness who testified
before this court who participated in
the proceedings that brought Tommy
Hamilton to death row.

And his credibility, his integrity,
and his honesty are not just
undisputed on this record. They are
beyond dispute, period. I am of course
referring to Judge Burney. Judge
Burney was a completely impartial
witness.

He presided over every trial
proceeding arising out of the death
of Lehman Wood. He saw and heard
the testimony pertaining to Tommy
Hamilton's involvement in the death of
Lehman Wood.

He saw and heard the testimony
pertaining to the involvement of
Janice Glasco, Tommy's sister, and

Debbie Gatlin Hamilton, Tommy's wife.
He saw the demeanor of the witnesses
and assessed their credibility.

He brought the experience of
twenty-five years on the bench to those
proceedings, and he brought that
experience to this court as well. And
I'd like to remind the court that but
for Judge Burney's retirement, Judge
Burney would be deciding this case
today, not you, Judge Suttle.

I submit to Your Honor that he left
no doubt as to how he would decide
this case today. He told the court
that he views Tommy's death sentence
as being disproportionately severe in
light of the sentences that were given
to Janice Glasco and Debbie Gatlin
Hamilton.

And he also pointed the court to
the real reason Tommy sits on death
row in Bessemer, Alabama, today: the
person truly responsible for the
events of the afternoon of July 11,
1984, Janice Glasco.

The Judge that sentenced Tommy to
die by electrocution has told this
court that Tommy was less responsible
for the death of Lehman Wood than a
woman who was given a maximum sentence
of ten years and is today free on
parole.

And where is she, by the way? This
is Tommy's sister we are talking
about. Does she care enough to even
be at these proceedings? Is she here
to support her family and her mother?
No. And you know why? Because the only
thing that Janice Glasco has ever
cared about since she set the entire
tragedy in motion, is Janice Glasco.

Judge Burney knew that, and that's
why he told this court that it would
be wrong to kill Tommy for a crime
that he never even would have been
involved in but for the influence of
a woman who is now free and released
from jail.

The Judge that tried these cases,
that knows them as well or better than
virtually anyone, does not believe
that Tommy should die for the murder
of Lehman Wood.

Judge Burney told this court that
if he were passing sentence on Tommy
today, he would not sentence Tommy to
die, even if the sentencing jury had
recommended such a sentence.

. . .

For these reasons, we believe that
great and indeed controlling deference
should be given by this court to the
conclusions in the testimony of Judge
Burney.

. . .

```
Thank you.
```

The closing argument presented by Ken Nunnelley on behalf of the state of Alabama was remarkably pedestrian. He largely asserted that our claims should be dismissed because: Tommy was a murderer; our claims could have been raised earlier—and therefore were procedurally barred; and Tommy was a murderer.

What substantive engagement Nunnelley offered with respect to the purchased, perjured testimony of Jimmy Dale Owens was skim milk:

```
        There is nothing at all in the
        record to suggest, as the petitioner
        claims, that Jimmy Dale Owens was
        released in return for testimony.
        There is nothing in the record that
        even suggests that Jimmy Dale Owens
        got out of the Lawrence County
        Jail under any circumstances other
        than those of the normal course of
        business.

            . . .

        What we did have at the Rule 20
        hearing in this case was William
        Eddie Oliver, who wouldn't even come
        to court, who insisted on filing a
        John Doe affidavit, whose identity was
        mightily sought to be protected from
        the state, all because William Eddie
        Oliver is afraid he's going to get
        some kind of adverse consequences for
        telling the truth.
        And that right there, Judge,
```

```
is why William Eddie Oliver isn't
a believable witness. He wouldn't
even come in this courthouse. He
insisted on testifying by videotaped
deposition. The last thing he said
was, "If I get called to court, I'll
probably tell the court the truth."
    Judge, I submit that William Eddie
Oliver lied.
```

Notably, Nunnelley made no mention of Anthony Winchester's testimony, which had corroborated Oliver's testimony—and was deemed so favorable to the defense that the state had to turn it over to us in advance of the hearing.

With respect to Judge Burney, Ken largely asked Judge Suttle to reconsider the admissibility of his testimony and ignore a rung bell:

```
    I'm not conceding that Judge
Burney's testimony is admissible.
I contend that it is not, because
it goes to the mental operations of
a trial Judge. Those are clearly
inadmissible.
```

Ken's fallback position appeared to be that Tommy's sentence wasn't too harsh; rather, the sentences given to Debbie and Janice were too lenient:

```
    My only shame in this case is that
Janice and Debbie didn't get the
sentences that they deserved.
    Tommy got the sentence he deserved.
```

While understandable as argumentation, in order to take the full measure of what Nunnelley was suggesting, one must remember that

Debbie, who was only fifteen years old when Lehman Wood was killed, agreed to serve a life sentence. I am not sure there could ever be enough death sentences in Alabama to satisfy Ken Nunnelley.

In conclusion, Ken attempted to press a home-court advantage by accusing Chicago lawyers of assassinating the character of Alabama attorneys:

> The only specific ground of
> ineffective assistance of counsel,
> Judge, that I really want to speak
> to directly, unless Your Honor has
> questions, is the claim that Mr.
> Lavender was somehow impaired in his
> ability to represent Tommy Hamilton
> because he was an alcoholic, whatever
> the terminology was.
>
> The testimony in this case from
> the person or persons in the best
> position to observe—and that's his co-
> counsel and the prosecuting attorney—
> established that Wes Lavender wasn't
> drinking during this trial in 1983
> or '84.
>
> . . .
>
> That's character assassination in
> the worst form imaginable, Your Honor.
> It's a professional attack, or rather
> it's an attack on an individual's
> professional competence, when that
> lawyer did everything he could to save
> that man's life.
>
> And the only reason he lost, and
> the only reason that Tommy Hamilton

```
got a death sentence was because he
was guilty of capital murder and he
deserved the death sentence.
     This court should uphold that
sentence.
```

Even though Luke and I had exceeded the fifty minutes we were granted at the outset, Judge Suttle allowed me ten additional minutes for my rebuttal, which did not pass without objection from Nunnelley:

```
The Court: Y'all have already used up
     all of your time. I'll give you ten
     minutes though.
Mr. Clark: We appreciate it, Judge.
The Court: Go ahead.
Mr. Nunnelley: Can I object?
The Court: Yes, sir. It won't do you any
     good.
Mr. Nunnelley: I didn't think it would.
     It never hurts to ask, though.
The Court: No, it sure doesn't. Go ahead.
```

I tried to make my rebuttal succinct:

```
     First of all, with respect to
procedural default, we have addressed
the procedural default issues at
length in our briefs. And I think that
we have established in those briefs,
based on the law as it exists in
Alabama, that a petitioner's claims
are not procedurally barred, or that
you are not necessarily required to
```

find that they are procedurally barred,
if you find that an injustice will be
done and that constitutional rights
have been violated.

It is uncontested that claims
regarding ineffective assistance of
counsel are not procedurally barred
and cannot be procedurally barred.

. . .

It's uncontested that claims
premised on newly discovered evidence
are not barred from consideration
in post-conviction proceedings. And
there's been no allegation that many
of the claims here are based on
anything other than newly discovered
evidence.

We were fortunate enough to be able
to find the evidence regarding this
perjury. We were fortunate enough to
be able to find the evidence regarding
the inducements that were extended to
Jimmy Dale Owens with respect to his
testimony.

Any of the claims that Mr. Hamilton
has presented that are based on
newly discovered evidence are not
procedurally barred. And this state's
Supreme Court has held that in *Ex
parte Womack*, again, a case dealing
with prosecutorial misconduct.

And the reason they are not
procedurally barred is because such
breaches of this state's judicial
system are difficult to find out. They
don't happen very often. And when
they do happen, they are difficult to
discover.

But this court, the state Supreme
Court, is upholding the integrity of
its judicial system and holding that
whenever such evidence comes to light,
this state's judicial system will deal
with it.

. . .

We have not invoked any harsh or
strange rules of law in an attempt to
spare the life of Tommy Hamilton.

And we object to any such rules of
law being invoked to kill him.

With respect to ineffective
assistance of counsel, Mr. Nunnelley
suggests that the representation
provided to Tommy Hamilton was
effective and that we can't second
guess the judgments that were made by
Mr. Lavender and Mr. Lovelace.

Well Mr. Lavender and Mr. Lovelace
testified, and they specifically told
you that decisions that they made
weren't based on tactics. They weren't
trial-strategy decisions whatsoever.
They just didn't think of the

arguments or didn't think the evidence was worth pursuing.

And one of the areas where that ineffectiveness is most blatant is with respect to the mental health issues. Judge Burney, on his own initiative, encouraged them to seek funds from him so that they would have the resources to get mental health expertise.

There was no tactical downside from them doing that. They could have taken the funds, talked to a psychiatrist or psychologist of their choosing. If that psychiatrist or psychologist told them, "There is nothing wrong with Tommy Hamilton, there's no mental health issue worth pursuing here," that never would have seen the light of day at court, and there was no tactical downside to them doing that.

But there was a definite downside to Tommy Hamilton because they didn't do that. If they'd done it, the evidence in this case is clear, that they would have found significant mental health mitigating issues.

Now Your Honor can weigh the evidence that has been presented by the experts on both sides and judge their credibility. But there is one piece of mental health evidence that

was not brought forth by an expert
for either side. And therefore, it is
irrefutable.

It was the EEG that was performed
by the University of Alabama Hospital,
independently of either side in
this case, and the report of that
hospital based on that independent
test specifically stated that Tommy
Hamilton's electrical brain function
is abnormal.

That evidence could have been
discovered by his trial counsel. That
evidence should have prompted further
inquiry in discovery by his trial
counsel. And the culmination of that
evidence should have been before the
jury and Judge making the life and
death decisions with respect to Tommy
Hamilton that they did.

I also felt I had to blunt what likely was an ever-present elephant in the room:

The conclusion that Tommy's trial
counsel were ineffective is not
the conclusion of two lawyers from
Chicago. It's the conclusion that is
shared by a prominent member of the
criminal trial bar of not only this
state but this region in particular.

Don Holt testified before Your Honor
that he had reviewed the actions taken

by these gentlemen, and that he found
them to be ineffective. And he told
you that you always, in any capital
case, seek out and obtain consultation
with mental health experts, no matter
what, because there is no tactical
downside in doing that.

And the conclusion that these men
were ineffective is not just the
conclusion of other lawyers. It's
their own conclusion. Barney Lovelace
told you that they sought outside
assistance in conducting their defense
of Tommy Hamilton, and that they
turned for assistance to the teaching
of others.

And one of those that they
considered authoritative were
publications regarding how you
try a capital case. They sought
this material. They considered it
authoritative. They looked to it for
guidance. And what did that material,
including Petitioner's Exhibit 33,
tell them?

It told them just what I have
told you and what Mr. Holt told you,
that you always seek out mental
health experts in a capital case. And
you always put the time and effort
necessary into obtaining mitigating
evidence.

Lastly, I needed to address Nunnelley's assertion that we had engaged in character assassination regarding Lavender's problems with alcohol:

> Another issue Mr. Nunnelley
> raises is with respect to Mr.
> Lavender's inability to fulfill his
> responsibilities as Tommy's trial
> attorney. I'm not in the business of
> making character attacks on anyone,
> let alone a fellow lawyer.
>
> Neither is my partner. Neither is
> Sister McKenzie. We did not bring this
> evidence to Your Honor lightly. We did
> not make the charge cavalierly. We
> did, only after we went out into the
> community and talked to several people
> about Mr. Lavender.
>
> And we did it only after we were
> convinced that there were credible
> people, willing to come forward in
> this courtroom and give Your Honor the
> facts with regard to Mr. Lavender.
>
> It's not something we enjoyed
> doing. The fact that there wasn't
> a bottle on counsel table during
> the trial is not the determinative
> standard. Indeed, your success in any
> trial is dependent not necessarily on
> what you do in the courtroom, but what
> you do out of the courtroom before you
> get there.

Mr. Lavender did nothing outside the courtroom. He did not seek out and talk to countless mitigation witnesses. He did not seek out and gather countless pieces of evidence that could have been brought forth in this case.

It is Mr. Lavender's inability to act outside the courtroom that is as much at issue as what he did inside the courtroom. And the evidence is that due to a disease of which he was afflicted, he was incapable of performing his obligations to his client.

That, I submit, is the reason Mr. Lovelace was involved in this case to begin with. He was brought in this case at the request of Mr. Lavender. He was delegated more than significant responsibilities by Mr. Lavender, because deep in his heart, Mr. Lavender knew that he wasn't in a position to discharge those responsibilities. He needed the help of somebody else.

. . .

The Court (interrupting): You have about two minutes.

Mr. Clark: It was in *Watts v. Indiana* when Justice Felix Frankfurter stated, "We are deeply mindful of

the anguishing problems which the
incidents of crime present to
the states, but the history of the
criminal law proves overwhelmingly
that brutal methods of law enforcement
are essentially self-defeating.

   "Whatever may be their effect in
a particular business, law triumphs
when the natural impulses, aroused
by a shocking crime, yield to the
safeguards which our civilization
has evolved for an administration
of justice, at once rational and
effective."

   May these words guide you in making
your decision.

      Thank you.

The issues having been fully briefed and argued, Judge Suttle took the petition for post-conviction relief under advisement on October 24, 1991. Telling us that he would issue his ruling "as expeditiously as possible," he added that "if I rule by Christmas, that would be expeditious."

To me, waiting for a decision—whether for a jury to return a verdict or for a Judge to make a ruling—is the most trying part of a case. In Tommy's case, months went by with no word from Judge Suttle. It is easy to convince yourself that the passage of time is a favorable sign, that it only takes a few minutes to write an order declaring "petition denied" but much longer to author the reasons why a condemned man should be given new legal life. But only the decision itself can put an end to the anxiety you feel while waiting. It must also be one of the worst times for the families and friends of trial lawyers, because we can never really be fully present for them until the waiting is over.

Tommy's days on death row were so isolated and boring that just waiting for Judge Suttle to rule likely animated them. In a waiting-to-die letter dated August 24, 1993, Tommy wrote, "I am gonna give yall a i deal ['y'all an idea'] on how a day is for me:"

> *So I got up at 9:30 a.m. to eat lunch i made my bed up and i got my ice put up in my cups, i miss the 45 minutes walk this morning because they came in here walking us at 6:30 a.m. So at 11.00 a.m. i will turn my tv on and watch a hour of local news then i will watch 3 hours of soap operas, and at 3.00 p.m. i will turn the tv off and wait on supper time around 3.30, And after that i will clean my cell up, and do my writing home, and wait on the mail to run, and every other day we will shower in the evening time, and at 5.00 p.m. i will watch the local news then the world news then the local news again. And from 6.30 till 10.00 i watch pretty much the top rated shows or movies, And i am always watching primetime and 20 20, i will also watch a lot of public tv, But at 10.00 i will watch the local news, And at 10.30 i always watch night line, then Jay Leno or whatever show has the best guess ["guest"] on it. And i may go on to bed at 12.30 But if it's a lot going on in the news i might stay on up and wait on that late night world news, You will see many things on there that the world news at 5.30 p.m. did not have the time to show, So as yall can see i am a news nut, But i have learned many things by watching shows like i watch, So that is pretty much a day and night from Tommy world.*

After twenty-two months had passed, I told Lynn that I should have asked the court, "At Christmas of which year should we expect the order?"

CHAPTER ELEVEN

The Order

More than two years after the completion of the hearing, in the fall of 1993, Judge Suttle broached the idea of the parties settling Tommy's case. An inquiry was made as to whether Tommy would drop his post-conviction appeals if granted a reduction in sentence to life without possibility of parole. The Alabama Attorney General's Office did not want to be viewed as the party initiating such an offer, but it also did not want to upset Judge Suttle in advance of his ruling on the pending petition. So the Attorney General's Office responded that upon receiving a letter from the prosecutor, Tim Littrell, requesting that the case be settled on such terms, it would make Tommy the offer suggested by Judge Suttle.

While I was not going to respond to an offer that had yet to be made, I was ecstatic at the possibility that Tommy's life might be saved. Tommy, however, was adamantly opposed to the potential deal. As he had told us from the beginning, the only thing he feared more than execution was spending the remainder of his life behind bars. He was not only angry; he was scared. Scared that declining such an offer would provoke Judge Suttle to impose it in his ruling on the pending petition. Scared that we would lose our enthusiasm for defending his interests as he defined them.

I could not blame Tommy for the emotions he was feeling. But I did not share his conclusion that electrocution was the lesser of two evils. Sister Lynn, Luke, and I implored Tommy's mother, Lucille, to persuade Tommy to seriously consider the deal should it be offered. She promised to see Tommy in person the following Monday and beg him to authorize us to accept such an offer.

After visiting with Tommy to discuss the prospective offer, Sister Lynn wrote him a letter that both urged him to reconsider his position and sought to coax his positive response. She wrote in part:

> To talk to someone about a decision of life & death is a very sensitive, awesome task. I can't imagine (though I can try) what it's like to be in your shoes.
>
> After we left you, as you know, we went to see your mother in Hillsboro. I kept thinking to myself as I saw the pain and anguish in her eyes & on her face that a mother should not have to go through this. She has been through so much. I am wondering how her visit, & those in your family who came with her, went yesterday. I'm sure these last several days have been very hard on you Tommy—emotionally draining.
>
> Ever since leaving you, there has been a scripture verse that keeps coming to me about all of this, & so I share it with you. It is from the book of Deuteronomy, in the Old Testament, chapter 30, verse 19:
>
> I have set before you life & death, blessings and curses. Choose LIFE.
>
> That's not coming from me, Tommy, but from God's Word. Perhaps you could pray over it.

Tommy responded to Lynn five days later. In an often rambling, grievance-filled seven-page letter, he wrote in part:

> I got your letter Thursday evening and I must say that I was happy to have received it, so thanks, And your

letter hit home on many things, so I know that you was able to see the pain and Im sure you also felt some of the pain, And I guess that at this time, it has been the hardest for me the first three days after seeing yall I've cryed and got myself maybe 3 hours of sleep I wrote to myself all night I fine that I am able to write my thoughts much better than speaking them. So yes those first 3 days really took me for a spin, but my visit went okay I was able to hold the tears and get back in control, but believe me I did keep an open mind on everything and I still have a open mind on this decision, but this is a choice that only I should have to make I will not let mother or anyone make it for me, I am not a man with out a brain.

. . .

And I wish to say that after spending 11 years in jails, a nut house, and prisons I do know much more than you think I do about prisons or the prison system I do know that 11 years ago I only had a drinking prob-lem I enter the prison system and got out after a year only to kill a man 3 months later so the system in my eyes made me crazier . . .

But its my life to and I know I did not get a fair chance to fight I got one drunk for a main lawyer and a lawyer as a back up, and all alone the DA making deals at the Sheriff house, and covering up his wrong turns, and I could go on and on but the point I wanted to make is that I can see all sides of my life, and at this point I wish to let yall know that I feel yall are looking at my life and case one sided, plus trying to force me into a deci-sion that will not effect yall but will effect me the rest of my life, in know way do yall have the power or should yall even want the power to help me make this decision that will effect the rest of my life, and sure I understand that yall are just telling me what yall feel is best, but please remember that yall don't know me, the me 11 years ago, yall don't know what it is like trying to live in a world that is full of madness, and homosexuals to show you care is looked at as weakness or to choose not to fight to avoid trouble is like telling them to go steeal anything they want, this is a world that is full of games, head games that yall could not deal with[.]

. . .

And never think that I have not looked at both side of this situation because over the last 11 years I have went over everything that I can remember in my life and I need a good reason to give up this fight and start a new one in a mad world down that hall, so I must end this letter but I really felt that I should try to let you see another side to this the side that yall chose not to see[.]

. . .

Also I looked the verse up and I went over the hold chapter 30 and to me, it meant that to choose life, is our only way out if we ever want peace and happiness, we had better choose life[.]

Lynn responded to Tommy on October 21:

Thanks so much for your letter which I received 1 week ago today. I very much appreciated the time and thought you put into writing it. Thank you for shar-ing with me your thoughts and feelings regarding your situation and the case in the posture that it is in. I'm writing today not so much as one of your lawyers, but as someone getting to know you and caring very much what happens to you.

As I read your letter, I was very struck with many of the things you said. I agree that, of course, you are the only one that can make the decision about whether to accept a potential offer of life without parole. I know that none of us has walked in your shoes and, therefore, none of us can really know what you have gone through, are going through and will go through. My own experi-ences in life are different from your own and we each have our own perspective on things. As I have thought and prayed about all of this, thinking of what you said, what we said, what your mother said, I must confess that I am not sure what I would do if I were in your place. Your statement, that we were trying to force you into a decision that will not affect us but will affect you for the rest of your life, hit me like a rock. I, nor Don or Luke, [do not] want to force you into anything. We want to make sure you are looking at all the options, understanding what they all might mean, and then make the decision yourself. We feel a heavy burden to advise you as fully and completely as we can. You're right, we are pushing hard for life without. It is hard for us not to. We don't want to think of you being strapped into the electric chair with your mother watching and dying a senseless death. But neither do we know or are we able to comprehend what you live in day after day nor what your life would be like in the general prison population. I do ask you to think about what we said, as well as all you have heard, as I know you have. Your saying you had cried and not slept for thinking of all that made me think hard. I have prayed for you and continue to pray for you. It is hard to know what else to say or do at this point.

District Attorney Littrell communicated that he would recommend reducing Tommy's sentence to a term of life in prison without the possibility of parole only if Tommy indicated in advance that he would agree to such an offer. I concluded that our efforts to persuade Tommy to accept this lifesaving deal, even bolstered by Lucille's pleas, would continue to be unsuccessful. But I also thought that hearing the recommendation from a different attorney might help persuade Tommy to accept.

On January 19, 1994, I enlisted the assistance of Bryan Stevenson, then the Executive Director of the Alabama Capital Representation Resource Center (thereafter, the Equal Justice Initiative). Bryan offered to have one of his staff attorneys, Kevin Martin Doyle, speak with Tommy.

Doyle had grown up in the Bronx and Rockland County, New York. His father was a police officer. Doyle obtained a Jesuit education at Fordham College and graduated from law school at the University of Virginia. He was a thirty-eight-year-old Irish American lawyer with Roman Catholic convictions who found the death penalty morally indefensible. After graduating from law school, Doyle enlisted with Stevenson and began representing capital defendants and inmates on Alabama's death row. In 1995, he returned to his native state to head New York's Capital Defender Office until it brought New York's death penalty to an end. Doyle could convey to Tommy an informed view of the merits of the possible offer. Littrell was pressing for an answer, and Doyle, who regularly visited other clients on death row, could arrange to see Tommy soon.

My "second opinion" strategy was also unsuccessful. Doyle met with Tommy on February 7, 1984, and he reported the results in a letter he mailed to us that day.

> *Dear Gentlemen:*
>
> *I saw Mr. Hamilton this afternoon and cannot report much progress on the plea front. He is about as entrenched an inmate as I have seen.*
>
> *He does not confess any safety concern about general population but simply refuses to consider a hopeless LWOP [life without parole] existence as living. Non-prison life is, amazingly, still a palpable memory for him, and that's a problem.*
>
> *Another problem is the lasting resentment over the d.a.'s (or court's) original insistence on a quick answer to the plea offer.*
>
> *Last, Don Holt recently communicated to Mr. Hamilton his judgment that Mr. Hamilton could avoid a capital conviction on retrial. Mr. Hamilton acknowledged that Mr. Holt was in no position to opine on this question. Indeed, at the end of the interview, Mr. Hamilton asked that I not repeat Mr. Holt's comment. I*

do so now only because this is literally a life-and-death
matter. Please do not bring this up to Mr. Hamilton. I
do not need a reputation as a sort of snitch on the row.
Still, Mr. Holt played right into the gross over-optimism
which stands between Mr. Hamilton and a rational
decision.

Anyway, I can only suggest that, as a last ditch
effort, you arrange for your client, his family, and
yourselves to meet. At such a meeting you could insist
everyone understand that Mr. Hamilton's election is
tantamount to suicide. In my experience, sometimes
an inmate's fantasy defenses weaken as he watches his
family accept the attorney argument he is rejecting.

Sincerely,
Kevin M. Doyle

"Disappointment" does not begin to adequately express my reaction. I was angry that Don Holt, Janice's trial attorney, had interjected his views, which were entirely premised on Tommy being granted a new trial. Unbeknown to Kevin Doyle, Tommy's family already embraced our view and, at our request, had conveyed their feelings to Tommy. Tommy's "walk me or fry me!" attitude was the quintessential symptom of his proclivity for self-destruction. I now had to agree with the sentiment expressed by Lynn in her last letter to Tommy: It was difficult to know what else to say or do at this point.

So I followed Tommy's wishes. We advised the court that its effort to broker a settlement of Tommy's claims had been unsuccessful. Judge Suttle was going to have to rule on our pending petition for post-conviction relief from Tommy's capital murder conviction and death sentence. Shortly thereafter, he did just that.

Judge Suttle issued a sixty-eight-page order on March 25, 1994.

In his order, Judge Suttle summarily rejected our claim that Tommy's defense counsel lacked the qualifications required by law in Alabama. He found that "[t]he statute provides for one lawyer with at least five years of experience. It is ludicrous to argue that one lawyer with five years of experience meets the statutory requirement, but if that same lawyer is given assistance, the statute is violated."

Despite Judge Suttle's assertion to the contrary, the statute does not say that a death penalty defendant is entitled to "one" lawyer with at least five years of criminal law experience. Rather, the statute says that "[e]ach person indicted for [a capital offense] who is not able to afford legal counsel must be provided with court appointed counsel having no less than five years prior experience in the active practice of law."

Nor had we made the argument that, if a lawyer meeting the statutory requirements is given assistance, the statute is violated. But Judge Suttle was just as dismissive of the argument we had made: "Hamilton argues that Lavender delegated too much responsibility to Lovelace. Such delegation could *de facto* violate the terms of the statute if the lead counsel abandoned the case to an associate. However, that was not the case here. Lavender was present throughout the trial, supervised and directed Lovelace's work, and was intimately involved in the preparation and trial of the case."

In my view, the law required more than just "presence" by a statutorily qualified attorney. I also thought that this stingy reading gutted the legislative promise by viewing the statutory requirements as having been fulfilled if the more experienced attorney participated merely to the minimum degree necessary not to constitute abandonment. Further, Judge Suttle managed to ignore the testimony that Barnes Lovelace was, effectively, the "designated driver" for Tommy's sentencing proceedings.

We were off to a bad start.

With respect to our contention that Tommy's sentence was disproportionately severe when compared to the sentences given to Janice and Debbie, Judge Suttle demurred. He said that such an assessment was an appellate-court function and that he was "certainly in no position to usurp or second-guess the appellate court's proportionality review" in this case.

But that did not stop him from editorializing. He gratuitously offered that he agreed with the observation made by the Court of Criminal Appeals in another case that "[i]n the sentencing phase of the trial, the fact that an alleged accomplice did not receive the death penalty is no more relevant as a mitigating factor for the defendant than the fact that an alleged accomplice did receive the death penalty would be as an aggravating factor against him." For good measure, he tossed in his belief that "there is no merit to this [disproportionate sentencing] claim."

Not everything in the order went against us. For example, Judge Suttle did note that, during the sentencing proceedings before the jury, prosecutor Tim Littrell directly implied that Tommy had previously engaged in another violent act by asking a witness whether he had heard about Tommy firing a shotgun at an unoccupied dwelling. As stated by Judge Suttle: "There was absolutely no factual basis for that question. Yet, the jury would have assumed that the prosecutor wouldn't have asked about it if it hadn't occurred. The jury was misled, and Hamilton was prejudiced by the prosecutorial conduct."

And Judge Suttle found that the final sentencing hearing before Judge Burney should have been continued so that the lawyer primarily responsible for the presentation, Barnes Lovelace, could have been present. He noted: "The lawyer who was present [Wes Lavender] did not even plead for his client's life at the final fateful hearing."

Importantly, Judge Suttle found that Tommy's court-appointed trial lawyers did not provide him effective assistance of counsel during the sentencing phase of his trial.

> Even with ineffective counsel, the jury only voted 10-2 to recommend the death penalty. A vote of 9-3 would have been considered a recommendation of life without parole. Judge Burney gave due consideration to the jury's verdict when he imposed the death sentence. Thus, if only one juror had voted differently, Hamilton may not have been sentenced to death. The question is what did Hamilton's lawyers do to try to convince the jury and then the Judge to spare his life? Sadly, the answer is "not much."

Judge Suttle specifically found that Messrs. Lavender and Lovelace fell short of this constitutional obligation in numerous respects, to wit: their failure to seek independent psychiatric or psychological evaluation of Tommy; their failure to present numerous mental health issues during the sentencing hearing; their failure to call available witnesses who would have testified to mitigating circumstances; and their failure to present available evidence of an abusive childhood at the hands of an alcoholic father.

> [W]hether all this evidence would have or should have made a difference in the jury's recommendation or the Judge's sentence is not the issue. Rather, the issue is, as the U.S. Supreme Court has stated:

> The benchmark for judging any claim of ineffectiveness must be whether counsel's conduct so undermined the functioning of the adversarial process that the result cannot be relied upon as having produced a just result.

> By that benchmark, it is this court's sorrowful decision that Hamilton did not receive such a sentencing hearing.

With respect to our claims that Jimmy Dale Owens's testimony was both perjured and purchased, Judge Suttle embraced wholesale our recitation of the relevant facts and legal standards governing these claims. Ironically, given the Alabama Attorney General's attempt to induce Judge Suttle to sign off on its ghostwritten order, Judge Suttle incorporated at least ten pages on this issue from our brief into his opinion. By doing so, he acknowledged that, in granting a new trial in a capital case based on an allegation of perjured testimony, the court must be reasonably well satisfied that 1) testimony given by a witness was false; 2) there is a significant chance that the jury, had it heard the truth, would have reached a different result; and 3) the defendant is not relying on evidence of which he was aware at trial and which he consciously decided not to use to challenge the testimony of the perjured witness.

Without hesitation, Judge Suttle found that our claims were premised on newly discovered evidence: "Hamilton is not relying on evidence which he consciously decided not to use to challenge the testimony of Jimmy Dale Owens. This information was not available to Hamilton's trial attorneys. They could not have been expected to discover it."

With respect to our claim that all of Jimmy Dale Owens's testimony was purchased perjury, Judge Suttle wrote: "The court is reasonably well satisfied that Owens' statements that Hamilton said: 'the son of a bitch deserved dying' and 'that he would do it again' were perjured. The court is *not* reasonably well satisfied that that the remainder of Owens' testimony was perjured." Specifically, Judge Suttle found that "[a]fter the trial, Owens told William Eddie Oliver, another Trustee, that he lied about the statements ('[Hamilton] would do it again if he had to' and 'the son of a bitch deserved dying')." But Judge Suttle also found that "Owens never told the other Trustee that he had lied about [the other testimony he gave at trial]."

He also found that "with the exception of denials [by law enforcement investigators] that they solicited testimony in exchange for a promise of lenient treatment, all of the evidence of record supports the conclusion that Jimmy Dale Owens testified against Hamilton in exchange for a recommendation from law enforcement that Owens would be released early from jail." Judge Suttle wrote:

> The investigators' denial that they "promised" Owens anything is merely playing with words. It is this court's firm conclusion from all the above facts that Owens was told in effect by investigator Ferris, "I can't promise you anything, but if you'll help us, I'll see what I can do." Or, "I'll tell the Sheriff or Judge you helped us, but I can't promise you anything." Such word games are intolerable all the time, much less when a man's, even a murderer's, life is being decided. Owens may not have been promised anything specific in terms of results, but he was promised their efforts. This is conclusively shown by the testimony and early release of Owens. As a result, Owens perjured himself by embellishing upon his conversation with Hamilton.

Judge Suttle's dilution of the evidence in this regard was curious. Oliver stated that law enforcement had promised Owens something "specific." He testified that Owens told him that law enforcement had promised to help him get out of jail early.

> Question: Now, what exactly, the best you
>   can recall, did Owens tell you when he
>   came back from his conversation with
>   Ferris and Weatherford?
> Answer: Well, first he kind of smiled.
>   He said, "After the trial I'll be a
>   free man. I'm going to Georgia," or
>   something to that effect. And I said,
>   "What do you mean?" He said, "I'm
>   going to testify for them."
>
>   . . .
>
> Q: Okay. Do you know why he did that? Did
>   he explain to you why he did that?
> A: Where he could get out of jail.
> Assistant Attorney General
>   (interrupting): I didn't hear your
>   answer. I'm sorry.
> A: Where he could get out of jail. They
>   told him that they would help him get
>   out early.
> Q: Mr. Weatherford and Mr. Ferris told
>   Mr. Owens that they would help him
>   get out of jail early if he gave this
>   testimony?
> A: Right.

Investigator Gandy's notes of his interview of cellmate Anthony Winchester documented that the offer went beyond efforts to get Owens released early, to the point of promising results.

Question: And Mr. Winchester also told
     you that Jimmy Dale Owens had said,
     quote, "They told me they would cut me
     loose if I testified for them against
     Tommy"?
Answer: I'm checking to see. Yes, sir,
     that's correct. Yes, sir. It's in my
     notes here.

Having satisfied himself on the third and first points raised in our brief about purchased perjured testimony, Judge Suttle proceeded to address the remaining element of our claim. He stated that "[h]aving found that Hamilton and his trial attorneys did not know of this perjury and that it did occur, the last issue is whether there is a significant chance that had the jury heard the truth, it would have reached a different result."

I had wanted a smart Judge. I had gotten one in Ned Michael Suttle. And after reading his order, I felt he was trying to outsmart me. Because on this element of our claim, Judge Suttle rendered a Solomon-like decision:

> There is no significant chance the jury would have reached a different verdict with regard to the capital murder charge. The truthful portions of Owens' testimony were corroborated and were proved by the rest of the State's case[.]

> . . .

> However, there is a significant chance that the perjury did affect the sentencing recommendation of the jury. The jury recommended death by 10-2; the absolute minimum allowed by law. If the vote of only one juror was affected by the perjured testimony of such mean, vicious, remorseless, cold, defiant, vindictive statements by Hamilton, then Hamilton was sentenced

to death by virtue of such perjury. Judge Billy Burney has testified that he gave due consideration to the jury's recommendation. Obviously, such statements by Hamilton would have affected all the jurors in their sentencing recommendation. Such statements would also have directly affected Judge Burney's decision, even if, somehow, miraculously, they had not affected the jury's.

Judge Suttle dismissed all of our other claims on Tommy's behalf, ruling that they could have been—but were not—raised at trial or on appeal; and that, in any event, they were without merit.

And so, Judge Suttle concluded: "Hamilton may deserve the death penalty and may yet receive it. However, if he is to be executed, he must receive a sentencing hearing where all reasonably available evidence is presented to the jury. The court, therefore, orders that Hamilton is granted a new sentencing hearing."

Was this a victory? Not in our client's eyes. Tommy had made it clear to me from the beginning that the only thing he feared more than being strapped into the electric chair was being incarcerated for the rest of his life. With his capital murder conviction having been affirmed, the only outcome possible from a new sentencing hearing was either another death sentence or a life sentence without possibility of parole. As far as Tommy was concerned, he had won nothing.

I was dissatisfied too. Judge Suttle was simply wrong. Eddie Oliver had testified that Owens had repudiated "*his testimony* against Tommy Hamilton" and "*the testimony* he gave at the trial of Tommy Hamilton," not just some portion of it.

```
Question: How many times did he make that
     statement to you that his testimony
     against Tommy Hamilton was false?
Answer: Well, after the trial is mostly
     when he did it. Because he was real
     nervous and upset, you know. And he
     was scared. He said, "I did the wrong
```

> thing." And, uh, he kept asking me
> what he should do. I said, "You're
> the one that's got to live with it
> now." He said, "Even after I did that
> they've lied to me."
>
> Q: Did he tell you on more than one
> occasion that the testimony he gave at
> the trial of Tommy Hamilton was false?
> A: Yes.

Moreover, even if Judge Suttle deemed credible a portion of Owens's testimony, he dismissed our claim that such evidence was obtained by Owens acting as a government agent. Judge Suttle found that "while the court is reasonably satisfied that Owens was induced to testify at trial, there is no evidence that the conversation with Hamilton was the result of an investigation by Owens."

Yet finding that there was *no* such evidence was simply to ignore the record. Eddie Oliver testified that James Ferris, the Sheriff's investigator, repeatedly encouraged Jimmy Dale Owens to "go up there and pick Tommy and see what you can find out and help us out here." Further, limiting relief merely to circumstances that constituted an "investigation" improperly circumscribed the constitutional protections extended to prisoners being kept in custodial interrogation. In *United States v. Henry*, government agents contacted the cellmate of an indicted defendant and promised him payment under a contingent fee arrangement if he would "pay attention" to incriminating remarks initiated by the defendant and others. The Supreme Court held that this violated the defendant's Sixth Amendment right to counsel. Even if the agents did not intend for the informant to take affirmative steps to elicit incriminating statements from the defendant in the absence of counsel, the agents must have known the result that would follow. In our case, Ferris did intend for Owens to take affirmative steps to elicit statements from Tommy ("go up there and pick Tommy and see what you can find out"). Judge Suttle's determination that these initiatives did not amount to an "investigation" was an exercise in misguided semantics. The actions of Ferris and Owens violated Tommy's right to be questioned only in the presence of counsel.

Lastly, and most importantly, all of Jimmy Dale Owens's testimony, including the portion that Judge Suttle specifically found to be perjured, was presented during the guilt phase of Tommy's trial, not the sentencing phase. The verdict, and not just the death sentence, was therefore tainted. Tommy was entitled to a new trial, not just a new sentencing hearing.

Nevertheless, Judge Suttle's ruling contained important findings of fact. He found that perjury had been committed during the guilt phase of Tommy's trial—and that evidence of the inducement for that perjury had been withheld from Tommy's defense counsel. Appellate courts do not lightly overrule findings of fact by a trial Judge, because it is the trial Judge who hears all the evidence and is in the best position to assess the credibility of witnesses presenting that evidence. We were now in the enviable position of being able to argue that Judge Suttle was right about crucial facts, even while being wrong on the legal ramifications of those facts.

We always knew Tommy's case would wind up in an appellate court one way or another. But we were going before that court in a strong position.

On April 13, 1994, shortly after Judge Suttle issued his order, Tommy wrote to me. He stated in part:

> *Yall, to me got me a good deal more from this Judge then most of these other cases in Alabama got, and I will hope that yall will continue to fight as hard for me on the guilt phase of this next appeal as yall have so far.*

I had no intention of letting Tommy down.

CHAPTER TWELVE

The Appeal

Clearly, we were going to appeal that portion of Judge Suttle's decision denying Tommy a new trial. To my surprise, the state of Alabama was not content with the prospect that in granting Tommy a new sentencing hearing, Judge Suttle's ruling could spare Tommy the death penalty, leaving him in prison for life with no chance of parole. The Alabama Attorney General's Office filed its appeal of Judge Suttle's ruling to the Alabama Court of Criminal Appeals on May 4, 1994, asking that the death sentence be affirmed. Our appeal followed a day later.

We filed our brief in support of our appeal with the Court of Criminal Appeals on September 23, 1994. Incorporating by reference all the issues we had raised in the post-conviction proceedings before Judge Suttle (along with more than four hundred pages of supporting briefs), we were able to adhere to the appellate court's rule limiting briefs to fifty pages. Our brief addressed four issues:

- Whether the lower court erred in concluding that although perjured testimony was presented during the

guilt phase of Tommy Hamilton's trial, Hamilton is not
entitled to a new trial.

- Whether the lower court erred in concluding that the
  failure of the prosecutor to disclose exculpatory and
  impeaching evidence, including the fact that a principal
  witness was testifying during the guilt phase in exchange
  for a promise of being released early from jail, did not so
  violate Tommy Hamilton's rights as to require that a new
  trial be held.
- Whether the lower court erred in concluding that the
  appointment of counsel who had less than five years prior
  experience in the active practice of criminal law and who
  was responsible for portions of Hamilton's defense, did
  not violate Alabama law and require that a new trial and
  sentencing hearing be held.
- Whether Tommy Hamilton's death sentence is disproportionately severe when compared to the sentences of
  his alleged accomplices and to the sentences imposed for
  other crimes.

We turned first to the issue of perjured testimony—and our argument was pointed.

> No other type of error is as pernicious and detrimental
> to the truth-seeking function of a trial and a just ver-
> dict as is perjury. Nor can the toxicity of this poison be
> so easily contained, as is suggested by the lower court's
> order. While Judge Suttle struggled to suggest that the
> perjured testimony of Jimmy Dale Owens only directly
> dealt with matters relevant to a sentencing determina-
> tion, and therefore that a new sentencing hearing alone
> would cure this ill, the fact of the matter is that Owens'
> false and fraudulent testimony was offered and admit-
> ted during the guilt phase of Tommy Hamilton's trial.

Turning next to our claim that Tommy was entitled to a new trial
because the prosecution failed to disclose the inducements offered to

Owens for the testimony he gave during the guilt phase of Tommy's trial, we cited the United States Supreme Court's recognition in *Napue v. Illinois* that:

> The jury's estimate of the truthfulness and reliability of a given witness may well be determinative of guilt or innocence, and it is upon such subtle factors as the possible interest of the witness in testifying that a defendant's life or liberty may be deprived.

We noted that prosecutor Timothy Littrell had represented to Judge Burney and Tommy's trial attorneys that he had disclosed all exculpatory evidence: "I think that the order was to give you anything that was exculpatory which I have done." The harm thus done by the failure of the prosecution to disclose the inducements offered to Owens was exacerbated by the fact that Owens testified during the guilt phase of Tommy's trial, stating during cross-examination by Tommy's lawyer that no inducements had been offered to him in connection with his testimony.

```
Attorney Lavender: Has anybody made you
    any promises about early parole or
    anything if you testified in this case?
Witness Owens: No sir.
```

Our third claim was that Judge Suttle had erred in concluding that the appointment of Attorney Lovelace did not violate Alabama's statutory requirement that only experienced defense counsel should be appointed to represent indigent capital defendants. We now argued that the findings made by Judge Suttle were inconsistent. On the one hand, he acknowledged that delegating significant defense responsibilities from a qualified attorney to an unqualified attorney might violate the terms of the statute; still, he found that there was no such objectionable delegation in Tommy's case. On the other hand, later in his order, Judge Suttle found error precisely because Lavender delegated to Lovelace responsibility for the sentencing proceedings, ruling that Judge Burney should have continued the sentencing hearing due

to Lovelace's unavailability. We argued that similar wholesale delegation of responsibilities to a statutorily unqualified lawyer had occurred
during the guilt phase of Tommy's trial.

For example, Lovelace 1) gave the opening statement to the jury
on Tommy's behalf; 2) was responsible for the cross-examination of
twelve of the prosecution's witnesses; 3) presented Tommy's motion
for acquittal at the conclusion of the state's presentation of its case; and
4) conducted the direct examination of half the witnesses called by
the defense. Accordingly, we argued that Tommy Hamilton deserved a
new trial, at which he could be represented as the Alabama legislature
had assured him he would be, before facing conviction for a capital
offense and being sentenced to die.

Finally, with respect to our claim that Tommy's death sentence
was disproportionately severe when compared to the sentences of his
alleged accomplices, we noted that the opinion in *Coulter v. State*, cited
by Judge Suttle, did not hold to the contrary. In that case, the Alabama
appellate court ruled that evidence of an alleged accomplice's sentence
is not relevant; therefore, it is not admissible as evidence to present *to
a jury* before *the jury* makes its sentencing recommendation. However,
the appellate court did not find that an accomplice's sentence was irrelevant *to an appellate court's review* of a sentence for disproportional-
ity. Indeed, that court stated:

> The consideration of accomplices' sentences, as well
> as sentences for those committing similar crimes, is
> a function properly reserved for the appellate courts.
> This "individualized" appellate review provides addi-
> tional assurance against possible arbitrary and capri-
> cious imposition of the death penalty.

We concluded by arguing that, should the appellate court determine that only sentencing relief was appropriate in Tommy's case,
no further sentencing hearing was necessary. Given that the severity
of a death sentence would clearly be disproportionate, the appellate
court should instead find a sentence of death to be unwarranted and
unconstitutional.

On the opposing side, the Attorney General's Office filed briefs seeking reversal of Judge Suttle's order granting a new sentencing hearing, while asking that the Judge's order denying a new trial be affirmed. The briefs argued that Judge Suttle committed reversible error when he found certain witnesses credible even as he rejected the testimony of other witnesses as not credible. The Attorney General's Office complained that it "does not understand" how Judge Suttle could have reached those determinations of credibility and that he gave "undue credence" to testimony presented on Tommy's behalf. We responded that Judge Suttle's findings were well supported by the evidence, noting that the Court of Criminal Appeals repeatedly had held that it would not reverse a trial court's credibility determinations. We also noted that assessments of the relative weights deserved by conflicting evidence are entitled to great deference on appeal.

As usual, the Attorney General argued that a claim for relief based on the inexperience of Barnes Lovelace had been waived because the issue had not been raised by Tommy's attorneys on their initial appeal following his trial. The gist of this argument was that an indigent capital defendant—the very person intended to benefit from a law ensuring he is provided with experienced defense counsel—can forfeit his rights under that law if his statutorily unqualified, court-appointed attorney fails to make an after-the-fact objection to his own appointment. We pointed out the paradox that would result from placing the responsibility for policing the statute in the very hands of the type of inexperienced lawyer the Alabama legislature believed should never represent a capital defendant in the first place.

In November of 1994, a very popular figure in Alabama, and a contentious one in some of the rest of the country, was elected the new Alabama Attorney General. He would now oversee the state's position in the Tommy Hamilton case.

Jefferson Beauregard Sessions III was born in Selma, Alabama, on Christmas Eve of 1946. Sessions, his father, and his grandfather were named after Jefferson Davis, a United States Senator and President of the Confederate States of America, and P. G. T. Beauregard, a Confederate general who oversaw the Battle of Fort Sumter that commenced the American Civil War. Sessions earned an undergraduate degree from Huntingdon College in Montgomery, Alabama, and received his law degree from the University of Alabama School of Law in 1973. In 1981, President Ronald Reagan nominated Sessions to be the United States Attorney for the Southern District of Alabama. In 1986, President Reagan nominated Sessions to be a United States District Court Judge. The nomination was never confirmed by the U.S. Senate, largely over concerns about racist comments attributed to Sessions. He continued as U.S. Attorney until 1993. In 1994, he won election as Alabama Attorney General. The harsh criticism he had received from Senator Edward Kennedy, who called Sessions a "throw-back to a shameful era" and a "disgrace," was considered to have won him the electoral support of Alabama conservatives.

Our request for oral argument was granted on February 8, 1995, and scheduled for the 21st of June.

At that time, the Alabama Court of Criminal Appeals was on the second floor of the Alabama Judicial Building in Montgomery, formerly a Scottish Rite Freemasonry temple. Originally built in 1926 and designed with an Egyptian motif, the three-story cream-colored limestone structure was renovated into a courthouse in 1938. Twenty-four stairs led from the sidewalk to the two-story-tall front door that was flanked by four columns, each standing three stories tall. The formerly imposing building has since been enclosed by a glass-fronted box that is part of a much larger modern office tower.

Luke DeGrand handled oral argument before the Court of Criminal Appeals. (If we needed to appeal further to the Alabama Supreme Court, I would present that argument.) Luke conferred with Bryan Stevenson on what we might expect, and we conducted mock oral arguments to prepare for the hearing. By June 21, Luke was ready.

As the five Judges paraded into the courtroom to take their seats, I soon feared that Luke would never get the chance to utter a word. Immediately after they seated themselves, Sam Wayne Taylor—the presiding Judge by virtue of seniority—turned to his colleagues and asked, with a laugh: "Should we decide now?"

I froze. Alabama's attitude toward the death penalty was firmly established. Getting the Court of Criminal Appeals to reverse a death case, especially a case that the court previously had affirmed, was rare. In fact, ten years ago it was Judge Taylor who had written this very court's unanimous opinion affirming Tommy's conviction and death sentence. Had the court already made up its mind? I very much feared that our appeal was over. Luckily, it turned out that it was just a matter of "Judge Taylor being Judge Taylor." He had a reputation for engaging in uncomfortable, even off-putting, remarks and behavior from the bench—and elsewhere.

Oral argument proceeded. Luke did an excellent job of highlighting the issues raised in our briefs. I remained uncomfortable, though, because only one of the five Judges asked any questions. Some lawyers are thankful when an appellate court is silent during oral argument because they then get to say, without interruption or diversion, everything that they had planned to say during the short time allotted. But judicial questioning during oral argument is invaluable to effective appellate advocacy. Just because you think something is important, if not determinative, in an appeal, it does not mean that the decision maker shares your view. A Judge's question is a window into what she or he thinks is important, and it's an invitation for you to address what you may be certain will factor into the court's final decision.

The one Judge who did engage was Sue Bell Cobb. Judge Cobb's questions were informed and incisive. She clearly had read the transcript of the evidentiary hearing before Judge Suttle. Her questions often focused on the actions of the prosecutors who had brought Tommy to trial. The remaining Judges, however, were poker players: attentive, stone faced, silent, doing nothing to tip their hands.

The Judge with the longest tenure on the court had started the oral argument in an unusual manner. Now, the most junior member on the five-Judge panel concluded it in a unique manner. As her colleagues left the bench and while the lawyers packed their briefcases, Judge Cobb walked across the courtroom to our counsel table. She shook our hands and thanked us for volunteering to "do this work."

Sue Bell Cobb was born on March 1, 1956, in Louisville, Kentucky. She graduated from the University of Alabama, first with an undergraduate degree in history, and then with a juris doctor degree in 1981. She was a third-year student at the law school in 1980, the year that Sister Lynn began her legal studies there. Cobb was appointed as a Judge of the Conecuh County District Court immediately after being admitted to the bar. At age twenty-five, she was one of the youngest Judges in the state. She was elected to the district court in 1982 and

reelected in 1988. She became the first female member of the Alabama
Court of Criminal Appeals in January of 1995, just a few months before
we appeared to present oral argument.

Responsibility for writing the court's opinion ultimately was
assigned to Judge Cobb, and on October 20, 1995, she issued the unanimous ruling of the Alabama Court of Criminal Appeals.

In a fifteen-page-long opinion and order, the appellate court agreed
with us.

Writing for all her colleagues, Judge Cobb stated that "[t]he primary
issue before this court is whether the court finding that the state's witness, Owens, perjured himself during his testimony was proper." After
summarizing all the evidence we had presented, Judge Cobb concluded
that "[b]ased on the above testimony, all of which supports Oliver's testimony, this court affirms the judgment of the trial court finding that
Owens's testimony was perjured. Ample evidence exists to support the
court's finding; thus, that finding was neither clearly erroneous nor
palpably wrong and must be affirmed."

The next issue before the court was whether Judge Suttle committed reversible error by remanding Tommy's case for only a new sentencing hearing, rather than a new trial on the merits.

The perjured testimony from Jimmy Dale Owens depicted Tommy
as a vicious, remorseless criminal who had murdered and robbed
Lehman Wood. This led Judge Cobb to reject Judge Suttle's conclusion
that there was no significant chance that the jury, if it had heard the
truth, would have returned a different verdict during the guilt phase
of the trial. She further ruled that had jurors known of the leniency
Owens received in exchange for his testimony, they could have fac-
tored his personal interest into the weight they afforded his testimony.

Judge Cobb, on behalf of all five Judges of the Court of Criminal
Appeals, concluded that granting a new sentencing hearing was not a
sufficient remedy.

> [G]ranting a new sentencing hearing is not an appro-
> priate remedy given the findings made by the Judge.
> The court found that the trial of Tommy Hamilton
> entertained perjured testimony and that the state
> withheld exculpatory evidence. In addition, the court

found that prosecutorial misconduct and ineffective assistance of counsel were factors in this trial. Given these findings, it is impossible to imagine that the petitioner received a trial that satisfied the minimum constitutional requirements for a fair trial as contemplated by and guaranteed under the United States and Alabama Constitutions.

She continued:

Clearly then the proper remedy, given the findings that a witness perjured himself during the guilt phase of the trial and that the perjured testimony was prejudicial to the defendant, is to remand the case for a new trial. Granting a new sentencing hearing is not a sufficient remedy for the violation of petitioner's due process rights as guaranteed by the Fifth Amendment of the United States Constitution, in light of the fact that petitioner's conviction was procured by illegal means.

. . .

In the present case, the lower court correctly found that the state's principal witness had perjured himself. However, the court also found that the perjured testimony did not affect the guilt phase of the trial and erroneously ruled that the petitioner was entitled only to a new sentencing hearing. This court holds that the perjured testimony tainted the petitioner's conviction; therefore, the petitioner is entitled to a new trial.

Judge Cobb went on to address our second principal issue on appeal:

The petitioner further asserts that the prosecution committed a [constitutional] violation by not disclosing to the defense that a promise of early release was bestowed upon Jimmy Dale Owens in exchange for his testimony against the petitioner. . . . In the present case, this important evidence was suppressed. . . .

She found that the suppressed evidence was material:

> The most damaging evidence presented against the petitioner was the testimony of the trusty, Jimmy Dale Owens, who had a compelling reason to lie. His testimony was the link between the murder and the robbery, and he falsely stated that the petitioner felt no remorse for his crime and that the petitioner was even proud of himself for the shooting. The most significant demonstration of the devastating effect of Owens's testimony is indicated by the fact that he did not testify at the trial of the petitioner's codefendant/sister, Janice Glasco, and she was convicted of the lesser offense of manslaughter and sentenced to ten years' imprisonment. This fact underscores the materiality of the suppressed evidence.
>
> . . .
>
> This case must be remanded for a new trial on the merits.

Because the court remanded Tommy's case for a new trial, it did not discuss the other contentions we had raised, including that Tommy's trial attorneys were ineffective and the sentence he received was disproportionately severe.

Judge Cobb concluded:

> For the foregoing reasons, this court finds that the petitioner in this case, Tommy Hamilton, did not receive a fair trial as guaranteed by both the United States and Alabama Constitutions. A new trial is the required remedy. Therefore, we reverse the lower court's denial of the petitioner's motion for a new trial. The judgment of conviction is reversed and this case is remanded for further proceedings on the merits.

REVERSED AND REMANDED.
All the Judges concur.

It was a stunning reversal and a huge victory for Tommy, but the case wasn't over yet. Under the leadership of Alabama Attorney General Jeff Sessions, the state decided it would not let the case go. On November 3, 1995, it filed a motion asking the Court of Criminal Appeals to amend and supplement its October 20th opinion by finding additional facts. It simultaneously filed an application asking the court to rehear the case.

In much the same way that his predecessor had tried to ghostwrite Judge Suttle's decision, Attorney General Sessions offered the court thirty pages of new findings of fact, effectively rewriting the court's fifteen-page-long opinion. The brief that he filed in support of the request for rehearing was stunningly aggressive. It asserted that "the trial court, and now this Honorable Court, have applied a misguided sense of justice to the facts of this case in order to allow Hamilton an opportunity to attempt to obtain a lesser conviction or sentence . . ." It argued that the "unfortunate result in this case" was the product of "an opinion of this court that is based upon erroneous findings and leaps of logic that are not supported by the record." It characterized the appellate court's opinion as the result of a "random picking and choosing of evidence" and complained that for the appellate court "[t]o reject the direct testimony of two law enforcement officers, a county Sheriff, and a District Attorney based upon the hearsay testimony of a multiple convicted felon is beyond understanding."

Though he denied it, the Alabama Attorney General implied that the appellate court had acted like a deity, creating something out of nothing:

> The Book of Genesis begins by telling of God's creation of the universe. The Hebrew term that is translated "create" has a particular meaning that implies creation *ex nihilo*, or "out of nothing." D. Robinson, *The Doctrine of Salvation*, Convention Press, Nashville, TN (1992).

> The state certainly is not alleging that this
> Honorable Court has any lofty, grandiose opinions
> of itself. However, this court certainly joined the trial
> court in a creation *ex nihilo* by its finding of a [consti-
> tutional violation] based upon an agreement that has
> never existed.

I do not know who in the Alabama Attorney General's Office
thought this would be a persuasive argument. And I wonder whether
it would have been made if the author of the appellate court's opinion
had not been a woman and the most junior Judge on the panel that
heard the case.

Judge Cobb and the Court of Criminal Appeals dealt swiftly and
deftly with the Alabama Attorney General's filings. Among the statements in Judge Cobb's opinion that the state took issue with was her
summation that "[t]he sentencing Judge (Judge Burney) testified that,
in retrospect, he did not believe that the petitioner deserved the death
penalty. . . ." On December 29, Judge Cobb and the court granted the
state's request to amend the opinion by making its explication of Judge
Burney's sentencing testimony more complete:

> The sentencing Judge testified that, in retrospect, if the
> petitioner had been tried after his codefendant's/sis-
> ter's trial (she received a manslaughter conviction and
> a 10-year sentence) he would not have sentenced the
> petitioner to death even if the jury had recommended
> the death penalty.

Otherwise, the court's opinion was unchanged. The application
for rehearing of the case was denied with the notation: "All the Judges
concur."

Either undeterred, clueless, or both, on January 12, 1996, the
Alabama Attorney General's Office filed a petition asking the Alabama
Supreme Court to hear the case and, in doing so, "vacate the judgment" of the Court of Criminal Appeals "and remand the case with
instructions that Tommy Hamilton's conviction for the offense of

capital murder and his sentence of death by electrocution be reinstated and affirmed." On May 31, 1996, the Alabama Supreme Court denied the state's request without issuing an opinion; instead, it issued a certificate of judgment in Tommy's favor.

In 1995, fifty-six people had been executed in the United States. This was the highest number of executions in a single year since the beginning of the modern death penalty era in 1976. Two lawyers from Chicago and a Ninja-nun from Alabama had seen to it that it did not rise to fifty-seven.

CHAPTER THIRTEEN

The Bargain

Every prisoner on death row leaves eventually. Few leave alive.
While Sister Lynn, Luke, and I had originally enlisted to try to save Tommy's life, our client's goal was more ambitious: he wanted to secure his freedom. The appellate court's decision to grant Tommy a new trial temporarily achieved everyone's goals. And yet, even with a new trial, as Judge Suttle had said in his ruling, "Hamilton may deserve the death penalty and may yet receive it."

By 1996, Tim Littrell, the District Attorney for Lawrence County who originally prosecuted Tommy for killing Lehman Wood, had moved on to private practice in Moulton. Governor Fob James appointed Jim Osborn, Littrell's assistant, to fill the remaining years of Littrell's term. Thus, it fell to Osborn to take up Tommy's case for the state of Alabama.

Jim Osborn had been an Alabama prosecutor since graduating from Cumberland School of Law in Birmingham in 1980. He'd served as an Assistant District Attorney in Morgan County before moving to Lawrence County in 1983.

When we met with Osborn, he tried to intimidate us, telling us that the decision by the Court of Criminal Appeals was of little moment. He said that he intended to retry Tommy for capital murder—and that Tommy would again be found guilty and again be sentenced to death.

I did not blink. I told Osborn to "go fry ice," the New England equivalent of "bless your heart" and a phrase I had learned from my mother-in-law. I explained to Osborn that any retrial of Tommy Hamilton would differ significantly from the original capital murder trial: we were staying on as Tommy's defense counsel.

After engaging in bravado and completing our obligatory posturing, we got down to the business of negotiating a just outcome.

Osborn eventually offered the terms Judge Suttle had suggested to us in 1993 before the evidentiary hearing: Reinstatement of Tommy's capital murder conviction and agreement to a sentence of life without the possibility of parole. This was a major concession, and, unlike the idea floated shortly before Judge Suttle's ruling, it was a firm offer. Tommy would be spared a death sentence. But we knew it was unacceptable to Tommy. He wanted a path to freedom. In his mind, a new trial offered the possibility of a "not guilty" verdict and therefore gave him that path. He could envision no upside to trading away this possibility—remote as it may have been—for the certainty of life imprisonment.

I told Osborn that exchanging death by electrocution for death by incarceration was a nonstarter. We would rather take the case to trial. I reminded Osborn that his predecessor District Attorney had secured a capital conviction and sentence of death. Osborn could either risk being known as the prosecutor who lost a retrial and allowed Tommy back on the streets of Moulton; or he could be known as the prosecutor who cleaned up the mess left by his predecessor—leaving it to someone else, namely, the Alabama Board of Pardons and Paroles, to decide whether Tommy would ever be freed.

What was the basis of Osborn's aversion to the idea of Tommy pleading guilty to the crime of murder—as opposed to capital murder—and agreeing to a sentence of life in prison with the *possibility* of parole? After all, this would be the maximum sentence possible for the commission of such a crime. The hang-up seemed to be that Tommy, under Alabama law, having already served more than ten years in jail and prison, would soon become eligible for parole.

Tommy resisted any life sentence, even with the technical possibility of parole, fearing the parole board would take the easy way out by denying his every application for parole. He viewed it as in effect agreeing to death by incarceration in disguise. We reminded Tommy that, at his original trial, he had already confessed under oath to killing Lehman Wood; he denied that he also had robbed him, which was the criminal element that had made his case eligible for the death penalty. Given the probability of Jason Glasco again testifying, this time as an adult, and the possibility of the state negotiating further with Tommy's child bride, Debbie Gatlin Hamilton—then still serving a life sentence—to obtain her testimony during a retrial, a jury would be unlikely to accept Tommy's theory of self-defense. In short, there was little chance that he would be found not guilty of murder during a retrial. Without doubt he would be incarcerated. We were now merely negotiating how long that incarceration might last.

Tommy needed some assurance that his chance at freedom would come within a reasonable period of time. Therefore, reminding Osborn that Tommy had already served almost ten years in prison, all of it on death row, I offered that Tommy might consider pleading guilty to murder and agree to serving an additional seven years before becoming eligible for parole. There did not need to be a guarantee of parole at the end of this agreed-upon period of incarceration, but, from that point on, Tommy could petition the Board of Pardons and Paroles. That board would have the final say as to when Tommy would be released, if ever.

Osborn was open to the idea, and we were elated that eligibility for parole seemed to be on the table. Maybe we would be able to obtain for Tommy the outcome he so badly wanted. After consulting with Lehman Wood's daughter, Charlotte Parker, Osborn grudgingly agreed to offer the deal. Perhaps our earlier outreach to her played a part in this acquiescence.

Selling Tommy on what was literally the deal of a lifetime proved surprisingly difficult. The jailhouse lawyers on death row gave unhelpful advice by urging that he hold out for a guaranteed release. We sought to reassure Tommy by having another lawyer who also had clients on death row speak to Tommy about the merits of the deal. And we enlisted the assistance of Lucille, who implored her son to agree.

Tommy's acquiescence was necessary both legally and morally. In the 1966 case of *Brookhart v. Janis*, the United States Supreme Court had held that a defendant cannot be forced to enter a plea against his will. The Court would expand this rule in 2018 in the case of *McCoy v. Louisiana* by holding that a lawyer may not admit guilt without the client's consent in a murder case eligible for the death penalty—even if the lawyer thinks that is the best way to spare his client from execution.

Eventually, Tommy agreed. With his consent, we presented the proposed plea agreement to Judge Suttle.

Even though he accepted the deal, Judge Suttle was beyond displeased, telling us that he would make certain his views were known to the parole board on every occasion that Tommy was considered for release. This is probably what gave District Attorney Osborn the confidence, when explaining the outcome to the local newspaper, that "we never expect to see him released."

Almost immediately after the ink was dry on the plea agreement, Tommy expressed his dissatisfaction with the outcome—and with us, whom he accused of selling him out. According to Tommy, we had denied him the new trial the court had said he was entitled to and the chance to be set free immediately. Lucille, on the other hand, was more than grateful.

———

Tommy served the minimum sentence he had agreed to, and then some. He was surprisingly productive during this time. He earned his High School Equivalency Certificate on June 16, 1998. He began working in the prison food-service operations. He also worked as a clerk in the prison warehouse. People within the prison took note. A few years later, Tommy and Debbie divorced.

Tommy's change in demeanor made an impression on some of the prison staff. One mentor named Barbara Holly would be instrumental in Tommy's parole board hearings. A brunette with big hair, big earrings, and a big smile, Holly bore a striking resemblance to Tommy's mother, Lucille Hamilton. On January 31, 2005, Barbara Holly retired from the Alabama Department of Corrections. Her coworkers gave her a cake with her "mug shot" on it and the inscription: E.O.S. 1-31-05. The notation, usually applied to inmates, meant "end of sentence, January 31, 2005." For Holly, it marked the final day of a twenty-four-year-long career in correctional food service—the first sixteen at Tutwiler Prison for Women and the last eight as food service administrator for the entire Department of Corrections, with responsibility for feeding the state's twenty-six thousand inmates daily. The previous summer she had completed a term as the President of the American Correctional Food Service Association.

Just eleven days after retiring, on February 11, 2005, Barbara Holly sent a memorandum to the Alabama Board of Pardons and Paroles. Holly wrote:

> *I am writing to recommend that inmate Tommy Hamilton be considered for parole. He does not work under my direct supervision, but I have worked with him on a daily basis since February 2004 until the time I retired on January 31, 2005. From my observation he is a conscientious and productive worker and should not have any problems with employment when released.*
>
> *I have talked with him about his crime. He freely admitted to what he had done and his comment to me was, "No one has the right to do what I did." He appears to have remorse for his actions and accepts responsibility for them. He does not display any violent tendencies and is even tempered. I believe the board could feel safe in the knowledge that inmate Hamilton would not be a threat to society.*
>
> *I realize that twenty years in prison cannot replace a human life, but inmate Hamilton has matured in prison and has maintained a disciplinary free record, which is no easy task for someone incarcerated. He has grown and matured and is no longer the same person who was convicted almost 21 years ago. He is looking forward to the day he can be released and become a productive citizen.*

In my 24 years with the department I have recom-
mended only one other person for parole, so you can see
that I don't enter this lightly. Thank you for your time
and attention to my request.

Two months later, on April 12, 2005, another longtime employee, Fay Carey, the warehouse superintendent for the Alabama Department of Corrections Institutional Services Division, also wrote to the Board of Pardons and Paroles on Tommy's behalf. She stated:

I have worked for the Dept. of Correction for 16 years,
2 years as a warehouse supervisor and 14 years as the
warehouse superintendent. Several inmate clerks have
worked in my office with me[,] handling daily duties
assigned to them.

Inmate Hamilton worked under my direct super-
vision since February 5, 2004 and has learned the
operation of the warehouse from receiving to final ship-
ment. He is a conscientious, responsible, and produc-
tive worker. He will have no problem with employment
when released.

We have discussed the seriousness of his case and
I find what he did was wrong, but he is remorseful and
excepts (sic) responsibility for his mistakes. Inmate
Hamilton has matured and grown in prison and is dif-
ferent than the boy that was sent to prison. I find him to
be honest and rehabilitated.

Inmate Hamilton has been incarcerated over 20
years and I know that can't replace life, but he has
thrived (sic) to be a better person and has a disciplinary
free record. He is looking forward to the day of his
release to prove he is a changed person.

In the 16 years I have worked for this dept. I have
never recommended any one for parole but feel inmate
Hamilton would not be a threat to society and would be
a productive citizen in the community. Thank you for
taking the time to read my request.

On February 10, 2006, the Alabama Board of Pardons and Paroles notified Tommy that it had scheduled a public meeting on the third of April to consider him for parole. At the conclusion of the meeting, the board issued its certificate of parole stating:

> It having been made to appear to the Alabama Board of Pardons and Paroles that Tommy Hamilton, 190163, is eligible to be paroled, that the Board is of the opinion that there is a reasonable probability that said prisoner will remain at liberty without violating the laws, that the release of this prisoner is not incompatible with the welfare of society, and that this prisoner will not become a public charge on release, the parole is hereby granted.

Tommy had been thinking about dying for more than twenty years. Now he could start thinking about living.

On May 1, 2006, Tommy was released to a residential facility in Thomasville, Alabama. He completed the eighteen-week Life Tech course that prepares inmates for reentry into society, and on December 8, 2006, while still subject to the terms and supervision of his parole, he became a free man.

Tommy moved into a trailer in the backyard of his mother's home. He worked hanging steel with his brother Jerry and married Tammy Sue Fagan on her birthday, October 15, 2009.

On April 27, 2011, a massive tornado ripped through Lawrence County—one of several "EF5" twisters to hit the state that day (EF5 is the highest rating on the Enhanced Fujita scale for tornado measurement). This event, with peak winds of 210 miles per hour, tracked across 106.9 miles of Lawrence County and was blamed for fourteen deaths in the county. It was the deadliest tornado to strike Alabama since the weather service began keeping fatality records in 1950. Thousands of hardwood and softwood trees were snapped, with a significant number of trees twisted and debarked, leaving only stubs of branches remaining. Many mobile homes were also destroyed, their frames mangled; and a single-family home was destroyed with the walls and contents strewn over an area greater than two acres.

Perhaps it was the stirring of the atmosphere that stirred things in Tommy. In any event, after almost six years without the confines and structured environment of prison, Tommy's impulsiveness apparently got the better of him.

Sometime in 2011, Tommy's niece, Lori Gray—the daughter of his sister Joyce—told her uncle's parole officer that Tommy was both using and selling pain pills. Tommy admitted as much. Rather than cite him for violating the terms of his parole, Tommy's parole officer directed him to attend Alcoholics Anonymous meetings.

When I first turned my thoughts to writing this book, I returned to Alabama and met with Tommy and Tammy at Lucille's home on October 6, 2012. He was in good spirits and seemed to have adapted well to life outside of prison.

But one year later, in October of 2013, Tommy's parole officer, Sid Slate, conducted a surprise visit to Tommy's trailer and discovered marijuana in the home. Tommy was charged with violating the terms of his parole and incarcerated in jail. A parole hearing was conducted in the jail on Halloween, with the hearing officer recommending that Tommy's parole not be revoked over this slight offense. Instead, Tommy was allowed to move to Florida to live with his maternal aunt, Geneva L. Norris. Tommy was sent to Kilby Correctional Facility in Mount Meigs, Alabama, to await completion of the interstate compact that would allow him to leave Alabama and move to Crawfordville, Florida.

Tammy refused to go with Tommy to Florida, so they separated. The terms of Tommy's parole included a requirement that he submit to periodic drug tests. In 2015, urinalysis indicted that Tommy had been using marijuana and methamphetamine. When advised that his urine test had come back dirty, Tommy failed to report to his parole officer to face the consequences as required. After being AWOL for three months, Tommy was apprehended, taken back to Alabama, and incarcerated in Kilby prison. A parole hearing was conducted at the prison, and it was generously recommended that Tommy's parole status once again be reinstated, with Tommy presumably being viewed as more of an addicted threat to himself than a threat to others. On March 10, 2016, Tommy was released and went to live with his Aunt Geneva at her new address in Gainesville in Alachua County, Florida.

During his time in Crawfordville, Tommy had fallen "in love" with Renee Haddock. Now he sought to be reunited with her. But the terms of his parole prevented him from leaving Alachua County, further restricting him to his aunt's home each day from 9:00 p.m. until 6:00 a.m. In search of more lenient terms on which to facilitate his pursuit of romance with Renee, Tommy returned to Alabama.

On July 8, 2016, Tommy was drunk in his trailer, and his niece again called the authorities to report him. He was arrested and charged once more with violating the terms of his parole. While in the back seat of a Sheriff's car en route to the jail in his inebriated state, Tommy allegedly threatened to kill his parole officer, Sid Slate. A parole hearing was held on July 18, 2016, in the Lawrence County Jail. Tommy was found guilty of making a terrorist threat, obstructing government operations, and failing to follow the instructions of his parole officer. It was recommended that his parole be revoked for one year. Tommy was taken to Kilby prison in Mount Meigs, Alabama.

Several months later, I received a Christmas card from Tommy's mother, Lucille. The printed card conveyed hope and good cheer: "May your heart and home be filled with happiness this Christmas." But Lucille's handwritten note spoke of resignation and despair:

> Tommy is back in prison.
> He is at Kilby prison, Alabama State prison.
> He got on Drugs & Alcohol bad.
> He got with a no good woman.
> I did all I could to help him.
> Thanks for all you did to help.
> You're the Greatest person I've ever know.

Tommy was in prison when Lucille Hamilton died on January 10, 2017.

The parole board ultimately extended Tommy's incarceration to five years for his latest parole violations. In March of 2018, he was transferred to the prison system's facility for the aged and infirm in Hamilton, Alabama. Since Tommy's alleged conduct not only violated the terms of his parole but also constituted new crimes, he was indicted for those crimes. On September 2, 2020, Tommy fired his court-appointed attorney and declined the state's offer of a ten-year sentence in exchange for a plea of guilty. As I write this, he awaits trial.

CHAPTER FOURTEEN

The Defense of the Guilty

There was never any doubt that Tommy Hamilton killed Lehman Wood on that hot summer day in 1984. Why then did I, a Chicago lawyer with no ties to rural Alabama, agree to spend years advocating on his behalf?

Lawyers defending the condemned have always played a pivotal role in the determination of which criminal defendants are sentenced to death. Indeed, the call for a lawyer to defend the most heinous among us, and the accompanying scorn for those lawyers who do so, has been with the profession since the founding of this country.

On December 4, 1770, a Boston jury passed judgment on a group of eight despised British soldiers in Captain Thomas Preston's Twenty-Ninth Regiment of Foot (what we would, today, call the Infantry). They were on trial for their lives after firing shots into a crowd that had gathered on March 5th outside Boston's Custom House. Five civilians—Crispus Attucks, Samuel Gray, James Caldwell, Sam Maverick, and Patrick Carr—were killed in what came to be known as the Boston Massacre. A defense attorney for the soldiers, future President John Adams, contended they had acted in self-defense after

being attacked by "a motley rabble of saucy boys." In his riveting closing argument, Adams—a devout patriot—told the jury that the endur-
ing value of the law lay in its neutrality and invulnerability to passion.
It was better, he said, that many guilty men go free than one innocent man be brought to the bar and condemned, "because it's of more
importance . . . that innocence should be protected, than . . . that guilt
should be punished." The jury acquitted six of Adams's clients and
found the other two guilty of the lesser offense of manslaughter.

Defending those that society has condemned is not an easy choice
for any attorney, and it can have real consequences for themselves and
their families. For his spirited and successful defense of his unpopular
clients, Adams was vilified and lost much of his law practice, but in the
long run the case enhanced his reputation. Years later, he characterized his defense of the soldiers as "one of the most gallant, generous,
manly, and disinterested actions of my whole life."

Josiah Quincy wrote the following upon hearing from neighbors
that his son, Josiah Quincy, Jr., had agreed to serve with John Adams
as co-counsel in defending those soldiers:

> *My Dear Son,*
> *I am under great affliction at hearing the bitterest*
> *reproaches uttered against you, for having become an*
> *advocate for those criminals who are charged with the*
> *murder of their fellow-citizens. Good God! Is it possi-*
> *ble? I will not believe it. . . . I have heard the severest*
> *reflections made upon the occasion, by men who had*
> *just before manifested the highest esteem for you, as one*
> *destined to be a savior of our country. I must own to you,*
> *it has filled the bosom of your aged and infirm parent*
> *with anxiety and distress, lest it should not only prove*
> *true, but destructive of your reputation and interest;*
> *and I repeat, I will not believe it unless it be confirmed*
> *by your own mouth or under your own hand.*

Josiah Jr. responded:

I have little leisure, and less inclination, either to know or to take notice of those ignorant slanderers who have dared to utter their 'bitter reproaches' in your hearing against me, for having become an advocate for criminals charged with murder . . . Before pouring their reproaches into the ear of the aged and infirm, if they had been friends, they would have surely spared a little reflection on the nature of an attorney's oath and duty. . . . Let such be told, Sir, that these criminals are not yet legally proved guilty, and therefore, however criminal, are entitled, by the laws of God and man, to all legal counsel and aid; that my duty as a man obliged me to undertake; that my duty as a lawyer strengthened the obligation. . . . This and much more might be told with great truth; and I dare affirm that you and this whole people will one day REJOICE that I became an advocate for the aforesaid 'criminals' charged with the murder of our fellow-citizens.

The elder Quincy wrote out of concern and love for his son; the younger Quincy responded with the courage of his convictions. These letters mirror a similarly motivated exchange that I had more than two hundred years later with my own father and others about representing Tommy Hamilton. Even today, far and away the most common question I am asked by family, friends, and even strangers is: "Would you have agreed to defend Tommy if, before you volunteered to represent him, you had known that he was guilty?"

My response is always, "Of course."

Too often, those asking the question view my response as a confession that I am akin to the driver of a getaway car. In their eyes, a defender who represents a guilty individual is an accomplice—morally, if not legally.

The underlying question being asked, and one that is entitled to a more complete answer, is "Why?"

First, it is important to note that a person can be "guilty" in two different senses: factual and legal. Factual guilt means the person committed the acts for which they stand accused. Legal guilt is a term of art. It means the government, while affording the accused the process due under our laws, has proven that the individual committed those acts beyond a reasonable doubt. The two overlap often, but not always. A person can be factually guilty, yet never be convicted of a crime. The converse is also possible: A person may be innocent but be convicted in a criminal proceeding.

A token of this distinction is the choice of pleas that a criminal defendant may tender in response to charges brought against her: "guilty" or "not guilty." A defendant is not required to plead innocence to compel a trial on the charges. By pleading "not guilty," a defendant informs the court that he or she is not willing to admit guilt for the crime she is accused of committing, which is to say, she chooses to require that the government meet its burden of proof.

To establish legal guilt, the government must comply with constitutional requirements, state and/or federal laws, and the rules of criminal procedure. These safeguards are put in place because our nation was founded, first and foremost, to secure the life and liberty of its citizens. To convict a citizen of a crime, and certainly to terminate a citizen's life, the government is held to the most exacting standards. No matter how heinous a crime the defendant is accused of committing, the end of punishing a defendant for such a crime does not justify the employment of unbounded means. A lawful result may not be achieved by unlawful means; and factual innocence should not be the paramount or exclusive value in constitutional criminal procedure.

Similarly, factual innocence is not a prerequisite for judicial relief even after trial. If it were, that would radically change the notion of wrongful conviction. Convictions are wrongful—even if the convicted person is factually guilty—when there is a demonstrable violation of the principles undergirding our notions of justice and fairness. This is not to say that the legal system should never take factual guilt into account, whether at trial or afterwards. Innocence can be relevant in several ways. For example, while the Supreme Court in *Herrera v. Collins* and its progeny has repeatedly declined to so hold, I believe that because death is different, a *prima facie* showing of innocence—a showing sufficient to raise a presumption of innocence unless disproved or rebutted—should always warrant consideration of awarding post-conviction relief. Similarly, as the Supreme Court did hold in

McQuiggin v. Perkins, factual innocence may serve as a "gateway" to overcoming some otherwise-applicable procedural obstacles to habeas relief. But factual guilt should not be the only consideration in criminal adjudication.

The protection against self-incrimination, the presumption of innocence, and myriad other constitutional protections embody the intent of our nation's founders to jealously guard their citizens' liberty. A bedrock principle of our justice system is well articulated by the notion that it is better the guilty should escape punishment than the innocent should suffer. That is because convicting an innocent person or setting a guilty man free are errors that differ in kind rather than merely in degree. The conviction of innocents is not the only possible flaw in a criminal *justice* system. We should not be hostile or even indifferent to other types of injustice.

I find myself aligned with dissents by Justice Thurgood Marshall from Supreme Court rulings that, at least implicitly, require a criminal defendant to demonstrate a reasonable probability of acquittal, if not factual innocence, in order to vindicate constitutional rights. In the landmark ineffective assistance of counsel case of *Strickland v. Washington*, the majority opinion required a showing of "a reasonable probability that, but for counsel's unprofessional errors, the result of the proceeding would have been different." In his dissent, Justice Marshall directly questioned the ascendancy of a requirement for verdict accuracy and the resulting diminishment of fair process:

> [T]he assumption on which the Court's holding rests
> is that the only purpose of the constitutional guaran-
> tee of effective assistance of counsel is to reduce the
> chance that innocent persons will not be convicted. In
> my view, the guarantee also functions to ensure that
> convictions are obtained only through fundamentally
> fair procedures. The majority contends that the Sixth
> Amendment is not violated when a manifestly guilty
> defendant is convicted after a trial in which he was
> represented by a manifestly ineffective attorney. I can-
> not agree.

Similarly, Justice Marshall's dissenting opinion in *United States v. Bagley* (this time joined by Justice William Brennan) took the court to task for creating too high a bar for relief from prosecutorial failure to disclose exculpatory and impeaching evidence to defendants. He argued that the structure of the adversary system and "equality of justice" depend on the government sharing exculpatory information with defendants, regardless of the outcomes of cases. And he urged that the "apparent" fairness of trials ought to matter, even when there is no showing that a defendant is either innocent or harmed by the government's misconduct. In urging automatic reversal for a prosecutor's deliberate failure to disclose exculpatory evidence, Justice Marshall argued that such misconduct is "antithetical to our most basic vision of the role of the state in the criminal process."

The role of the criminal defendant's lawyer specifically is to make sure that the defendant is convicted only if legal guilt can be fairly found and if all the constitutional and procedural rules are faithfully followed. The benefit of having legal counsel should not depend on whether the lawyer believes the client is innocent. Such a criterion would transform the lawyer from an advocate to a fact-finding Judge or jury. To deny anyone a robust defense—even someone who may be factually guilty—would be to put everyone's liberty at risk. Only when counsel vigorously challenges charges against the defendant will prosecutors and Judges take precautions to ensure that only valid cases are brought. Thus, by defending the guilty, the defense attorney protects the freedom of the innocent.

As stated by criminal law Professor Abbe Smith:

> The more we focus on those who can actually be proved innocent, the more we undercut the right of everyone to be presumed innocent unless the state proves otherwise. Our system of justice emphasizes proof, not truth, because of the value we place on individual liberty and our abiding skepticism of state power. To check that power we give the benefit of every reasonable doubt to the accused even if he or she *did it*. Thus, if the proof is lacking, a factually guilty person may nonetheless be legally not guilty. A single-minded

focus on factual innocence threatens this important
safeguard, this check on the hubris of power.

While the primary duty of the prosecutor is, in principle, to seek
justice within the bounds of the law rather than merely to convict,
defense counsel plays an important role in ensuring adherence to that
duty. Thus, in practice, the criminal justice system requires undivided
partisanship by defense counsel. Because the prosecutor, with resources
of the government behind him or her, may almost single-mindedly
present the state's case, the defender must concentrate entirely on
the accused individual's case and present it as forcefully as possible.
Despite prosecutorial standards that incorporate limiting principles,
political pressures or unjust motivations may influence prosecutors
to charge a defendant with multiple crimes or choose the most serious crime to charge the defendant with. One crucial role the defender
plays is to keep the prosecution honest by resisting overcharging or by
arguing vigorously that the facts support only a less serious crime (for
example, manslaughter versus murder). I suspect that Tommy's next
defense counsel will have something to say about an inebriated rant
in the back of a Sheriff's car resulting in a criminal charge of making
a terrorist threat. Likewise, when a prosecutor presses for the harsh-
est sentence, the defender highlights facts that point toward leniency.
Without the defender, prosecutors have less incentive to be careful in
their charging decisions and sentencing recommendations.

This is particularly true in a death penalty case, where the state
seeks to impose the most extreme penalty known to the law. Assessing
guilt is largely a factual question, whereas punishment determinations
often include subjective judgments. The law says that even a defendant
who is factually guilty of murder—and therefore eligible for imposition of the death penalty—still might not deserve a death sentence.
Sentencing is not a cause-and-effect equation amounting to "if this,
then that." Indeed, the Supreme Court has specifically held that man-
datory death sentences for those convicted of murder are unconstitutional. While some may argue that the purpose of the death penalty is
to deter others from committing capital offenses, it should be universally agreed that it is the role of defense counsel to deter prosecutors

from violating constitutional rights and to argue about the appropriateness of the range of punishments that may be applicable.

In many capital trials, inadequate representation results in recommendations of death sentences from jurors and sentences of death imposed by Judges, when mitigation options, if they had been properly investigated and presented by counsel, might have secured different outcomes. While inadequate representation is often viewed solely as a problem for the poor and indigent, all citizens can potentially be subject to bias from the legal system. Clarence Darrow, for example, was a famous Chicago lawyer who often argued that the justice system persecuted the poor. However, when defending two teenage thrill killers in what was billed as the "Trial of the Century," on August 24, 1924, Darrow paradoxically beseeched Judge John R. Caverly to spare the lives of the killers because they were not poor but rather the sons of millionaires. Nathan F. Leopold, Jr., and Richard A. Loeb had set out to prove they could commit the perfect crime, kidnapping and killing fourteen-year-old Bobby Franks. Knowing that a jury would show little sympathy for perpetrators of such horrendous acts, Darrow had his clients plead guilty and waived a jury for sentencing. "[H]ad this been the case of two boys of this age, unconnected with families who are supposed to have great wealth, that there is not a state's attorney in Illinois who would not at once have consented to a plea of guilty and a punishment in the penitentiary for life," Darrow told Judge Caverly. "We are here with the lives of two boys imperiled, with the public aroused. For what? Because, unfortunately, their parents have *money*. Nothing else." The argument must have been effective, as Judge Caverly sentenced the teenage killers to a term of life in prison plus ninety-nine years.

The Supreme Court, recognizing the important role that defense counsel plays in the criminal justice system, has held that criminal defendants have a constitutional right to be represented by counsel at trial. While the Court has not held that the appointment of an attorney to represent a death row inmate in post-conviction proceedings is constitutionally required, I believe that death is different; therefore, post-conviction counsel is necessary, in my view, to ensure that the capital conviction and resulting death sentence were properly imposed. We must be equally committed to doing justice retrospectively as we are to doing it prospectively.

It mischaracterizes the efforts of post-conviction counsel to view them as attempting to secure judicial relief based merely on technicalities or procedural irregularities. Insisting that law enforcement not suborn perjury; ensuring that the prosecution discloses exculpatory and impeaching evidence that is material to guilt or punishment; and challenging whether the accused received effective assistance of counsel—these are efforts to guarantee that constitutional principles will be upheld not only in a given case, but in every case. Ensuring that criminal proceedings are free of constitutional defect is as much a criminal defense attorney's job as arguing about factual guilt or innocence.

Did Tommy Hamilton ambush Lehman Wood and kill him in cold blood? Yes, he did. Most death row inmates probably committed the crime for which they were sentenced to die. This creates a difficulty for Judges in post-conviction proceedings. These Judges are being asked by convicted murderers to protect their constitutional rights, even as the victim's friends and family, as well as some of the public, demand retribution—claiming that since the murderer did not care about the rights of the victim, no one should respect the murderer's rights either.

Death penalty attorney David Dow has noted that it no doubt is difficult for a Judge to preside over the post-conviction appeal of a death row inmate whom the Judge believes to be factually guilty. It is not easy for a Judge to rule that, because the inmate's rights were violated, he must receive a new trial or sentencing hearing. Yet, that is what Judges ought to do. And death penalty lawyers are needed in order to persuade them that it is what they *must* do. Not only because that is the Judge's job, not just because the Judge has sworn an oath to enforce constitutional standards, but because our legal system depends upon Judges doing the right thing—even when it is difficult. It is a death penalty lawyer's job to remind Judges that it is their duty to honor the law.

And as Dow has stated:

> Death penalty lawyers like me are not needed to teach
> that there is murder and evil in the world. [They] . . .
> are needed to remind everyone that these inmates are,
> in fact, human, and to illuminate a tragic phenomenon
> . . . too often in death penalty cases, we have abandoned

our principles . . . The tragedy of contemporary death penalty litigation is [that we use the murder of innocents] as excuses to violate our constitutional values.

To defend against the death penalty is not to be dismissive of crime. It is not to be callous toward victims. Tommy Hamilton was not innocent, but he was unconstitutionally sentenced to death. Our arguments in Tommy's case had a sound constitutional basis, while accounting for the needs of law enforcement and the protection of the public. Tommy's lawyers failed to meet the constitutional requirement of providing effective assistance of counsel while representing Tommy at his sentencing hearing. I was not so much defending the man and what he had done as I was defending the law under which he should have been tried in the first place. This may be a difficult duty for a lawyer in the case of the factually guilty client, but it is necessary for our free society nonetheless.

I did not put Tommy Hamilton back on the streets. Local law enforcement made that possible by violating the constitutional rights of a citizen, sullying the justice system, and overreaching to secure a death sentence. The Alabama Board of Pardon and Paroles put Tommy back on the street, having determined that it was appropriate and just under the circumstances.

Did I win the Tommy Hamilton case?

Ever since my representation of Tommy, I have tried to eschew such binary assessment—indeed, binary thinking in general. After Tommy, litigation became less of a sport. Outcomes were no longer singularly experienced or categorized.

It is more complete to say that, while I alone did not put Tommy Hamilton back on the streets, I played my part in Tommy's eventual release. And, at the end at least, it was a part that went beyond advocacy about legal guilt and the enforcement of constitutional norms. Indeed, it went beyond what I had been retained to do.

The law rightfully, and to a great extent mechanically, dictated that a new trial was required to determine the proper outcome in Tommy's case because of the constitutional violations that occurred during the original trial. But it did not determine what that outcome should be.

I had been retained to serve as Tommy's attorney for his post-conviction proceedings. Once the Alabama Supreme Court declined to review the order by the Court of Criminal Appeals awarding Tommy a new trial, that job was finished. At that point, I could have walked away. The Lawrence County court would have appointed an attorney to represent Tommy during a new trial, and the result of that trial would not have involved me.

But I did not walk away. I extended my representation of Tommy beyond merely ensuring a fair process to determine the proper outcome of his case; I signed up for the determination of the outcome itself. That determination remained a very human endeavor, and, by participating in a negotiated plea and sentence, I undeniably injected my own humanity into the equation.

As a human being, Tommy's factual guilt does matter to me. But because I continued my legal representation of Tommy and negotiated the plea bargain, I had the opportunity to legally guarantee that Tommy would not be executed for his crime. No statute dictated that Tommy should not be put to death for murdering Lehman Wood. No law or regulation prescribed that a minimum sentence of about seventeen years of incarceration with the possibility of parole thereafter was the appropriate consequence for Lehman Wood's death. These were human judgments that I found personally and professionally acceptable enough to recommend that Tommy agree to them.

I am opposed to the death penalty in all cases except for treason, and in Tommy's case these personal beliefs aligned with my client's self-interest. While it is true that lawyers give advice but clients make decisions, still it is undeniable that my advice to Tommy carried significant weight. I will not diminish my responsibility for what happened. And I am at peace, personally and professionally, with the outcome.

But, as always, some will ask the question repeatedly until an answer is given: did I win the Tommy Hamilton case? It might be more accurate to say that I prevailed.

———

Though my efforts to save Tommy Hamilton's life were successful, many other wrongfully sentenced prisoners currently face the death penalty in America. Still, the nationwide trends bode well for the future. Statistics from the Death Penalty Information Center show that the death penalty in America is dying. In 1976, when the United States Supreme Court reinstated the death penalty in America, only twelve states did not provide for that punishment. Today, twenty-three states have abolished the death penalty, and three others have a formal moratorium on executions.

But not Alabama. Alabama continues to sentence more people to death per capita (.956 per 100,000 people) than any other state. In June of 2006, the American Bar Association published the results of its own assessment of Alabama's death penalty system. The Alabama Death Penalty Assessment Team identified several areas in which the state falls short in its efforts to afford every capital defendant fair and accurate procedures. These include inadequate indigent defense services at trial and on direct appeal; lack of defense counsel for state post-conviction proceedings; inadequate proportionality review in determining death sentences; the lack of effective limitations on finding the "heinous, atrocious, and cruel" aggravating factor in determining a death sentence; and capital-juror confusion.

In 2008, Philip Alston, a law professor at New York University School of Law reporting to the United Nations on such things as arbitrary executions, looked at Texas and Alabama—two of America's death penalty leaders—and found similar problems. In Texas, at least he found "significant recognition" that changes needed to be made. Not so in Alabama. Alston found it entirely possible that Alabama had already executed innocent people, but that officials would rather deny this fact than confront flaws in its criminal justice system. In Alston's report, one particular problem in Texas and Alabama was cited: Shoddy systems for providing criminal defense lawyers for those accused of death penalty crimes.

The Equal Justice Initiative recently issued a damning assessment of the state's approach to the death penalty. It reported that at least 170 Alabama death sentences have been reversed by state or federal courts and resulted in exoneration, lesser conviction, or a reduced sentence.

Alabama appears largely unmoved by these assessments. In 2017, Alabama finally eliminated the ability of a Judge, by imposing a sentence of death, to override a jury's recommendation of life in prison;

but the law was not made retroactive, and thirty-five people who had
been sentenced to death in that manner remained on death row.

In 2011, Alabama executed Jason Williams by lethal injection,
using a secret combination of drugs after the original set of drugs
was confiscated by the Drug Enforcement Administration. In 2018,
Alabama joined Oklahoma and Mississippi in authorizing executions
by nitrogen gas, a method that has never been used before anywhere
in the world.

Hugo Bedau, a philosopher who opposed the death penalty and
whose seminal work, *The Death Penalty in America*, was so influential
to me, died of complications from Parkinson's disease on August 13,
2012. In a pamphlet he coauthored for the American Civil Liberties
Union, he wrote:

> The history of capital punishment in American society
> . . . shows the desire to mitigate the harshness of this
> penalty by narrowing its scope. Discretion . . . has been
> the main vehicle to this end. But when discretion is
> used . . . to mark for death the poor, the friendless, the
> uneducated, the members of racial minorities and the
> despised . . . discretion becomes injustice. Thoughtful
> citizens . . . must condemn [capital punishment] in
> actual practice.

That same year, the National Research Council concluded that in
the three decades since the death penalty moratorium had been lifted,
no reliable research had emerged on whether capital punishment has
served as a deterrent.

Yet, as I finished this book, the outgoing Trump administration,
after a nearly twenty-year pause in federal executions, engaged in an
unprecedented effort to carry out the federal death penalty against as
many prisoners as possible. Donald Trump saw more prisoners executed in a single year (2020) than any other President in history. And
breaking a long-standing norm not to carry out federal death sentences during a lame-duck period, five federal executions were scheduled during the waning weeks of Donald Trump's time in office.

I believe that the current system of capital punishment in America needs significant reform, and as a lawyer it is my duty to advocate on behalf of those facing injustice from such broken institutions. The legal profession should not be defined or bound by statutes and cases, rules and regulations. Ours is a profession that should not be lashed to the law alone.

Of all the titles used to describe lawyers—such as attorney or esquire—my preferred title is counselor-at-law. That is because, often, I have found that the greatest service we can perform for our clients is to provide them with good advice, or "counsel." Certainly, counsel should be given with the law in mind. But good counsel should also take into consideration who the client is, what the client believes, and what the client stands for.

That is what I tried to do for Tommy Hamilton, and it saved his life.

EPILOGUE

Where They Are Now

Sometime in 2019, **Tommy Hamilton** allegedly was in possession of drugs in violation of the terms of his parole and was arrested. While in the backseat of a Sheriff's car being transported to the Lawrence County Jail, he was allegedly overheard threatening to kill his probation officer. At the time of this writing, he is incarcerated in the Department of Corrections' Aged & Infirmed Center in Hamilton, Alabama, awaiting trial on the resulting criminal charges.

Upon the dissolution of the Knight & Griffith law firm in 2012, **Sister Lynn Marie McKenzie** became a mediator of workers' compensation disputes for the state of Alabama's Department of Industrial Relations; she also was made President of the Benedictine Sisters of the Federation of St. Scholastica, a union of twenty monasteries in the United States and Mexico. In 2018, she was elected Moderatrix (leader) of the Communio Internationalis Benedictinarum, a worldwide confederation of Benedictine women.

Luke DeGrand formed his own law firm, DeGrand & Wolfe, in 2006 and continues to practice law in Chicago.

Janice Glasco, Tommy Hamilton's sister and codefendant, lived in Oklahoma City and Hillsboro, Alabama, after being released from prison. She married Thomas "Tommy" Edwin Letson on February 1, 2014. He died of lung cancer on September 11, 2018.

Debbie Gatlin Hamilton, Tommy's (first) wife and codefendant, literally grew up in prison. She was only sixteen years old when, on October 25, 1985, she pled guilty to the crime of murder and accepted a sentence of life in prison.

On April 28, 1998, Judge Billy Burney asked the Alabama Board of Pardons and Parole to release her. He stated: "I was the Judge that presided over Ms. Hamilton's trial many years ago. When this event occurred, she was very young, as was the young man (Tommy) involved. The sister of the man was older and in my opinion was the instigator of what happened. . . . Down through the years I have kept in touch with Debbie and her family. What she did was a terrible act, but in my opinion you should look at her age at the time and the circumstances involved; she has paid for what she did, and deserves to be paroled."

On November 9, 1999, Lehman Wood's daughter, Charlotte Parker, and his granddaughter, Cheri Parker, also wrote in support of parole for Debbie.

On November 29, 2005, Timothy Littrell—who prosecuted Tommy at the original trial—joined the chorus of those asking for parole on behalf of Debbie: "It was, and is, my personal opinion, based on my handling of all three cases, that in ranking culpability, that of Debbie Hamilton would have been less than that of her two co-defendants."

Finally, after serving more than twenty years in prison, Debbie was granted parole in 2007. I met with her in the fall of 2013.

At the time of this writing, her whereabouts and circumstances are unknown.

Jason Glasco, Janice's son and a testifying witness during Tommy's trial, got married, moved to Cullman, Alabama, and became a maintenance technician for Southern Energy Homes.

Lucille Looney Hamilton, Tommy's mother, died on January 10, 2017. She donated her body to medical research.

In 2007 Judge **Sue Bell Cobb**, author of the Alabama Court of Criminal Appeals opinion that overturned Tommy's capital conviction and death sentence, became the first female Chief Justice of the Alabama Supreme Court. As Chief Justice, she championed the Juvenile Justice Reform Act of 2008. Cobb served as Chief Justice until her resignation in August of 2011. Her work, and the work of others, on behalf of abused and exploited children is recounted in her book, *There Must Be a Witness.* In 2018 she unsuccessfully ran for Governor of Alabama. At the time of this writing, she is the founder of Justice Earned—a group dedicated to providing legal representation for prisoners seeking parole.

On January 31, 2009 Judge **Ned Michael Suttle**, who presided over Tommy's post-conviction proceedings, retired after twenty-four years as the Presiding Circuit Court Judge of Lauderdale County. He then practiced law in Florence, Alabama.

Retired Judge **Billy C. Burney**, who presided over Tommy's capital murder trial and sentenced him to death, initially established a solo private law practice in Decatur, Alabama. In 1992, he began to practice law with his two sons under the firm name of Burney & Burney. At one point he was appointed a Special Justice of the Alabama Supreme Court. He died on November 3, 2018.

After serving twenty years as the Circuit Court Judge for Lawrence County, **Judge A. Philip Reich II** retired on January 31, 2009, and went into private law practice, sharing office space with former District Attorney **Timothy Dean Littrell**.

Wesley M. Lavender, Tommy's principal defense attorney, overcame his problems with alcohol and became an Assistant District Attorney and then a Judge. He died in 2011, at the age of sixty-three, after battling cancer.

Barnes F. Lovelace Jr., Tommy's additional defense attorney, is the managing partner of the Harris, Caddell & Shanks law firm in Decatur, Alabama.

William Edward "Eddie" Oliver died of a drug overdose on April 15, 1999.

Jim Osborn, Tim Littrell's successor as District Attorney for Lawrence County, Alabama, retired from that office on February 8, 2012. During his career he prosecuted ten capital murder cases.

Donald Eugene Holt, Janice's defense attorney, was widely regarded as the best criminal defense attorney in northwest Alabama. He was a charter member of the Alabama Criminal Defense Lawyers

Association and a President of the Lauderdale County Bar Association. In 1992, he received the Roderick Beddow Sr. Award, which is given by the Alabama Criminal Defense Lawyer's Association for outstanding achievements in criminal law. He died of cancer on May 26, 2006, just forty-two days after the death of Betty, his wife of more than forty-five years.

Alabama Attorney General **Don Siegelman** was sworn in as Governor of Alabama in January of 1999. In 2006, while serving in that office, he was convicted by a federal jury of bribery and other charges. On August 3, 2012, after exhausting his appeals, he was sentenced to more than six years in prison.

Alabama Attorney General **Jefferson Beauregard Sessions** became a United States Senator from Alabama. He was appointed Attorney General of the United States in the Trump administration, resigning on November 7, 2018, at the President's request.

Ed Carnes, the head of the Alabama Attorney General's death penalty division at the time of Tommy's post-conviction proceedings, became the Chief Judge of the United States Court of Appeals for the Eleventh Circuit.

Soon after the conclusion of Tommy Hamilton's appellate case, **Kenneth Nunnelley** became the Senior Assistant State Attorney General dedicated to representing the state of Florida in post-conviction death penalty cases.

Daniel Webster "Snooks" Ligon lost his bid for reelection and a third term as Sheriff of Lawrence County (1971–75; 1983–87) on November 4, 1986, and he died on December 30, 2003.

Investigator **Ed Weatherford** left the Lawrence County District Attorney's Office in 1994 and became the Chief of Police of Moulton, Alabama, a position he held until he retired in 2005. Thereafter, he became the Director of the Lawrence County 911 system.

Charlotte Wood Parker, Lehman Wood's daughter, died on March 27, 2015, almost thirty-six years after her father was murdered and not quite two years after she was orphaned by the death of her mother on February 23, 2013.

ACKNOWLEDGMENTS

According to the *Oxford English Dictionary*, the term "acknowledge" means "to accept or admit to the truth of" a thing, and "to recognize the fact or importance or quality of it." In writing this book, I have accumulated many intellectual and personal debts to several individuals. I am glad to have the opportunity to acknowledge them here. Much of what is good in this manuscript is due to these talented and supportive friends and members of my family, whereas errors in form or substance are mine.

Sister Lynn McKenzie guided me through the Alabama legal system, taught me that it is important to "howdy" with people, and served as a moral guidepost. She and her sisters at the Sacred Heart Monastery in Cullman also provided room and board during my visits to the Yellowhammer State.

Luke DeGrand, my law partner for almost a decade, worked tirelessly on the extraordinarily challenging Tommy Hamilton postconviction proceedings.

As always, my administrative assistants over the years—Mary Bray, Renee Campanella, Debbie Glass, Kim Johnson, Katie McCarthy-Cushing, Heather Smith, Barbara Tousignant, and Wendy Zunker—made my efforts look good.

Justice Sue Bell Cobb and Judge Ned Michael Suttle were as friendly and welcoming in reflecting on the Tommy Hamilton case after the fact as they were professional and courteous during the legal proceedings.

Professor Perry Dane helped me articulate my views on the importance of defending the guilty.

Attorney Kip Purcell helped me develop the media rights authorization for my former client, Tommy Hamilton.

Numerous readers of my earliest efforts, including Mary Munday, Elizabeth Dilley, Margaret Fogelman, Ed Furman, Debra Hilton, Alice Hunt, Heather Kimmel, Harry Teinowitz, and Lisa Zook, provided helpful reactions to one or more chapters and important encouragement to "keep writing."

Even during my always prudent and at times forced isolation on a Hawaiian island in the Pacific Ocean during the 2020 global coronavirus pandemic, the manuscript for this book was not the product of solitary effort. The Hualalai Writers' Group—Cyndi Muscatel and Debby Webster—provided encouragement and accountability for the drafting of many chapters.

Just before we attended game three of the 2013 Stanley Cup Final between my Chicago Blackhawks and his Boston Bruins, I asked Mark Vershbow—my college roommate—if he would serve as first editor of my memoir. At that time, he said that he would. Seven years later, I emailed him the manuscript, and he promptly completed this generous and invaluable service. He is a talented editor and a man whose word is his bond.

My manuscript would not have gone further than my desktop without the expert assistance of the folks at Girl Friday Productions: Karen Upson, Alex Rigby, and Georgie Hockett. Independent publishing offers the possibility of partnership in bringing a book to print, and the folks at GFP made it a reality.

I also want to acknowledge the humble hands and invisible minds that might otherwise go unnoticed. The developmental editing of Dan Crissman helped me see the forest for the trees. It is said that you should never judge a book by its cover. But just in case, Paul Barrett designed an excellent one. Corinne Moulder at Smith Publicity, and Beth Silverman at the Silverman Group, were skilled at bringing this story to the attention of others.

I owe a special thank-you to my mother for her steadfast love. I love you, Mom.

My children, Bethany and Alex, are a source of constant support and unflagging devotion, for which I am deeply grateful.

Finally, I have long owed the greatest thanks and appreciation to my wife, Ellen, an extraordinary partner in the writing of this memoir, as she is in every way that matters.

BIBLIOGRAPHY

CHAPTER ONE—THE ATTORNEY

Emerson, Jason. *Giant in the Shadows: The Life of Robert T. Lincoln.* Carbondale: Southern Illinois University Press, 2012.

Goff, John S. *Robert Todd Lincoln: A Man in His Own Right.* Norman: University of Oklahoma Press, 1969.

Smith, Carl S. *Chicago's Great Fire: The Destruction and Resurrection of an Iconic American City.* New York: Atlantic Monthly Press, 2020.

Gideon v. Wainwright, 372 U.S. 335 (1963).

Murray v. Giarratano, 492 U.S. 1 (1989).

CHAPTER TWO—THE CLIENT

Stancil, Clyde. "Chief Retires After 33 years in Law Enforcement: Weatherford Did 'A Great Job' for Moulton." *Decatur Daily,* July 31, 2005.

"Hen Talk." *Moulton Advertiser,* October 10, 1957, 5.

"L'rence Gets CD Director." *Decatur Daily,* February 15, 1977, A1.

"Lehman Wood Gets Nod As New Carrier." *Moulton Advertiser,* June 20, 1957 at 1.

"Lehman Wood Named School Trustee." *Moulton Advertiser,* August 23, 1962, 7.

"Moulton Boat Club Plans Season of Special Events." *Moulton Advertiser,* May 14, 1959, 1.

"Tarred and Feathered Woman Marries Anyway." *UPI,* March 27, 1981.

"3 Charged in Shooting of Lawrence County Official." *Montgomery Advertiser,* July 14, 1984, 16.

"Hamilton Guilty of Murder Charge." *Anniston Star,* September 1, 1985, 18.

"Suspect Convicted in Lawrence Slaying." *Anniston Star,* October 28, 1985, 6.

"Three Charged in Director's Death." *Selma Times-Journal,* July 13, 1984, 12.

"Woods Find Moulton Good Place to Live." *Moulton Advertiser,* August 30, 1956, 11.

Moulton Advertiser, May 7, 1959, 7.

Southern Democrat (Oneonta, AL), June 30, 1955, 14.

State of Alabama v. Tommy Lee Hamilton, No. CC-84–131 (Circuit Court of Lawrence County, Alabama 1985).

Hamilton v. State, 520 So. 2d 155 (Ala. Cr. App. 1987).

Ex parte Tommy Hamilton, 520 So. 2d 167 (Ala. 1987).

Hamilton v. State of Alabama, 488 U.S. 871 (1988).

CHAPTER THREE—THE PUNISHMENT

Baker, David V. "American Indian Executions in Historical Context." *Criminal Justice Studies* 20, no. 4 (December 2007): 315–73.

Baker, David V. "A Descriptive Profile and Socio-Historical Analysis of Female Executions in the United States: 1632–1997." *Women & Criminal Justice* 10, no. 3 (1999): 57.

Barbour, Philip L. "Captain George Kendall: Mutineer or Intelligencer?" *Virginia Magazine of History and Biography* 70, no. 3 (July 1962): 297.

Canan, Russell F. "Burning at the Wire: The Execution of John Evans." In *Facing the Death Penalty: Essays on a Cruel and Unusual Punishment,* edited by Michael L. Radelet, 60. Philadelphia: Temple University Press, 1989.

Brotman, Barbara. "Law Firm's Liquidation Solidifies End of a Legal Era." *Chicago Tribune,* August 11, 1988.

Bedau, Hugo Adam. *The Death Penalty in America: An Anthology.* Chicago: Aldine, 1964.

Banner, Stuart. *The Death Penalty: An American History.* Cambridge, MA: Harvard University Press, 2002.

Bohm, Robert M. *Deathquest: An Introduction to the Theory and Practice of Capital Punishment in the United States.* Cincinnati: Anderson, 1999.

"Bolts of Fire: It Burned Out a Soul: Veins are Turned to Charcoal." *Boston Daily Globe,* August 7, 1890, 1.

Chester, Alden and Edwin Melvin Williams. *Courts and Lawyers of New York: A History, 1609–1925.* 310–16. New York: American Historical Society, 1925.

Demos, John Putnam. *Entertaining Satan: Witchcraft and the Culture of Early New England.* 346. New York: Oxford University Press, 1982.

Essig, Mark. *Edison and the Electric Chair: A Story of Light and Death.* 98. New York: Walker, 2003.

"Far Worse Than Hanging: Kemmler's Death Proves an Awful Spectacle," *New York Times,* August 7, 1890, 1.

Galliher, John F., Gregory Ray, and Brent Cook. "Abolition and Reinstatement of Capital Punishment During the Progressive Era and Early 20th Century." *Journal of Criminal Law and Criminology* 83, no. 3 (1992–93): 538–41, 573–76.

Grizzard Jr., Frank E. and D. Boyd Smith. *Jamestown Colony: A Political, Social and Cultural History.* 108–10. Santa Barbara, CA: ABC-CLIO, 2007.

Hearn, Daniel Allen. *Legal Executions in New England: A Comprehensive Reference, 1623–1960.* 7–9, 54. Jefferson, NC: McFarland, 1999.

Keedy, Edwin R. "History of the Pennsylvania Statute Creating Degrees of Murder." *University of Pennsylvania Law Review* 97, no. 6 (May 1949): 759, 769–71.

Konig, David Thomas. "'Dale's Laws' and the Non-Common Law Origins of Criminal Justice in Virginia." *American Journal of Legal History* 26, no. 4 (October 1982): 354.

Mandery, Evan J. *A Wild Justice: The Death and Resurrection of Capital Punishment in America.* New York: W. W. Norton & Company, 2013.

Preyer, Kathryn. "Crime, the Criminal Law and Reform in Post-Revolutionary Virginia." *Law and History Review* 1, no. 1 (Spring 1983): 56–70.

Records of the Court of Assistants of the Colony of the Massachusetts Bay, 1630–1692. Vol. 1. 199. Boston: Count of Suffolk, 1901.

Robinson, Conway. "Notes from Council and General Court Records, 1641–1659." *Virginia Magazine of History and Biography* 13, no. 4 (April 1906): 389–90.

Schiff, Stacy. *The Witches: Salem, 1692.* New York: Little, Brown, 2015.

Randa, Laura E., ed. *Society's Final Solution: A History and Discussion of the Death Penalty.* Lanham, MD: University Press of America, 1997.

Warden, Rob and Daniel Lennard. "Death in America Under Color of Law: Our Long, Inglorious Experience with Capital Punishment." *Northwestern Journal of Law and Social Policy* 13, no. 4 (Spring 2018).

"Couple Escapes From Jail Using Broom Handle as Gun." *Alabama Journal*, October 16, 1984, 3.

"Police Recapture Pair Charged with Murder." *Montgomery Advertiser*, October 17, 1984, 21.

"Suspect Convicted in Lawrence Slaying," *Anniston Star*, October 28, 1985, 6.

New York Herald, July 23, 1874.

Coke v. Georgia, 433 U.S. 584 (1977).

Crampton v. Ohio and *McGautha v. California*, 402 U.S. 183 (1971).

Ford v. Wainwright, 477 U.S. 399 (1986).

Furman v. Georgia, Jackson v. Georgia, and *Branch v. Texas*, 408 U.S. 238 (1972).

Gregg v. Georgia, 428 U.S. 153 (1976).

Hopper v. Evans, 456 U.S. 605 (1982).

Hubbard v. State, 274 So. 2d 298, 300 (Alabama 1973).

Jurek v. Texas, 428 U.S. 262 (1976).

Norris v. Alabama, 294 U.S. 587, 598 (1935).

People ex rel. Kemmler v. Dunston, 119 N.Y. 569, 576–79 (1890).

Powell v. Alabama, 287 U.S. 45, 68–69, 72 (1932).

Proffitt v. Florida, 428 U.S. 242 (1976).

Trop v. Dulles, 356 U.S. 86 (1958).

Woodson v. North Carolina, 428 U.S. 280 (1975).

CHAPTER FOUR—THE LEGAL TEAM

Baldwin v. Alabama, 472 U.S. 372 (1985).

Beck v. Alabama, 447 U.S. 625 (1980).

Hopper v. Evans, 456 U.S. 605 (1982).

Marshall, Steven T. and Andrew L. Brasher. "Assistant Attorney General Ed Carnes from 1980 to 1985." *Alabama Law Review* 69, no. 3 (2018): 651–61.

CHAPTER FIVE—THE INVESTIGATION

"Hamilton-Harper Plans Announced." *Decatur Daily*, May 19, 1974, C10.

Daily Records, Marriage Licenses. *Decatur Daily*, February 20, 1975, A-3.

Daily Records, Marriage Licenses. *Decatur Daily*, February 24, 1976, 7.

Phillips, Martha Ann. "Martha Ann's Valley." *Decatur Daily*, October 3, 1976, F-10.

Glasco v. State, 513 So. 2d 54 (Ala. Crim. App. 1987).

State of Alabama v. Janice Glasco, No. CC-84-132, Circuit Court of Lawrence County, Alabama.

CHAPTER SIX—THE PETITION

"Alabama Executes Man in Death of a Widow." *New York Times*, May 27, 1989.

"2 Electric Jolts in Alabama Execution." *New York Times*, July 15, 1989.

"Murderer of Woman is Executed in Alabama." *New York Times*, November 18, 1989.

"Alabama Man, 43, Is Executed for Killing Girl with Pipe Bomb." *New York Times*, August 19, 1989.

Penry v. Lynaugh, 492 U.S. 302 (1989). In 2002, the Supreme Court found that a national consensus had developed and thus execution of the mentally disabled was deemed unconstitutional. *Atkins v. Virginia*, 536 U.S. 304 (2002).

Earley, Pete. *Circumstantial Evidence: Death, Life and Justice in a Southern Town*. New York: Bantam Books, 1995.

Stevenson, Bryan. *Just Mercy: A Story of Justice and Redemption*. New York: Spiegel & Grau, 2015.

Roberts, Russ. "Littrell New Lawrence DA." *Decatur Daily*, February 19, 1976, A1, A5.

CHAPTER SEVEN—THE PERJURY

"24 Hours on Death Row: Description of Alabama's Electric Chair." May 26, 2011. YouTube video, 3:47. https://www.youtube.com/watch?v=_oC_fQpn6cM.

Hrynkiw, Ivana. "This is How Alabama Executes Inmates: Court Releases Details on Drugs, Process." AL.com. Last modified October 17, 2019. https://www.al.com/news/montgomery/2019/10/alabama-execution-protocol-details-on-drugs-process.html.

Bailey, Stan. "Retired Executioner Says He Has No Regrets." *Tuscaloosa News*, August 3, 2002. https://www.tuscaloosanews.com/article/DA/20020803/News/606113080/TL.

"City Hall Shot Up." *Montgomery Advertiser*, May 3, 1978, 12.

Doty, John. "Lawrence Corruption Charge Draws Grand Jury Challenge." *Decatur Daily*, August 23, 1974, A1.

Harris v. New York, 401 U.S. 222, 225 (1971).

Holman, Steele. "Four Escape Lawrence Jail; Three Recaptured." *Decatur Daily*, February 16, 1977, A1.

"State Patrol Searches for Escapees." *Montgomery Advertiser*, January 10, 1976, 9.

"Teenage Gunman Shoots Up Town, Then Wounds Self." *Alabama Journal*, May 2, 1978, 1.

"Witnesses Describe 'Revolving Door' Jail." *Selma Times-Journal*, October 25, 1989, 2.

CHAPTER EIGHT—THE HEARING

Annie Lee Hughes, as Administratrix of the Estate of Jimmy Dale Owens, et al. v. Dan Ligon, Sheriff, et al., 5:87-cv-05519-JHH (N.D. Alabama 1987).

Tommy Hamilton v. State of Alabama, CC-84-131.60, Circuit Court for the County of Lawrence, 36th Judicial Circuit.

CHAPTER NINE—THE ESCAPE

Ortega-Rodriguez v. United States, 113 S. Ct. 1199 (1993).

Tommy Hamilton v. State of Alabama, CC-84-131.60, Circuit Court for the County of Lawrence, 36th Judicial Circuit.

CHAPTER TEN—THE ARGUMENTS

Brady v. Maryland, 373 U.S. 83 (1963).

Chapman v. California, 386 U.S. 18 (1967).

Ex parte Frazier, 562 So. 2d 560 (1989).

Gideon v. Wainwright, 372 U. S. 335 (1963).

Massiah v. United States, 377 U.S. 201 (1964).

Spano v. New York, 360 U. S. 315 (1959).

Strickland v. Washington, 466 U.S. 668 (1984).

Tommy Hamilton v. State of Alabama, CC-84-131.60, Circuit Court for the County of Lawrence, 36th Judicial Circuit.

United States v. Bagley, 473 U.S. 667 (1985).

United States v. El Paso Natural Gas Company, 376 U.S. 651 (1964).

United States v. Henry, 447 U.S. 264 (1980).

Woodson v. North Carolina, 428 U.S. 280 (1976).

CHAPTER ELEVEN—THE ORDER

Tommy Hamilton v. State of Alabama, CC-84-131.60, Circuit Court for the County of Lawrence, 36th Judicial Circuit.

CHAPTER TWELVE—THE APPEAL

"Magistrate Refuses to Release Records." *News Courier* (Athens, GA), June 18, 1999, 6A.

"Ex-Judge Accused of Sexual Harassment." *Montgomery Advertiser*, February 14, 1997, 21.

"Harassment Complaint Made Against Former Judge." *Selma Times-Journal*, May 2, 1997, 2.

"Women File Suit Against Judge." *Montgomery Advertiser*, May 2, 1998, 13.

State of Alabama v. Tommy Hamilton, 93-1357, Alabama Court of Criminal Appeals.

Tommy Hamilton v. State of Alabama, 93-1377, Alabama Court of Criminal Appeals.

CHAPTER THIRTEEN—THE BARGAIN

Brookhart v. Janis, 384 U.S. 1 (1966).

McCoy v. Louisiana, 584 U.S. ___ 138 Sup. Ct. 1500 (2018).

Weisberg, Karen. "Barbara Holly: Making Corrections." *Food Service Director*. Last modified March 29, 2005. https://www.foodservice-director.com/people/barbara-holly-making-corrections.

CHAPTER FOURTEEN—THE DEFENSE OF THE GUILTY

Abrams, Dan and Fisher, David. *John Adams Under Fire: The Founding Father's Fight for Justice in the Boston Massacre Murder Trial.* New York: Hanover Square Press, 2020.

American Bar Association. "Evaluating Fairness and Accuracy in State Death Penalty Systems: The Alabama Death Penalty Assessment Report." (June 2006): 117–20.

Dow, David R. *Executed on a Technicality: Lethal Injustice on America's Death Row.* Boston: Beacon Press, 2005.

Farrell, John A. *Clarence Darrow: Attorney for the Damned.* 333–60. New York: Doubleday, 2011.

McCullough, David. *John Adams.* 67–68. New York: Simon & Schuster, 2001.

Smith, Abbe. "In Praise of the Guilt Project: A Criminal Defense Lawyer's Growing Anxiety About Innocence Projects." *University of Pennsylvania Journal of Law and Social Change* 13, no. 3 (2010): 315–30.

Herrera v. Collins, 506 U.S. 390 (1993).

McQuiggin v. Perkins, 569 U.S. 383 (2013).

"Funerals." *Gadsden Times,* April 17, 1999.

INDEX